Revival of Maoism in Reform-Era China

Lin Le

Revival of Maoism in Reform-Era China

Bo Xilai in Chongqing, 2008-2012

palgrave
macmillan

Lin Le
Independent Scholar
Menlo Park, CA, USA

ISBN 978-981-92-4605-2 ISBN 978-981-92-4606-9 (eBook)
https://doi.org/10.1007/978-981-92-4606-9

This Palgrave Macmillan imprint is published by the registered company Springer Nature Singapore Pte Ltd.
The registered company address is: 152 Beach Road, #21-01/04 Gateway East, Singapore 189721, Singapore

To the people of China,
who deserve better

Acknowledgments Writing a book is like a lonely pilgrimage undertaken to fulfill a divine mission in response to one's inner calling. The completion of this book would not have been possible without the providential support and help from many sources, to whom I wish to express my sincere gratitude.

This book received generous funding from Cornell University, including the C. V. Starr Fellowships in East Asian Studies through the East Asia Program and a research grant from the Qualitative and Interpretive Research Institute, as well as support from the Clements Center for National Security at the University of Texas at Austin and the America in the World Consortium. The book was also supported by Stanford East Asia Library Travel Grant through the International and Foreign Language Education (IFLE) program; the contents of this book were developed under grant #P015A220015/84.015A from the U.S. Department of Education. However, those contents do not necessarily represent the policy of the U.S. Department of Education, and readers should not assume endorsement by the Federal Government.

Intellectually, I am indebted to Alice Miller, Jeremy Wallace, Richard Bensel, Kenneth Roberts, and the anonymous reviewers for their constructive feedback on earlier versions of the manuscript. I feel especially grateful to all those in Cornell's Department of Government who worked to maintain and provide a nourishing environment of academic freedom during my years of study—one that enabled and encouraged graduate students to think, explore, and write without mind shackles.

My thanks extend to Jacob Dreyer, Senior Editor of Economics, Business and Finance at Palgrave Macmillan, who played an indispensable way-making role in turning this project from manuscript into book.

It was the emotional support and companionship of my parents and my wife that gave me the courage and perseverance to have walked this far.

Ultimately, thanks be to God, who delivers and provides. Isaiah 6:8 has always brought me strength whenever I felt weary.

Competing Interests The author has no competing interests to declare that are relevant to the content of this manuscript.

Contents

List of Figures

List of Tables

CHAPTER 1

Introduction: Turning Left

Why has there been a sea change in China under Xi Jinping?[1] Rather than Xi's own ambition or ideological disposition, or both, as conventional wisdom suggests, an alternative theory points to a collective force of conservatism, or leftism in the context of communist China.[2] This force, with which Xi identified and sided from the very beginning, drove China backward after decades of reform.

Some of Xi's major policies, in fact, had already been on full display in the years leading up to his fateful accession to power in 2012. In particular, many of these policy prototypes were closely associated with Bo Xilai, the son of a preeminent first-generation party revolutionary and once Xi's political rival during Hu Jintao's final years in office. When Xi later rolled out a wide range of policy initiatives and campaigns—such as the anti-corruption drive, ideological education, cadre rectification, the crackdown on organized crime, poverty alleviation, and the so-called Common Prosperity program—they appeared to be little more than a reprise of what Bo had implemented while serving as party secretary of Chongqing from 2008 to 2012.

Perhaps, Xi simply learned from Bo. Or perhaps there is a deeper connection between what Bo and Xi did?

The goal of this book is to uncover this deeper connection by focusing on what happened in the critical period immediately preceding Xi's rise to power. Drawing heavily on official Chinese-language documents and relevant government publications, the book reconstructs a historical

L. Le, *Revival of Maoism in Reform-Era China*,
https://doi.org/10.1007/978-981-92-4606-9_1

narrative of what Bo Xilai did in Chongqing between 2008 and 2012 and explains why.

In his quest for power, Bo Xilai adjusted his political orientation in response to shifting winds at the top. He aligned himself closely with conservative forces, turning Chongqing into a local battleground for the left–right struggles unfolding within the central leadership. Theoretically, Bo's open campaigning for power offers a vivid illustration of how authoritarian leaders strategically use public information for intra-elite struggle, challenging the conventional wisdom that elite politics in autocracies is typically hidden in a black box. The book also presents additional theoretical perspectives to illuminate the political significance of Bo's use of mass mobilization. First, against the backdrop of China's post-Mao rectification, it shows how mass mobilization under Bo broke established political taboos, thereby revealing both his political ambition and the extraordinary nature of the political situation. Second, through the lens of the "party–people relationship," it analyzes the structural reasons why Bo's attempt to revive Maoist practices ultimately backfired and was hijacked by radical Maoist forces.

1.1 Who Is Bo Xilai?

If we were to compare Bo Xilai to a character from *Game of Thrones*, who would be the closest match? Ned Stark, perhaps? In late 2024, more than a decade after Bo Xilai was purged and imprisoned on corruption charges, his son, Bo Guagua, shared an AI-generated comparison on the social media platform X, explicitly endorsing the analogy.[3] According to this AI narrative, Bo and Ned Stark share several "thematic parallels," outlined as follows.[4]

> Integrity and Fall: Both were seen as figures of integrity but ultimately fell from grace due to political machinations. Bo was convicted of corruption and murder, while Ned was executed for treason.
>
> Charisma and Leadership: Bo was known for his charisma and populist policies in Chongqing, akin to Ned's respected leadership in the North.
>
> Family Legacy: Both had significant family legacies; Bo was a "princeling" with a revolutionary father, and Ned was from the ancient Stark lineage.
>
> Tragic End: Their stories both end tragically due to the complexities of power and betrayal.

In short, both men were blameless and popular, yet fell victim to political persecution—an illustration of the "often tragic nature of political power." Speaking through the voice of AI, Bo's son sought to vindicate his father's downfall: he was a casualty of power struggles, and the corruption charges against him were entirely unfounded.

Bo's fall from power in 2012 was widely seen at the time as the most significant political upheaval in Communist China since the Tiananmen crisis—or perhaps even since the Lin Biao incident and the purge of the Gang of Four during the Mao era.[5] Only the recent sweeping purge in the military, particularly the downfall of Central Military Commission Vice Chairman Zhang Youxia, can be said to represent an episode of intra-elite turmoil of comparable, or even greater, magnitude. Once again, the fierce internal power struggles and factional divisions within the Chinese Communist Party (CCP) were laid bare. The political rifts had grown so deep that the usual behind-the-scenes maneuvering could no longer conceal the discord. The image of a unified, infallible Party leadership collapsed in full view of the public, dealing a serious blow to the CCP's political legitimacy. The peaceful power transition from Jiang Zemin to Hu Jintao had once been hailed as a milestone in the institutionalization of Chinese politics during the reform era. But Bo's dramatic downfall underscored the enduring dominance of personalized rule, and the deep unpredictability, at the heart of the Chinese political system.

Bo Xilai was born into a prominent revolutionary family. His father, Bo Yibo, was a first-generation CCP leader who once served as China's vice premier. Bo Yibo was also one of the so-called Eight Immortals—a group of party elders that included figures like Deng Xiaoping and Chen Yun.[6] From the early 1980s through the early 1990s, these elders wielded substantial political influence during a period of leadership transition and regime transformation. Bo Yibo supported Deng Xiaoping's economic reform and opening-up policies but firmly opposed political liberalization. He criticized Hu Yaobang for promoting "bourgeois liberalization" and backed Deng's decision to remove him from office. He is also believed to have endorsed the Tiananmen Square crackdown.[7]

Bo Xilai's political rise is widely believed to have been aided by the stature and influence of his father, Bo Yibo. The elder Bo reportedly leveraged political deals and his residual clout to secure key promotions for his son. Bo Yibo was considered a key supporter of Jiang Zemin in the 1990s. When Deng Xiaoping attempted to replace Jiang in 1992, it was Bo Yibo who strongly defended him. Later, after Hu Jintao was named successor,

Bo again backed Jiang's decision to retain the chairmanship of the Central Military Commission for an additional two years. In return, Jiang is believed to have extended significant political favors to Bo Xilai, smoothing his path to higher office.[8]

Bo Xilai's political career began in northeastern China, where he held a series of increasingly prominent positions in Liaoning Province. He served as mayor of Dalian from 1993 to 2000, during which time he gained national attention for transforming the port city into a modern, cosmopolitan hub. Under his leadership, Dalian underwent significant urban beautification, economic development, and infrastructure expansion. He also helped establish a top-tier professional soccer team, which contributed to his popularity and image as a dynamic, hands-on leader. In 2001, Bo was promoted to governor of Liaoning Province, a post he held until 2004. He was then appointed Minister of Commerce, serving from 2004 to 2007, where he cultivated a reputation as a charismatic and media-savvy politician on the national and international stage.

In 2007, Bo Xilai was promoted to the Party's Politburo, but was simultaneously reassigned to serve as the party secretary of Chongqing. This move was widely interpreted as a de facto demotion. Compared to China's other three centrally administered municipalities—Beijing, Shanghai, and Tianjin—Chongqing was less economically developed and held lower political prestige. At age 58, Bo's prospects for further elevation seemed dim, especially given his assignment to a region far from the political center in Beijing.[9] Age plays a significant role in career advancement within the reform-era CCP hierarchy. Since the late 1990s, an unwritten rule known as "seven up, eight down" (*qi shang ba xia*) has guided elite promotions: Politburo members may be promoted at 67 but are expected to retire at 68.[10] Based on this convention, Bo's political future appeared limited. When the next generation of top leaders was to be selected at the Eighteenth Party Congress in late 2012, Bo would have been 63, making it unlikely that he would be appointed to a key post for only one five-year term before mandatory retirement.

Bo Yibo's death in January 2007, shortly before the Seventeenth Party Congress, appeared to confirm just how much Bo Xilai's political ascent had relied on his father's clout. Once the patriarch was gone, so too was Bo's powerful backing.[11] Beyond the loss of his patron, Bo Xilai's own personality was often cited as an obstacle to further promotion.[12] His flamboyant, attention-seeking style, including a penchant for grandstanding and courting foreign media, left a negative impression on some senior

Party officials who valued discretion and conformity. Bo's reputation for ruthlessness also raised concerns among his peers, who saw him as a potential threat. According to widely circulated accounts, during the Cultural Revolution, Bo Xilai physically attacked his father during a public denunciation session, reportedly beating the elder Bo so severely that he broke three of his ribs. The act was meant to prove his unwavering loyalty to Mao and the Party. Paradoxically, Bo Yibo later praised his son for doing what was necessary.[13]

In stark contrast to Bo Xilai's fate after the Seventeenth Party Congress, Xi Jinping was clearly being groomed as the next party leader around the same time.[14] Xi's rise was marked by his unprecedented direct promotion to the Politburo Standing Committee without prior service on the broader Politburo. Simultaneously, he was appointed executive secretary of the Party Secretariat, a role that allowed him to oversee party affairs and build an extensive network of political relationships. Building on this foundation, Xi was named president of the Central Party School in December 2007, an influential institution for training party cadres. In March 2008, he was appointed China's vice president. It is said that Xi's status as successor was bolstered by a high score in an intra-party "democratic" straw poll at the time.[15] His position as heir apparent was further confirmed in 2010, when he was named Vice Chairman of the Central Military Commission during the Fifth Plenum of the Seventeenth Central Committee.

Clearly, Bo Xilai did not give up. His series of bold initiatives in Chongqing quickly made both him and the city the center of attention. He aggressively promoted investment and urban development, and launched his famous "Sing Red and Strike Black" campaigns—mobilizing the masses to sing revolutionary songs while cracking down on organized crime. He sent local party cadres to rural areas to serve the people, or practice the Maoist Mass Line, and championed the egalitarian slogan of "common prosperity." Bo demonstrated a strong talent for political propaganda and mass mobilization. His personal charisma, combined with populist policies, earned him widespread popular support. It seemed that Bo sought to showcase his governing abilities as a way to vie for higher political office—an unprecedented form of open political competition in China's authoritarian system.

Bo Xilai's political ambition was widely seen as aiming for a seat on the Politburo Standing Committee—or even higher. The most sensational rumors claimed he was vying directly with Xi Jinping for the top position of the Party's general secretary.[16] Some of Bo's supporters openly declared that he could become the next premier, even comparing Bo and his aide Huang Qifan to Mao Zedong and Zhou Enlai.[17] More seriously, there were rumors that Bo conspired with Zhou Yongkang, then a member of Politburo Standing Committee and head of the Central Political and Legal Affairs Commission, in a failed coup attempt.[18] Zhou's subsequent downfall, coupled with the intensified official denunciations of "political conspiracies" under Xi, fueled these speculations further. Xi personally criticized Bo and Zhou, accusing them of letting "their political ambition swell," "engaging in political intrigue," and "collaborating to undermine and divide the party." Xi charged that some leading cadres "think of themselves as number one, and they take wherever the Party sends them as their own independent kingdom."[19]

Just as Bo Xilai was enjoying immense popularity in Chongqing and his future seemed bright, he was unexpectedly removed from his position in early 2012. This occurred following a series of dramatic, Hollywood-style events—an aspect that attracted the most attention from Western media.[20]

On November 15, 2011, British businessman Neil Heywood was found dead at the Lucky Holiday Hotel in Chongqing. Heywood had business ties with the Bo family. Shortly before his death, Heywood met with Bo Xilai's wife, Gu Kailai. Initially, the police attributed his death to excessive alcohol consumption, but it was later confirmed that he had been poisoned with cyanide.

In January 2012, Wang Lijun, Chongqing's police chief, discovered that Gu Kailai was suspected of murder and reported this to Bo Xilai. Wang played a key role in implementing Bo's "Strike Black" campaign targeting local gangsters and criminal organizations. At that time, the Party's Central Discipline and Inspection Commission had already launched an investigation into Wang's alleged corruption during his time in northeast China. It is believed that Wang sought Bo's protection. However, his request was rejected, and Wang was reportedly slapped by Bo. On February 2, Bo dismissed Wang from his post as police chief and reassigned him as vice mayor of Chongqing, in charge of education, environment, and science and technology. Officially, it was announced that Wang was on medical leave for health reasons.

Fearing for his safety, Wang fled to the U.S. Consulate in Chengdu on February 6, 2012, where he sought political asylum. Bo Xilai attempted to forcibly bring Wang back and surrounded the consulate with armed personnel. The central government eventually intervened.

On March 15, 2012, immediately after attending the National People's Congress session in Beijing, Bo Xilai was announced to have been relieved of his duties as Chongqing's party secretary. Gu Kailai was sentenced in August 2012 to death with a two-year reprieve. On September 24, 2012, Wang Lijun was sentenced to 15 years in prison by the court on charges of dereliction of duty, defection, abuse of power, and bribery. On July 25, 2013, Bo was formally charged with bribery, corruption, and abuse of power. On September 22, 2013, he was convicted and sentenced to life imprisonment.

Some say that if Wang Lijun hadn't gotten into trouble, Bo Xilai might have secured a seat on the Politburo Standing Committee at the Eighteenth Party Congress. But could a scandal alone have brought about Bo's downfall? Or was it his brazen challenge to the Party's rules that led to his removal? If his defeat was the result of a power struggle, who were Bo's allies, and who were his adversaries?

1.2 What Bo Xilai Wanted

A thorough empirical update on Bo's Chongqing saga has been long overdue.[21] The empirical foundation of our current knowledge of what Bo did and why was laid mainly by those analyses published around 2012 when Bo was purged.[22]

More importantly, these existing, decade-old explanations provide limited insight because they are uniformly *negative* answers only, concerning what it is *not*, as opposed to what it *is*. Measured against some conventional theoretical frameworks widely shared by analysts at the time—local officials competing for promotion, rule-based succession, and factional power balancing under partial institutionalization in reform-era China—Bo is depicted as an anomaly, an outlier, and an unexpected disrupter in Chinese politics.

First, departing from the presumption that Bo Xilai was competing for political advancement with other local officials in a "promotion tournament," a common negative explanation suggests that while Bo wanted to play by the rules, he did *not* play it well. According to the vast literature that searches for the systemic pattern of China's political mobility,[23] party cadres are generally rewarded by delivering good results in developing the localities under their rule, although their political careers unsurprisingly depend more fundamentally on political connection and networks, especially for those of higher rank. Thus, some analysts argue that the

"Chongqing Model-Guangdong Model" debate appeared highly politicized primarily because the strong incentives for promotion drove Bo Xilai and his Guangdong counterpart Wang Yang to stage an eye-catching public contest, while the policy substance itself amounted to nothing more than an apolitical exploration of alternative development strategies.[24]

Given this overarching framework, what Bo did is arguably nothing but his effort to impress the Party's central leadership with something new and bold. But unfortunately, Bo bungled his plan, as the negative explanation suggests, by being overly pompous and aggressive.[25] Bo was believed to have misjudged his political communication strategy.[26]

However, this explanation is obviously oversimplified, with two major puzzles remaining unsolved. First and foremost, if Bo was consciously playing by the rules, why did he opt to make some controversial moves that would potentially hurt his chances? For example, the red culture movement. Indeed, one of Bo's policy aides publicly dismissed this "promotion" perspective by pointing out that if Bo the Good Communist really cared about his political career, he would have avoided "poking the beehive," namely launching the Mao-style mass campaigns.[27] In addition, it is unclear why the high-profile contention over developmental models, best captured in the so-called Cake Debate, was even possible in the first place.[28] Open expression of political ambition by high-ranking politicians is rare,[29] not least because in authoritarian China elite-level differences are supposed to be hidden away from the public. Hence, all the unusual and dramatic elements suggest something much bigger than competition for promotion.

Second, as an effort to iron out these puzzles with a more coherent view, another popular negative explanation suggests that instead of playing by the rules, Bo Xilai was actually playing *against* the rules. That is, Bo was *not* following the informal rules that the Party had stipulated and put in place for regulating political succession and promotion in the spirit of political institutionalization.

Indeed, a quick comparison between Bo and the other two Politburo members who were purged in China's post-Deng era, namely Chen Xitong and Chen Liangyu, helps to bring in sharp relief Bo's unusual defiance of promotion rules in particular and of the Party's hierarchical order in general. Admittedly, Bo might not be so different from the two Chens in certain ways—i.e., all these cases concerned a problem of how the Party could control local officials,[30] and all involved removing an irritant to top leaders in the name of anti-corruption.[31] Nevertheless, the similarities in structural, procedural, and legalistic aspects appear to be overshadowed by striking differences from a political perspective. In particular, Bo challenged the Party's central leadership and the existing rules for selecting leaders with his own ideological programs and populist mass mobilization.[32]

It is worth noting that this story of Bo Xilai acting out of line has two versions: Bo did it either intentionally or unintentionally. One variant of the latter version describes Bo as wholeheartedly striving to innovate "socialism," or the Party's ruling mechanism, and taking measures that did look radical, but actually did not go beyond official parameters.[33] According to this account, Bo did challenge the Party politically simply because some disruption is inevitable for any reform. Another variant of the "unintentional" theory suggests that what appeared to be Bo's deliberate quest for popularity may be driven by considerations other than political ambition—i.e., Bo's charisma grew out of his own control, or Bo sought mass support only defensively, primarily as political protection, or Bo miscalculated and attracted the attention he didn't want.[34] In short, this "unintentional" theory basically takes us back to the "promotion" model, suggesting that Bo was playing by the rules but somehow did not get it right. The puzzles remained unsolved, unless we are willing to accept that Bo was a rare good communist who acted idealistically and then stumbled due to his political imprudence, and that the bizarre public debate between Chongqing and Guangdong leaders simply happened idiosyncratically without some bigger structural force at work that made it possible in the first place.

In contrast, the "intentional" theory appears more persuasive, arguing that Bo Xilai was driven by his ego and ambition. But it begs the question of what made Bo believe that he could possibly realize this ambition by what he was doing. To rephrase it, what was Bo's basis of power? Considering that Bo was a seasoned Party insider who should know well the risk of playing against the rules,[35] what was Bo counting on to protect himself from being cashiered? Moreover, in what sense could the powerless masses in authoritarian China help Bo in elite politics? No answers to these questions would possibly come from a negative theory, from which the best conclusion seems to be that Bo was ambitious insofar as he was an anomaly against some systemic patterns. Then, Bo's political demise ultimately testifies to the robustness of the Party's collective leadership and maturing political institutionalization.[36]

Third, this is where a factionalism approach comes into the picture, arguing that Bo Xilai's political campaigning in Chongqing was part of the factional struggle at the top. However, it is a *positive* explanation with numerous different, conflicting versions that end up making it *negative*—i.e., Bo seemed to belong to *none* of the established factions.[37] Once again, Bo became an anomaly.

A quick glimpse of the existing literature would tell that identifying Bo's factional affiliation requires getting the broad factional landscape right in the first place, which, unfortunately, has been elusive. The issue hinges on understanding the relationships between the Party's top leaders, especially Hu Jintao, Wen Jiabao, Jiang Zemin, and Zeng Qinghong. Who was against whom? In addition, how much power did retired Party leaders still have,[38] and whether the so-called Youth League Faction or Shanghai Gang had ever existed?[39] Finally, who did Bo side with? There are multiple interpretations, which inevitably lead to many combinations and hypotheses.[40] Stories about where Bo positioned himself in the grand chessboard of Chinese elite politics vary according to one's presumption about Bo's relationships with key political players. Specifically, who were Bo's supporters and who were his rivals? Whether Hu Jintao was for or against Bo,[41] whether Jiang Zemin was backing or opposing Bo,[42] and to what extent other top party leaders viewed Bo as a political asset or liability?[43] While factional infighting seemed undeniably present, the conventional analytical framework that presumes the existence of some major factional groupings led by top party leaders brought only confusion. Given this general paradigmatic incapacity, it was once argued that Bo Xilai was a special case in China's factional politics, where factional defection and cross-factional conspiracies are not impossible.[44] However, simply acknowledging that the relations between Bo and the members of the Party leadership were complicated—conditioned and influenced by unknown emotions of idiosyncratic mutual likes and dislikes that permeate the criss-crossing networks of patronage and political blue blood—provides little analytical clarity and insight.[45]

To be sure, how to accurately discern factional ties is a perennial problem that haunts the factionalism approach like a specter. Analysts typically identify factional linkages and networks through party leaders' résumés and biographies, assuming that certain types of relationships—such as shared birthplace, kinship, friendship, educational background, and, most importantly, work experience—bind them together politically.[46] However, observable indicators of potential factional groupings do not necessarily reveal real factional ties, which are often unobservable. Moreover, politicians possess multiple identities that may place them in different factions. Worse, factional affiliation is a matter of choice and may change over time, as the power structure at the top leadership is constantly reconfigured and realigned.[47]

In short, from these existing negative explanations we see a Bo inflated with ambition, who turned out to be an anomaly, an outlier, and an unexpected disrupter in Chinese politics. But it is an oversimplified sketch. Additional issues abound.

One important question is why Bo chose a *conservative* path? A popular view is that Bo's Chongqing story had nothing to do with a conservative-reformist struggle. Instead, it was essentially an interest-driven fight over political seats.[48] Political actors were motivated by ambition, personal loyalty, and unresolved feuds. It follows that Bo's policy choices were mainly strategic. In particular, Bo's leaning to the left was a response to the structural demands of Chinese politics at the time—the Party's anxious search for new grounds of political legitimacy, the widespread socioeconomic injustice and inequality that caused Hu-Wen's policy shift, and the intellectual undecidedness about how to balance the role of the state versus market economy.[49] In this light, Bo's use of ideological elements was purely instrumental. The Maoist revolutionary language proved to be a convenient tool for political mobilization, effective in stirring up and exploiting public anger, as it reminded the people of class enemies and revolutionary ideals.[50] Bo's left-turn then seemed to be a predetermined choice. It aligns well with not only the political culture of communist China in general, but also a major prudential rule in Chinese politics—i.e., it's better to stay with the Left than with the Right (*ning zuo wu you*),[51] pointing to the long shadow of Mao's legacy.[52]

However, structural conditions and strategic considerations do not necessarily lead to one particular ideological inclination. Indeed, the embrace of political conservatism would be a self-defeating choice if reformism still remained the unchallengeable ideological hegemony in China. Would not a reformist profile be equally or even more attractive in the reform era? Furthermore, a close scrutiny shows that Bo's Chongqing policy programs were not purely leftist in the early days; there was something for everyone.[53] Then, why this mixture?

Another question is whether Bo was purged simply because he was who he was—a political maverick, arrogant, disruptive and uncontrollable, who flagrantly broke the rules, too openly exposed socio-political problems to the public, threatened fellow elites and major vested interests, and played with fire by reviving Mao-style mass movement?[54] But are these reasons sufficient for shooting Bo down, given the high political cost of making elite division public? Why purge, and why not simply sidelining Bo?

In fact, Bo's fall from power was quite unusual, considering that the Party usually extends privileges and protection to the children of its founding revolutionaries, or the "red descendants" (*hongse houdai*) who believe that they are born with the right to rule China.[55] Unwittingly highlighting his political high caste, Bo stressed in his trial that he and Xu Ming, who was charged with participating in Bo's corruption scheme, "are not on the same level."[56] Interestingly, despite being so disparaged by Bo, Xu Ming chose to leave his foreign sanctuary and flew back from Australia, even after Bo was arrested in 2012, believing that Bo could survive and their business would go back to normal eventually.[57]

Relatedly, was the Wang Lijun scandal by itself serious enough to be the last straw that unified the factionalized party leadership and made the purge doable?[58] Rather than being a mere incident, Wang's scandalous flight into a U.S. consulate was arguably an unexpected trigger for a bomb that had already been set to blow Bo up. Before moving against a political opponent, capturing their key allies is a common tactic in Chinese political struggles. In fact, an investigation into Wang's criminal record had been underway for some time as he desperately sought protection from the Americans. This was a strong sign of a factional scheme to target Bo through Wang, his top aide in Chongqing.[59] In this light, although the Wang Lijun scandal occurred immediately before Bo's fall, the former alone was not powerful enough to cause the latter.

Finally, how can we explain the bizarre pattern of *open* political communication in China during Hu Jintao's final years and Bo's time in Chongqing? Political views from the Left and the Right clashed with one another; arguments that deviated from, questioned, criticized, or even rejected the Party's past and current policies emerged one after another. This peculiar openness at the time prompted one observer to describe the situation as China's "quasi-democratic" era without democratic institutions and rules.[60] Another salient phenomenon was the wide circulation of political rumors, many of which, paradoxically, were later verified as true. Western media played an indispensable role in this picture. Chinese political insiders strategically used foreigners to get their messages out, spreading both true and false information.[61] China's internet firewall was even briefly disabled soon after Bo was removed from the political stage, making overseas information on Bo accessible to the Chinese public.[62] Further adding to the perplexing nature of this brief period of openness was the peculiar timing of the *New York Times'* report—months after Bo was stripped of his Chongqing title—on the "hidden riches" of the family of Wen Jiabao, then Chinese Premier, who was commonly believed to be one of Bo's opponents.[63]

All these clues suggest something bigger going on behind the scenes. In other words, what were the *structural* conditions necessary for Bo to exercise his egoistic agency? Bo is widely believed to have been the mastermind who started everything: he sensed the social grievance, seized the opportunities, exploited available resources, and took proactive actions.[64] But is that really the case? Was Bo directing the drama or simply dancing to the music?

Ironically, all these *negative* frameworks went bankrupt soon after Bo fell from power in 2012, when Xi Jinping became the Party's general secretary. Xi's strongman rule has effectively put an end to the paradigm of institutionalization that once dominated the study of Chinese politics. A peculiar coincidence here is that the de-institutionalization of Chinese politics under Xi in effect made Xi look like another anomaly against these institutionalization frameworks, just like Bo. It suggests that the historical connection between Bo and Xi, who came after Bo was purged, probably goes much deeper than the temporal level. Indeed, a revisit to the Bo Xilai story is worthwhile, not only for its own sake but also because it may shed new light on Xi's rise. Ultimately, we need a new, *positive* understanding of Bo's political behaviors.

1.3 Arguments

The main empirical finding is that Chongqing under Bo experienced major policy adjustment three times and went through four different phases: reformism, leftism, Maoism, and finally, opportunism. It suggests that Bo's political maneuvering was not a premeditated plan he simply rolled out upon his arrival in Chongqing, and that Bo did not begin his Chongqing tenure already firmly committed to the path of political conservatism. Instead, his factional identity evolved and his political orientation shifted over time. But *to what* was Bo responding?

The book argues that Bo's political show in Chongqing was a local chapter of the factional infighting at the central level between two political coalitions: the reformers and the conservatives.

The point of departure for this narrative is the observation that Xi's eventual centralization of power has its origin in a long decade of left–right struggles spanning the entire Hu Jintao era and Xi's early years.[65] This reform–conservative contestation can be seen as a continuation of the struggle that began in the early 1980s over the political and ideological direction of China's reform. After his 1992 Southern Tour, Deng Xiaoping decisively suppressed conservative opposition and pushed forward market-oriented economic reform, but he was neither willing nor able to eradicate leftist forces entirely. For the party leadership, full-scale reforms risked undermining the vested interests of party elites and even threatened the Party's ruling position. Deng's reformist spirit never went that far.[66] In 2002, the Sixteenth Party Congress report delivered by Jiang Zemin proposed a relatively progressive plan for further political and economic reforms, but after Hu Jintao came to power, the leftist backlash intensified. Initially, the struggle started as a *policy* dispute, concerning China's state-owned enterprise (SOE) reform, but gradually shifted into a *political* contention. The key issue, in a nutshell, was the political direction of "Socialism with Chinese Characteristics"—should it emphasize *Chinese* particularity to break away from the socialist model, or should it uphold *socialism* as the guiding framework for China's reform? Political conservatism soared and the left–right contention intensified sharply during Hu's second term (2007–2012). Chinese leftists emphasized ideological supremacy of socialism and fiercely criticized the reformist camp's embrace of "universal values." Bo Xilai's political programs rolled out in Chongqing can be seen as the most forceful expression of the conservative backlash: it not only elevated leftist rhetoric to a Maoist level, but also translated leftist ideals into concrete policies and mass mobilization in the streets. China's reformist force regained the upper hand around the Eighteenth Party Congress held in 2012 but the comeback turned out to be ephemeral. A final defeat of the reformers by the conservative coalition occurred around 2015, followed shortly by Xi's formal inauguration as the Party's "core" leader in 2016.

This is the political wind at the top to which Bo was responding. The Seventeenth Party Congress held in 2007 still sent mixed political signals. A reformist call for further reform appeared in the central place in the congress report, although it turned out that the framing of the agenda reflected a conservative takeover. Hu Jintao introduced the idea of "Ten Combinations," emphasizing the unity of reform and political loyalty. Leftist theorists began to propagate the idea that it was Mao, not Deng, who truly initiated the reform and opening-up era. They promoted the "Two Thirty Years" thesis, which sought to rehabilitate the Mao era by presenting it as equally valuable as the post-1978 reform period, effectively whitewashing its disasters. Jiang Zemin's "Three Represents" theory was demoted—it failed to achieve the status of the "third great leap" in the "sinicization of Marxism," and was instead grouped together with Deng Xiaoping Theory and Hu's Scientific Outlook on Development under a broader theoretical framework of Socialism with Chinese Characteristics. The underlying message was that the *socialist* framework that had been loosened during the Jiang era was being reinstated. However, after the Seventeenth Party Congress, Guangdong's party secretary Wang Yang launched a sweeping campaign of "mind emancipation," inspiring other provinces to follow suit and giving the impression that a new wave of reform was gaining momentum.

This is why Bo's Chongqing policies initially followed the reformist playbook in 2008 (Chap. 2). The policies Bo put forward in his early days prioritized the Dengist reform over pro-poor objectives. Bo launched a pompous campaign to promote the idea of "mind emancipation," a term strongly symbolic of reformism. Bo's "Sing Red" movement was initially framed in a non-ideological fashion.

The following years, or Hu Jintao's second term, saw a rising tide of leftism against further political and economic liberalization. Politically, the Fourth Plenum of the Seventeenth Central Committee revisited the same party-building theme discussed five years earlier, signaling that reformist proposals for professionalism and technocratic governance had stalled. Economically, SOE reform came to a halt and began to reverse, accompanied by the rise of the so-called China Model, which emphasized the success of state-led development. Ideologically, leftist defenders of political orthodoxy spoke out loudly about safeguarding the dominant position of Marxist theory and socialist ideology. They often invoked the Soviet Union's collapse as a cautionary tale about the importance of maintaining ideological conviction, while denouncing the reformist narrative as "historical nihilism" and blaming it for distorting and maligning the CCP's past. Leftist theoreticians also sought to highlight Deng Xiaoping's more left-leaning positions—his concern about socioeconomic inequality in his final years—and began promoting the idea of "common prosperity." Some went even further, openly challenging core reformist principles. For instance, whereas Deng had urged the Party to guard primarily against "leftist" tendencies, the leftists insisted that the main threat now came from the right, i.e., the reformist camp.

In Chongqing, there came an observable shift in Bo's political orientation from reformism to leftism (Chap. 3). Bo's "Sing Red" movement went through an ideologized re-framing that now emphasized socialist values. Chongqing's urban planning project also became ideologized, with the focus shifted from development to socialist spirit. In the realm of economic policy, redistribution was given higher priority than growth. Party cadres' technocratic ability was de-emphasized as Bo sent local officials down to villages to reconnect with the masses. Bo launched the "Strike Black" campaign, reminiscent of the campaign-style political purges from the Mao era.

During the 2010–2011 period, Bo moved away from his earlier role as a *follower* who had advanced leftist policies within the limits set by central guidelines and recast himself as a Maoist *vanguard*, making a series of bold moves that challenged the political paradigm of reformism (Chap. 4). Bo's signature programs included a call for "common prosperity" and the "Chongqing Model." Indicative of a peculiar connection between Bo and the conservatives force at the central level, Bo's revival of "mass spontaneity" in mass mobilization was later replicated in central-level rectification campaigns. Highly unusual was the reversed flow of political initiative and guidance from a locality to the party center.

However, toward the end of Hu's final years, the balance of power seemed to be shifting against the conservatives. At the Sixth Plenum of the Seventeenth Central Committee, a party conference dedicated to the agenda of developing "socialist culture," the reformers effectively downplayed the Marxist ideological elements and put greater emphasis instead on forging solidarity to achieve modernization. In his "July 1" speech commemorating the Party's 90th anniversary in 2011, Hu Jintao focused on the "scientification" of party building, highlighting the reformers' continued political strength and persistence in pushing for technocracy and institutionalization. On the eve of the Eighteenth Party Congress, Jiang Zemin made a rare public appearance at an event commemorating the historical formulation of the "socialist market economy" concept in the early 1990s, using the occasion to call for continued reform. The transient reformist fightback at the time is evidenced by the progressive agenda on economic and political reforms later put forward at the Eighteenth Party Congress held in 2012, and the subsequent third and fourth party plenums convened in 2013 and 2014, which focused on the "decisive" role of the market and "governance according to law," respectively.

In response, Bo had to adjust his posture with both caution and opportunistic acumen (Chap. 5). On the one hand, around late 2011, Bo had decided to temper the Maoist momentum of his political campaigning. This is evident from Bo's public denial of pursuing a "Chongqing Model" and from his last-minute effort to reframe and truncate some of his major policy programs. On the other hand, Bo still held onto his general alignment with the leftist camp. Bo signaled his determination by putting the Common Prosperity blueprint into practice—i.e., extracting wealth from private entrepreneurs and redistributing it to the poor in the name of developing the private sector.

In short, by correlating Bo's shifting political orientation in Chongqing with the bigger picture of left–right contestation within the party leadership, the book offers a *positive* explanation of what Bo did and why: Bo's Chongqing adventure *is* part of the two-line-struggle at the time among the party oligarchs. Figure 1.1 illustrates this argument. By providing an alternative framework that more accurately maps the political landscape than the narrative of political institutionalization in reform-era China, this conservative-versus-reformist perspective effectively turns what is conventionally believed to be abnormal into something that reflects the undercurrent of Chinese elite politics. This perspective also allows us to locate the bigger force behind Bo's agency. It is observed that the Maoist revival at the time appeared to be a broad political climate change, with political endorsement from above, rather than Bo Xilai's personal initiative.[67] Moreover, the purge of Bo in early 2012 didn't restrain the conservative party theoreticians from continuing to talk about common prosperity, suggesting that it was something beyond Bo's individual strategy.[68] It seems more likely that, rather than the leftist forces hitching a ride on Bo's campaign, it was Bo who chose to ride the coattails of the former.

We can find further corroboration for this positive explanation by looking at Bo's peculiar invocation of "mass spontaneity" in the context of China's post-Mao rectification campaigns (Chap. 6). The fact that Bo deliberately sought to revive rhetoric that called for the autonomy of the masses, or bottom-up input, in mass campaigns that he in fact launched from the top down, though largely at the level of symbolism rather than genuine implementation, marked a conspicuous break with the reform-era tradition of political demobilization. Moreover, the timing of Bo's taboo-breaking move testified to its extraordinary political significance. It occurred during a period of fierce political infighting, as illustrated by a longitudinal view of the varying political intensity of China's reform-era

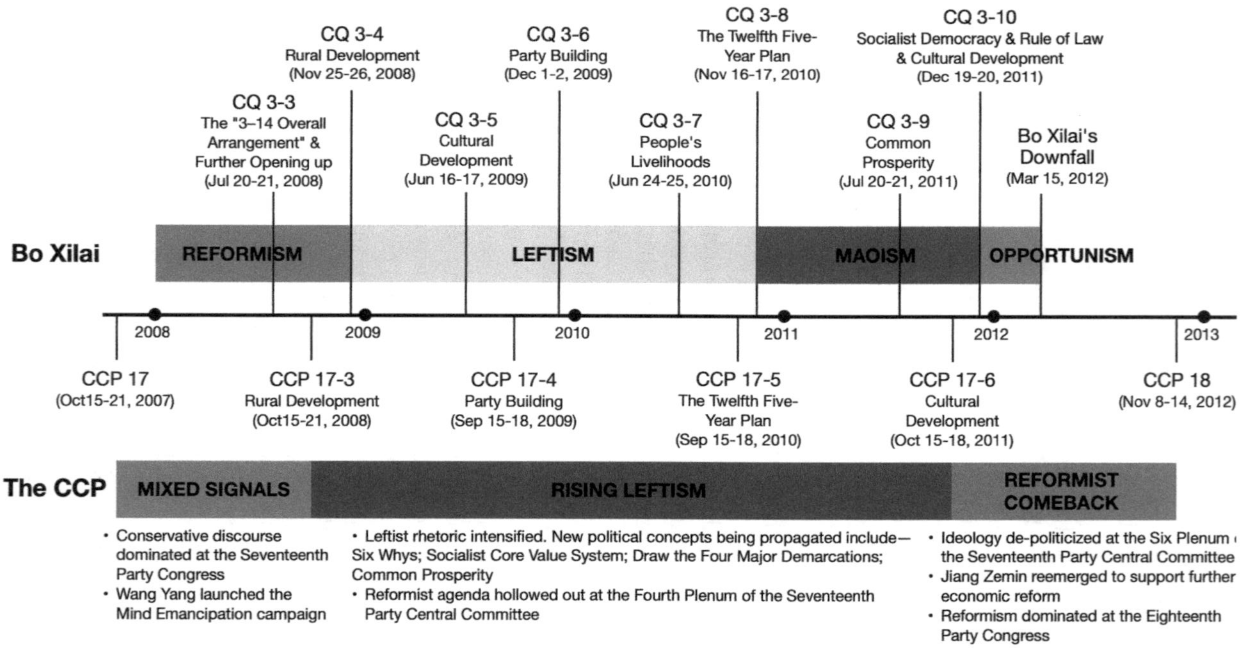

Fig. 1.1 Bo Xilai's shifting political orientation in relation to central-level political struggles. Note: Each CQ X-X refers to a specific party conference held by the Chongqing Party Committee. Each CCP X-X refers to a specific party conference held by the CCP at the central level. For example, CQ 3-3 is the Third Plenum of Chongqing's Third Party Committee; CCP 17 is the Seventeenth Party Congress; CCP 17-3 is the Third Plenum of the Seventeenth Party Central Committee. Conference themes and dates appear below the conference titles

rectification campaigns, which can be negatively correlated with the intensity of elite power struggle.

Playing the mass card is taboo, however, for a reason. The crux is the Party's conceptual manipulation of the party-people relationship and its unintended consequence in the current age of democracy (Chap. 7). The Chinese autocrats constantly face a dilemma: how to maintain political domination over the people while persuading the latter that they are the master. In communist China, the Party engineered a murky idea of party-people "oneness" to tackle this problem. But crises arise whenever political elites mobilize the masses in power struggles. Invoking the spirit of popular sovereignty always sows the seeds of political enlightenment that can make the ruled realize their rights vis-à-vis the ruler. In this sense, Mao's Great Proletarian Cultural Revolution delivered the first lesson to the Chinese masses through a limited exercise of Maoist "big democracy." Inspired by the Mao-era "rebels," China's neo-Maoists, who yearned for a second Cultural Revolution, sought to hijack Bo's conservative project, even as Bo tried to distance himself from these radicals. Bo's call for mass spontaneity did, to some extent, backfire.

1.4 Primary Sources

This book presents a historical narrative of Bo Xilai's Chongqing story in chronological order, beginning with his assumption of power in Chongqing in early 2008 and concluding with his political downfall in early 2012. The analysis is grounded in extensive reading and parsing of political texts.

The most important primary source is *Chongqing ribao* (or *Chongqing Daily*, December 2007 to June 2012), the official mouthpiece of the Chongqing Party Committee. The author was fortunate to access the print editions of this newspaper during fieldwork in China. Unlike the heavily censored electronic versions available in online databases, the print editions provide a complete and uncensored view of this key political text. *Chongqing Daily* was reportedly edited, vetted, and approved by Bo Xilai himself prior to daily publication.[69] Therefore, the content it conveys is regarded as an accurate reflection of Bo's political will.

Complementing the *Chongqing Daily* is *Jinri Chongqing* (or *Chongqing Today*, issues from 2008 No. 1 to 2012 No. 6), a political and external publicity magazine supervised and guided by the Chongqing Propaganda Department and managed by the *Chongqing Daily* editorial team. While there is some overlap between *Chongqing Today* and the *Chongqing Daily* on key political events, the former often features more vivid, pictorial reporting. Like the *Chongqing Daily*, the digital version of *Chongqing Today* is also subject to censorship and control; the author relied on paper copies to access its full content.

Academic journals published by Chinese research institutions also constitute an important source of information. Local Chongqing publications include *Tansuo* (Exploration), overseen and published by the Chongqing Party School; *Gaige* (Reform), managed and published by the Chongqing Academy of Social Sciences; *Chongqing xingzheng* (Chongqing Administration), supervised by the Chongqing government and published by the Chongqing Academy of Administration; and the *Chongqing Blue Book* series, edited by the Chongqing Academy of Social Sciences. The texts selected for analysis cover publications from 2008 to 2012 that focus on Bo Xilai and related political and policy issues. The study also draws on special-issue articles on Chongqing published in journals not based in Chongqing, such as *Renmin luntan* (People's Forum).

In addition, the author collected a wide range of official propaganda materials related to Chongqing politics between 2008 and 2012 through various channels. These materials fall into several main categories: (1) promotional booklets published by the Chongqing Propaganda Department that outline and elaborate official policies; (2) anthologies of articles or papers presented at academic conferences held in Chongqing that focused on the city's politics and policies, as well as monographs written by scholars or research teams on topics such as the "Chongqing Model" and "common prosperity"; and (3) internal official documents not intended for public distribution. Some of these materials were accessed through local libraries in Chongqing, while others were obtained from secondhand book sellers and flea markets. Owing to political censorship, some serialized publications are incomplete, and only individual volumes could be acquired.

Finally, online writings also serve as an important source of information. In addition to publicly available newsletters and interviews, particular attention is given to the online commentary of Su Wei, a scholar at the Chongqing Party School. Su Wei's online writings are often far more radical and direct than those found in official media outlets. Some of his pieces elaborate on Bo's decisions, while others defend them forcefully. With regard to discourse from the radical Maoist camp, the primary sources are articles published on the grassroots Maoist website Wu You Zhi Xiang (Utopia) and in its online periodical *Dianzi Ban Yue Kan* (Digital Biweekly Journal).

Drawing on these textual materials, this book traces the shifts in Bo Xilai's political orientation during his tenure in Chongqing. The focus is on the political and policy dimensions of his rule rather than on excavating the previously unknown details of the scandals that preceded his downfall. The book also seeks to explore Bo's political motivations—the ideas and logic behind his policies and behaviors. Of course, these are necessarily inferences based on limited evidence, not definitive conclusions. As such, whenever the narrative points to Bo Xilai's intentions or thinking, it should be understood as an interpretation rather than a factual claim. As more historical materials become available in the future, the account offered here may be revised or corroborated accordingly.

1.5 Autocrats Going Public

From a theoretical perspective,[70] Bo Xilai's dramatic political campaigning—marked by opportunistic policy shifts and large-scale mass mobilization reminiscent of Mao-era politics—is a quintessential case of "autocrats going public," a concept that describes how elite-level political struggles in authoritarian regimes strategically use public information. Bo's actions illustrate the political logic behind making internal power struggles deliberately visible. Elite infighting under autocracy, though often shrouded in deep secrecy, is not entirely a black box. Precisely because those in power control the public information space, the publicization of political discourse and actions becomes a means of leveraging autocratic power—a strategic tool for elites engaged in power struggles. Authoritarian elites must signal strength and rally allies by releasing public cues, which, ironically, offers outside observers rare glimpses into the regime's inner workings.

1.5.1 Authoritarian Politics and Information

The existing literature on the role of information in authoritarian politics tends to focus more on *state-society* relations than on *intra-elite* politics. Specifically, it examines how authoritarian rulers control the flow of information to manage, monitor, and suppress social forces in order to maintain regime stability.[71] This includes: (1) political propaganda and thought control,[72] as well as censorship and surveillance;[73] (2) displays of power to deter rebellion by projecting elite unity or an image of political invincibility[74]—thereby discouraging opposition by suppressing expectations of change, eliminating focal points for mobilization, and intimidating potential challengers.[75] Public political rituals also serve to enforce behavioral compliance[76] and prevent the emergence of oppositional signals or grassroots foundations.[77] (3) At times, authoritarian rulers intentionally allow limited expressions of popular discontent as a way to gauge public sentiment and monitor local officials,[78] helping to bridge the regime's information gap.[79]

In contrast, how authoritarian elites manipulate information in the course of internal power struggles for political communication and collective action purposes remains undertheorized and understudied. One obvious reason is factual: autocratic politics is nontransparent by nature, which makes observation from the outside difficult. Another reason, however, is analytical—the "dictator" is often assumed to be a single individual while it is often a collective body.[80] The latter depiction aligns with empirical realities, where persistent infighting among authoritarian elites often determines the fate of regimes. Most theories start from the widely cited premise that the dictator does not rule alone. However, this simple dichotomy between the dictator and other ruling elites obscures key political dynamics—a theoretical negligence that echoes the literature's emphasis on state-society relations. The internal structure of the top leadership is itself a variable, ranging from a single paramount leader to an oligarchic body composed of multiple actors with comparable power.

Due to the non-transparent nature of authoritarianism, scholars have to look at something observable. Existing research on the role of information in leadership politics under authoritarianism has largely focused on how *institutions* help address the central structural problem of power sharing.[81] Specifically, how can authoritarian rulers ensure adherence to established power-sharing arrangements without resorting to force? This centers on the problem of credible commitment—a challenge present in all human organizations but especially acute under autocracy,[82] where no third-party enforcer exists to uphold agreements, and violence remains the final arbiter of disputes.[83] Political secrecy, in this context, is more than just an expression of autocratic obsession with control. While secrecy allows leaders to shield themselves from internal threats, it also imposes a strategic "blindness" that affects all players. This opacity simultaneously empowers and weakens everyone involved, locking them into a suboptimal dynamic where trust is scarce and fear is constant.

This is where institutions come into play. Scholars have argued that information and publicity can help mitigate the credible commitment problem. Regularized interactions and formal rules—such as legislatures and term limits—facilitate information sharing and enhance transparency. These mechanisms reduce unnecessary misunderstandings, enable negotiation, lower transaction costs, mediate conflicts, curb individual ambition, and help orient all actors toward long-term cooperation.[84] Moreover, formal rules serve as publicly observable signals; they provide monitoring tools that make deviations from or noncompliance with power-sharing arrangements more detectable.[85] (Of course, scholars acknowledge that it is ultimately the balance of power—not informational mechanisms alone—that sustains such arrangements.)[86]

However, the institutional approach to authoritarian elite politics is limited in two key respects. For one thing, this approach offers a static view only. It theorizes the conditions under which power-sharing commitments may become credible, while power struggles are inherently dynamic processes that evolve over time. More importantly, it largely overlooks a more intuitive and observable form of information: what autocrats say, write, and do in *public*.[87]

1.5.2 Authoritarian Politics and Publicity

Indeed, contrary to intuitive presumption, authoritarian power struggles often involve the strategic use of *public* information, rather than operating entirely in *secrecy*. This calculated openness serves multiple functions: rallying and mobilizing political allies, demonstrating political strength, and lobbying for support within the elite and from the public through persuasion.[88]

First, making one's voice heard in public is itself a demonstration of power; silence, by contrast, signals weakness. This is because the authoritarian public sphere is fundamentally a field of power. The varying authoritativeness of media outlets often reflects the distribution of political power; in such systems, it is not merely about *what* gets published, but *who* has the right to publicize. Gaining access to these platforms requires political strength. The ability to make one's political stance visible corresponds directly to one's rank within the power structure, to the type of media involved, and to the purpose it serves. In short, the regime's control over the information space means that the content circulating publicly can be read as a faithful reflection of what is politically salient at a given moment.[89]

From the standpoint of a unified state, elite disunity is undesirable and potentially destabilizing. However, when internal channels of influence and bargaining no longer suffice—when rival elites are too divided to resolve disputes behind closed doors—they are compelled to go public. In such cases, publicizing power struggles becomes a way to tap into the authority and influence embedded in the authoritarian public sphere.

Second, publicized information on key issues is often politically encrypted: internal conflicts are concealed from the general public while signals are still communicated to insiders. This is achieved through the use of political jargon. On the surface, such language may appear vague or formulaic, but its true meaning lies in its context and in the historical evolution of its usage. Typically, high-level official documents employ ambiguous terms that tend toward balance and compromise, while more direct political signals and discourse appear in lower-level outlets. Strong political signals do, of course, sometimes appear in top-tier official media, usually indicating that one faction has gained the upper hand. When power is evenly balanced, politicians may create new channels to convey their messages. Together, high- and low-level information channels form a comprehensive political communication system characterized by mutual contextualization. By interpreting political discourses, observers can assess political trends and the relative strength of factions. Ironically, such informed conjecture is made possible precisely because autocrats feel compelled to publicize certain messages themselves.

Last but not least, beyond language, there are actions: political mobilization—organizing people to take to the streets—is a more direct form of political signaling and a demonstration of power. This relates to the notion of "mass support" in authoritarian politics. We often speak of elites seeking mass support or of the masses rising up to back particular leaders. But what, precisely, can the masses contribute to political elites in their power struggles?

Mass mobilization often appears to imply a notion of power rooted in physical strength. Scholars frequently cite examples where street protests have overcome military repression and even toppled regimes.[90] However, this perspective overlooks a critical factor: the strength of the regime or, more specifically, the state's capacity for repression. Put simply, mass support appears politically influential largely because the ruling regime lacks sufficient power—often due to an unstable relationship between the dictator and the military—to effectively deter mass mobilization and, crucially, prevent its escalation.[91]

More importantly, the primary significance of mass support and mass mobilization lies in their *informational* function. Whether mobilization occurs signals the strength or weakness of those in power.[92] For opposition forces, mass movements shape expectations, affect the unity or disunity of ruling elites, and help political elites coordinate their decisions to overcome collective action problems.[93] A key factor in political calculations about whether to defect is elites' perception of the regime's survivability and the associated uncertainty about their future benefits.[94] The informational role of mass mobilization is also reflected in the legitimacy it represents; popular dissatisfaction points to a potentially correct political alignment.[95]

Of course, mass mobilization is not always spontaneous; it can be orchestrated. In cases where the party-state has achieved a high degree of social penetration, many mass campaigns and movements are state-organized. This kind of top-down mobilization rarely permits autonomous actions or free expression of ideas by mass participants, although it is possible for state-led movements to resonate with the genuine normative orientations and preferences of the people.[96]

In sum, autocrats do go public. Elite power struggles in authoritarian regimes often unfold through the strategic use of publicity (i.e., through public discourse and mass mobilization), rather than remaining entirely secret. The sphere of public information under the state control is essentially a field of power, allowing political actors to signal strength, rally support, and influence factional dynamics.

This is the theoretical lens through which we may better grasp the political nature and significance of what Bo Xilai did in the context of Chinese politics. Set against the backdrop of China's left right struggles, Bo's deliberate framing of political discourse and orchestration of mass campaigns reveal how authoritarian elites in China strategically wield and manipulate public information to serve their internal power struggles.

Common explanations attribute the apparent political pluralism during the Hu Jintao era to China's decades of opening up to the outside world and advances in information technology—factors said to exceed the Party's control—and they often see Bo's Maoist mass campaigns as only possible due to the increasing institutionalization of competition within China's political system. What few have considered is that this fleeting period of openness may actually have resulted from internal party disunity that led to the party-state's momentary loss of control over the public sphere. What we witnessed was not genuine openness, but rather authoritarian rulers exploiting public information channels to send political signals during intense elite conflict.

1.6 Political Identities in Chinese Politics

The core argument of this book engages with a range of political labels associated with Bo Xilai's multiple ideological shifts, including reformist, leftist, conservative, and Maoist. This section provides a brief overview of these key terms.[97]

The meanings of "left" and "right" in the politics of communist China differ significantly from their Western counterparts. The Chinese Left is rooted in the global communist and socialist movements and is closely linked to class struggle. Broadly speaking, the Chinese Left symbolizes support for proletarian revolution. During the Mao era, counterrevolutionaries were labeled "rightists," a term with strongly negative connotations. Functionally, *left* and *right* serve primarily as positional labels distinguishing allies from enemies, and their specific political meanings shift with changing political circumstances. Since the 1990s, the boundary between *left* and *right* in China has centered on several key political divides: ideologically, whether China's development should adhere to Marxism–Leninism–Maoism principles or embrace universal values; politically, whether the Party or the law holds primacy; economically, whether market forces or state control should dominate; socially, whether the Marxist tenet of class struggle remains relevant; and in governance, whether political legitimacy derives from revolutionary spirit or technocratic competence.

The Chinese Left champions socialist principles. Those who advocate abandoning the socialist path are labeled rightists by the Left. The Chinese Right, by contrast, usually call themselves *reformers*, emphasizing support for the reform and opening-up agenda. To be sure, a reformist identity does not necessarily entail a commitment to transforming China into a liberal democracy. Support for liberalization—a market economy, openness to the world, and limited political reform—can coexist with support for one-party rule. Reformers sometimes call the Left *conservatives* because the Left seeks to preserve the socialist doctrines inherited from the Mao era. These leftists are often referred to as the "Old Left," in contrast to the "New Left," a group of Chinese intellectuals who emerged during the reform era and are known for their critical views of capitalism from the perspective of Western postmodernism and neo-Marxist thought.[98] However, the New Left has no substantive political base comparable to that of the Old Left.

Leftists generally embrace the Left label far more readily than reformers accept being called rightists. This is because the Left has been a symbol of political correctness and revolutionary legitimacy in the CCP's political culture since its inception. That said, leftist elites seldom openly proclaim their leftist identity. The Left label is also burdened politically by its association with Mao's Cultural Revolution, which is seen as a liability during the reform era. Those who nostalgically support Mao's Cultural Revolution are typically called Maoists or radical leftists. While many senior party officials harbor Maoist sympathies, Maoists are more widespread among the general population. Ordinary people who grew up during the Mao era, who gained little from the reform era, and who witnessed the widening wealth gap and deepening official corruption, sometimes look back fondly on the Cultural Revolution's anti-bureaucratic spirit.

Given the presence of Maoists, distinguishing between orthodox leftism and radical leftism—without undermining the political legitimacy of the Left—is an important issue. The CCP's official approach is to refer to Mao's Cultural Revolution as a special case of "leftism" with quotation marks. These quotation marks signal a boundary: it is the radical leftism that must be criticized, not the true revolutionary leftism. This allows the CCP leadership to take a middle path—supporting the genuine leftism, opposing Mao's radical leftism, and resisting liberalizing tendencies on the right.

The political struggle between *left* and *right* is officially termed "line struggle" within the Party's official discourse. Victors are typically portrayed as having discovered and led the correct line, while deviations are labeled as leftist or rightist "errors." The political backdrop of Bo Xilai's story, as depicted in this book, is precisely such a left–right line struggle between the conservatives defending socialist fundamentalism and the reformers advocating liberalization—that unfolded during Hu Jintao's final years over the issue of China's reform direction. This conflict is essentially a continuation of the left–right struggle that began in the early 1980s.

1.7 Populism in Authoritarian China

Beyond the political identities discussed above—left and right, conservative and reformist, and variants of Maoism—another political image has also been active in modern Chinese politics: populist. Although not indigenous to China's political culture, it has repeatedly surfaced throughout the Party's political history. Populism is more typically associated with democratic systems, or at least with polities that feature electoral institutions and some space for opposition. Yet even within China's highly authoritarian system, it has a discernible presence.

In the case of Bo Xilai, while many China scholars and journalists call Bo a *populist*, it is left unclear what it exactly means by referring to what Bo did in Chongqing as *populism*.

In this book, the terms "populist" and "populism" are used to refer to a specific type of political behavior, when political leaders frame political struggle, either explicitly or implicitly, as a moralized confrontation between "us" and "them," or between good and evil; claim to embody the true will of the people; present themselves as rooted in the grassroots; and utilize mass mobilization to signal factional alignment and project political strength. In some cases, such strategies may even involve the instrumental use of popular anger and mobbish action to target political opponents.

This definition fits well within the three major mainstream approaches to populism. Chinese politics sometimes looks unambiguously populist. In particular, wherever party leaders mobilized the Chinese masses against the "counter-revolutionary" capitalists and the "enemies" of the people, we can see the *ideational* spirit of populism at work in a battle between the pure people versus the corrupt elite, based on a Manichaean divide within the society between those who stand for popular sovereignty and those against it.[99] Mao's Cultural Revolution is probably the best manifestation of populism *strategically* defined in the Chinese context: a personalistic leader seeks or exercises power based on direct and unmediated support from the unorganized masses,[100] though such uninstitutionalized political mobilization is by and large a general feature of China's political system where power is unconstrained and hierarchically distributed, and by no means Mao's one-time invention. Finally, a *sociocultural* conceptualization of populism, i.e., "flaunting of the low,"[101] is visible from time to time in Chinese politics where the Party self-claims to represent the interests of the oppressed proletariats against the capitalist upper class. This sentiment is best captured in a Mao quote that "the lowly is the cleverest, while the noble is the most stupid."

Certainly, populism in authoritarian China differs fundamentally from its counterparts in democratic settings, even if they share common definitional elements. However, as a general concept, populism should be able to travel across contexts. Variation in its manifestations does not entail a corresponding shift in its conceptual core, which should remain stable. The key question, then, is: *how is it possible* in communist China? How can anti-establishment opposition, which is by definition a central element of populist politics,[102] exist under a regime that suppresses dissent both from below and within? Research on populism under full authoritarianism remains limited, likely because such regimes typically operate through political *demobilization*, a logic at odds with populist mobilization.

Unfortunately, a growing literature on populism in Chinese politics remains largely detached from the broader populism scholarship, particularly in its lack of engagement with the crucial "how is it possible" question. Many researchers proceed by uncritically labeling authoritarian phenomena as populist, simply matching empirical fragments to definitional elements derived from democratic contexts. While certain rhetoric, discourses, and behaviors under authoritarianism may sound and look populist, this alone does not establish the existence of populist politics if we cannot explain how it could operate in such a setting. The result is a risk of conceptual stretching and misidentification.[103]

A major problem is that much of the literature is not actually about populism as a distinct political phenomenon. Instead, "populism" is used as a catch-all label for disparate issues—legal responsiveness to public opinion,[104] rural protest against inequality and corruption,[105] or state paternalism vis-à-vis the global trend of neoliberalism.[106] What unites these usages is a vague appeal to "the people." So-called populist authoritarianism often simply refers to a governing technique rooted in the Maoist tradition.[107] Closely related is the tendency to conflate populism with other ideologies, especially nationalism.[108]

Even studies explicitly addressing populism in China generally fail to explain how anti-establishment opposition can exist under authoritarian rule. One approach is to find a surrogate for "anti-establishment" while asserting that Chinese populism is different.[109] For instance, populism in China is viewed as a governing technique for maintaining authoritarian control over society.[110] The Chinese party-state adopts "populist" rhetoric to legitimize its rule by claiming that the Party never forgets its accountability to the people, and deliberately creates a mirage of "enemies" to reward compliance and threaten dissenters with punishment. Yet this "localization" hollows out populism's core meaning. If it merely denotes authoritarian responsiveness in democratic guise,[111] then virtually the entire history of communist China could be labeled populist.[112]

Another approach locates populism in cyberspace, identifying people-centric and anti-elite rhetoric in online discourse.[113] While this "virtualization" makes Chinese populism appear closer to the ideational definition, it is problematic. Online expression is shaped by censorship, and many anti-elite narratives, usually in the form of anti-capitalism discourse, align with the Party's official propaganda. More importantly, this view ignores the *strategic* dimension of populism: the absence of leaders, organization, and sustained mobilization suggests that populism does not truly exist. Treating netizens as substitutes for charismatic leadership overstates their political significance.[114]

What is analytically at stake is less *which* mainstream definition of populism to adopt than *what* is lost by ignoring its mobilizational dimension. In democratic contexts, contention is institutionally embedded; in authoritarian systems, it is not. Recasting "populism in China" as "Chinese populism," or locating it primarily in cyberspace, obscures this issue and risks trivializing the concept by conflating it with long-standing expressions of popular grievance under authoritarian rule. If populism lacks a concrete political vehicle, it becomes indistinguishable from ordinary dissent.

What, then, explains the persistent failure to identify populist opposition in Chinese politics? First, the prevailing understanding of China's elite politics is outdated. It rests on the assumption that, since Tiananmen Square protests of 1989, China has undergone increasing political institutionalization, rendering elite competition more rule-based—at least until Xi Jinping. The lesson drawn by the Party leadership from 1989 is that open elite conflict risks regime stability by enabling mass mobilization; hence, power struggles must remain behind closed doors. This institutionalization thesis, reinforced by the regime's carefully maintained image of elite unity, creates the impression that unrestrained power struggles have disappeared. Although elite competition persists, it is seen as occurring within the bounds of collective leadership—an inner-circle process of bargaining and maneuvering. As a result, Chinese elite politics is typically portrayed as a closed-door game with no space for popular participation. Starting from this premise of a unified authoritarian leadership intolerant of open dissent, it is unsurprising that scholars fail to find anti-establishment forces.

Second, while scholars often search for populism in China's cyberspace, they have largely overlooked two major cases where populist leadership and anti-establishment mobilization are more clearly observable. One is the era of mass mobilization under Mao Zedong, especially the Cultural Revolution. Earlier scholarship tentatively linked Maoism to populism,[115] but recent studies tend to sideline this line of inquiry, instead treating Mao-era practices (e.g., the Mass Line) as a cultural legacy that informs a top-down governing technique.[116] The other case is Bo Xilai's open political campaigning between 2008 and 2012. Although frequently described as "populist," his political practices are rarely examined systematically as a case of populism.[117]

Theoretically, for populist anti-establishment forces to exist under full authoritarianism, two conditions must be met. First, populist elites must be able to mobilize supporters openly against rivals without creating a visible elite split that could invite broader dissent and threaten regime stability. Second, followers must be sufficiently mobilizable such that their collective action can persist without being swiftly suppressed.

Under full authoritarianism, where the regime exercises near-total control, the second condition can be met when mobilization is initiated from above. During intra-elite power struggles, competing elites may temporarily sustain mass mobilization as a political instrument, until a final outcome is reached and losers are subdued. In this sense, what is institutionalized as open opposition in democratic systems may intermittently emerge in authoritarian settings when elite unity breaks down.

The first condition, however, presents a deeper puzzle. How can competing elites signal strength and resolve through public channels while preserving a facade of unity to deter regime-threatening dissent from below? Relatedly, why do autocrats not confine their struggles entirely behind closed doors, given the risks of public exposure?

Because populist strategies, such as "us-versus-them" rhetoric and visible mass mobilization, require elites to "go public," explaining populism under authoritarianism depends on understanding how elites strategically use public information in power struggles. Empirically, elite conflicts do sometimes spill into the public sphere, often alongside state organized mass campaigns. Yet systematic patterns remain understudied. Existing scholarship on authoritarianism focuses primarily on how elites control information to govern society, rather than how they deploy public signals in intra-elite competition. This gap is precisely what the concept of "autocrats going public," discussed earlier, seeks to address.

Returning to the central question: how is populism possible under authoritarianism? The cases of Mao Zedong's Cultural Revolution and Bo Xilai's Chongqing campaign suggest the following preliminary answer. First, populism under authoritarianism is closely tied to top-down mass mobilization during intra-elite power struggles and requires competing elites to "go public." This entails deploying antagonistic, moralized framings of politics and publicizing orchestrated mass movements. In this sense, authoritarian populism can be understood as a special form of elite contestation that strategically uses public information. Second, populism under authoritarianism rests on an ideological precondition: the normative dominance of popular sovereignty as the ultimate source of political legitimacy. Even autocrats seek to present themselves as ruling with popular support. This normative hegemony explains how authoritarian politics can assume a populist form despite the absence of representative democracy.[118] In effect, political authority is asserted as both derived from and immediately transferred by the people, without meaningful participation. One important implication is that populism becomes a double-edged instrument for autocrats. While invoking popular sovereignty and mobilizing the masses can strengthen an elite's position against rivals, such strategies also risk fostering political awareness among the populace. Mobilization may expose subjects to the idea that they possess rights vis-à-vis rulers.

The Chinese case of populism suggests that it cannot serve as a corrective to democracy.[119] Neither Cultural Revolution nor Bo Xilai's Mao-style political campaigns aimed at genuine democratization; rather, the masses were mobilized to advance political ambitions under the banner of serving the people. Although such populist manipulation may produce unintended, potentially pro-democratic effects, it is conceptually dubious to characterize these top-down campaigns as democratizing.

The Chinese case also shows how populism obstructs democratization by sustaining the illusion that the people are already perfectly represented. Under populist logic, leaders claim to embody the people in opposition to constructed enemies, locking democratic aspirations into a false sense of empowerment and thereby reinforcing authoritarian rule. If the preservation of democracy ultimately depends on a robust democratic consensus, then meaningful democratization in a fully authoritarian system such as China requires not only institutional change but also a transformation in how democracy is understood,[120] including a rejection of the populist notion of "mass democracy." Just as scholarship has demonstrated the corrosive effects of populism in *government* on democratic institutions, the Chinese case offers a preview of what populism in *power* can do when democratic foundations are entirely eroded under authoritarian rule.

Notes

1. The contents of this book were developed under grant #P015A220015/84.015A from the U.S. Department of Education. However, those contents do not necessarily represent the policy of the

U.S. Department of Education, and readers should not assume endorsement by the Federal Government.

2. Lin Le, "Chinese Politics since Hu Jintao and the Origin of Xi Jinping's Strongman Rule: A New Hypothesis," *Texas National Security Review* 6, no. 4 (2023): 37–78, https://doi.org/10.26153/tsw/48844; Lin Le, *China's Conservative Turn: The Origins of Xi Jinping's New Era* (Lynne Rienner Publishers, 2025).
3. The answer was provided by Grok, an AI chatbot developed by Elon Musk's xAI.
4. Kuangyi (Guagua) Bo, "Bo Xilai as Ned Stark," *X*, December 23, 2024, https://x.com/BoKuangyi/status/1871275984621850691.
5. Cheng Li, "The Bo Xilai Crisis: A Curse or a Blessing for China?" Brookings Institution, April 18, 2012, https://www.brookings.edu/on-the-record/the-bo-xilai-crisis-a-curse-or-a-blessing-for-china/.
6. There are different opinions on who these eight persons are. See Xu Qingquan, "'Ba lao' yu 1980 niandai zhengtan gaoceng geju" [The "Eight Immortals" and the Political Structure of Top Leadership in the 1980s], *Duli zhongwen bihui*, July 29, 2018, https://www.chinesepen.org/blog/archives/107417.
7. Joseph Kahn, "Bo Yibo, 98, Leader Who Helped Reshape Chinese Economy," *The New York Times*, January 17, 2007, https://www.nytimes.com/2007/01/17/world/asia/17bo.html.
8. John Garnaut, *The Rise and Fall of the House of Bo* (Penguin, 2012), 31–33.
9. Joseph Fewsmith, "Bo Xilai Takes On Organized Crime," *China Leadership Monitor*, no. 32 (Spring 2010).
10. Of course, from a historical perspective, this age limit has never been a binding rule, but rather a tool used to serve political maneuvering. Its very origins demonstrate this point: at the Fifteenth Party Congress, Jiang Zemin introduced the retirement age of 70, which was later lowered to 68 at the Sixteenth Party Congress. Reportedly, this adjustment allowed Jiang to force two of his political rivals into retirement. Although the age rule was followed at the Seventeenth Party Congress, its application has always been politically contingent. See Joseph Fewsmith, "The 17th Party Congress: Informal Politics and Formal Institutions," *China Leadership Monitor*, no. 23 (Winter 2008); Alice Miller, "The 18th Central Committee Politburo: A Quixotic, Foolhardy, Rashly Speculative, but Nonetheless Ruthlessly Reasoned Projection," *China Leadership Monitor*, no. 33 (Summer 2010)
11. "Profile: Bo Xilai," *BBC*, September 22, 2013, https://www.bbc.com/news/world-asia-china-19709555.
12. Alice Miller, "The Politburo Standing Committee under Hu Jintao," *China Leadership Monitor*, no. 35 (Summer 2011).

13. Paul Roderick Gregory, "Making Sense of China's Bo Xilai Earthquake," *Forbes*, April 10, 2012, https://www.forbes.com/sites/paulroderick-gregory/2012/04/10/making-sense-of-chinas-bo-xilai-earthquake/.
14. Alice Miller, "The Problem of Hu Jintao's Successor," *China Leadership Monitor*, no. 19 (Fall 2006); Alice Miller, "China's New Party Leadership," *China Leadership Monitor*, no. 23 (Winter 2008).
15. Alice Miller, "The Case of Xi Jinping and the Mysterious Succession," *China Leadership Monitor*, no. 30 (Fall 2009).
16. Jaime A. FlorCruz, "China's Bo Xilai trial: A show or serious test of Communist Party reforms?," *CNN*, August 18, 2013, https://www.cnn.com/2013/08/18/world/asia/china-bo-xilai-trial-analysis.
17. Li, "The Bo Xilai Crisis."
18. Bo Zhiyue, "Were China's Corrupt Officials Plotting a Coup?" *The Diplomat*, April 13, 2015, https://thediplomat.com/2015/04/were-chinas-corrupt-officials-plotting-a-coup/.
19. Joseph Fewsmith, *Rethinking Chinese Politics* (Cambridge University Press, 2021), 154.
20. For a more detailed account of these dramas, see Garnaut, *The Rise and Fall*; Pin Ho and Wenguang Huang, *Zhongguo quangui de siwang youxi: Bo Xilai shijian mimi baogao* [A Death in the Lucky Holiday Hotel: Murder, Money, and an Epic Power Struggle in China], trans. Li Tianxin (Lingxiu chubanshe, 2013); Jamil Anderlini, "Bo Xilai: Power, Death, and Politics," *Financial Times*, July 20, 2012, http://www.ft.com/intl/cms/s/2/d67b90f0-d140-11e1-8957-00144feabdc0.html.
21. Recent scholarly work on Bo Xilai either focuses on some trivial topics—such as measuring to what extent Bo's leftist policies had real effect and evaluating whether they lived up to the leftist principles—or uses Bo Xilai as a special case that offers certain inferential leverage for other research topics, such as censorship, propaganda, legal system, anti-corruption, state-business relations, and the effect of political uncertainty on asset price. See Roderic Broadhurst and Peng Wang, "After the Bo Xilai Trial: Does Corruption Threaten China's Future?" *Survival* 56, no. 3 (2014): 157–178, https://doi.org/10.1080/00396338.2014.920148; Christopher Cairns, "Microblog Dissent and Censorship during the 2012 Bo Xilai Scandal," in *Handbook of Protest and Resistance in China*, ed. Teresa Wright (Edward Elgar Publishing, 2019), 361–376, https://doi.org/10.4337/9781786433787.00037; Christopher Connery, "The Chongqing Way," *boundary 2* 46, no. 2 (2019): 163–188, https://doi.org/10.1215/01903659-7497088; Bei Guo and Ying Jiang, "Analyzing the Coexistence of Emerging Transparency and Tight Political Control on Weibo: Case Study of Weibo Broadcast of the Bo Xilai Trial," *The Journal of International Communication* 21, no. 1 (2015): 78–108,

https://doi.org/10.1080/13216597.2014.998700; Norman P. Ho, "Addressing Corruption and the Trial of Bo Xilai: Historical Continuities, Rule of Law Implications," in *China's Socialist Rule of Law Reforms Under Xi Jinping*, ed. John Garrick and Yan Chang Bennett (Routledge, 2016), 109–121; Francis L. F. Lee, "Political Scandals under Responsive Authoritarianism: The Case of the Bo Xilai Trial in China," *International Journal of Communication* 12 (2018): 3048–3066; Laura Xiaolei Liu et al., "The Impacts of Political Uncertainty on Asset Prices: Evidence from the Bo Scandal in China," *Journal of Financial Economics* 125, no. 2 (2017): 286–310, https://doi.org/10.1016/j.jfineco.2017.05.011; Ben Self, "The Bo Xilai Trial and China's Struggle with the Rule of Law," *Washington University Global Studies Law Review* 14, no. 1 (2015): 155–180; Jonathan R. Stromseth et al., *China's Governance Puzzle: Enabling Transparency and Participation in a Single-Party State* (Cambridge University Press, 2017); Yang Zhou, "Do Ideology Movements and Legal Intervention Matter: A Synthetic Control Analysis of the Chongqing Model," *European Journal of Political Economy* 51 (2018): 44–56, https://doi.org/10.1016/j.ejpoleco.2017.03.010.

22. Mei Xiao's book is likely the most in-depth study in recent years of Bo Xilai's "sing red" campaign in Chongqing. However, it has two key limitations: (1) it employs a postmodern framework to interpret Chinese authoritarian politics, the applicability of which is questionable; and (2) its narrative is entirely detached from elite-level power struggles. See Xiao Mei, *Chongqing's Red Culture Campaign: Simulation and Its Social Implications* (Routledge, 2017); Xiao Mei, "Why Chongqing's Red Culture Campaign Was Not a Real Mass Campaign," *International Journal of Politics, Culture, and Society* 30 (2017): 63–81, https://doi.org/10.1007/s10767-016-9217-7.
23. Hongbin Li and Li-An Zhou, "Political Turnover and Economic Performance: The Incentive Role of Personnel Control in China," *Journal of Public Economics* 89, nos. 9–10 (2005): 1743–1762, https://doi.org/10.1016/j.jpubeco.2004.06.009; Chenggang Xu, "The Fundamental Institutions of China's Reforms and Development," *Journal of Economic Literature* 49, no. 4 (2011): 1076–1151, https://doi.org/10.1257/jel.49.4.1076; Victor Shih, Christopher Adolph, and Mingxing Liu, "Getting Ahead in the Communist Party: Explaining the Advancement of Central Committee Members in China," *American Political Science Review* 106, no. 1 (2012): 166–187, https://doi.org/10.1017/S0003055411000566; Pierre F. Landry, Xiaobo Lü, and Haiyan Duan, "Does Performance Matter? Evaluating Political Selection along the Chinese Administrative Ladder," *Comparative Political Studies* 51, no. 8 (2018): 1074–1105, https://doi.org/10.1177/0010414017730078.

24. Carolyn Cartier and Luigi Tomba, "Symbolic Cities and the 'Cake Debate'," in *China Story Yearbook 2012*, ed. Geremie R. Barmé, chap. 2 (Australian Centre on China in the World, 2012); Lance L. P. Gore, "The Fall of Bo Xilai and the Seduction of the Chongqing Model," *East Asian Policy* 4, no. 2 (2012): 53–61; Dan Steinbock, "Guangdong and Chongqing: Two Sides of the Same Coin," *China US Focus*, December 11, 2012, http://www.chinausfocus.com/uncategorized/guangdong-and-chongqing-two-sides-of-the-same-coin/; Kean Fan Lim and Niv Horesh, "The Chongqing vs Guangdong Developmental 'Model' in Post-Mao China: Regional and Historical Perspectives on the Dynamics of Socioeconomic Change," *Journal of the Asia Pacific Economy* 22, no. 3 (2017): 372–395, https://doi.org/10.1080/13547860.2016.1263044; Anna Zakharzhevskaya, "The Chongqing Model—Socialist Alternative or Propaganda Cliché?" *Research in Political Economy* 32 (2017): 227–252, https://doi.org/10.1108/S0161-723020170000032013; Chunhua Chen and Bruce Dickson, "Coping with Growth in China: Comparing Models of Development in Guangdong and Chongqing," *Journal of Chinese Governance* 3, no. 2 (2018): 197–222, https://doi.org/10.1080/23812346.2018.1430998.
25. Dimitar D. Gueorguiev and Paul J. Schuler, "Keeping Your Head Down: Public Profiles and Promotion under Autocracy," *Journal of East Asian Studies* 16, no. 1 (2016): 87–116, https://doi.org/10.1017/jea.2015.1.
26. Chengju Huang, "Power, Ambition, and Arrogance: Lessons of Bo Xilai's 'Singing Red Song' Campaign as a Political Communication Project," *Global Media Journal (Australian Edition)* 8, no. 1 (2014): 1–13.
27. Su Wei, "Yu san pi faguo jizhe tan Chongqing 'chang hong', 'da hei'" [A Talk with Three Groups of French Journalists about Chongqing's "Singing Red" and "Striking Black"], *Wu You Zhi Xiang*, June 21, 2011, https://www.wyzxwk.com/Article/shidai/2011/06/234683.html.
28. The core issue of the Cake Debate was whether China's primary task should be to make the cake bigger or to divide it more fairly, reflecting a broader debate between prioritizing economic growth and prioritizing redistribution.
29. Yawei Liu, "Bo Xilai's Campaign for the Standing Committee and the Future of Chinese Politicking," *China Brief* 11, no. 21 (2011): 8–11; François Godement et al., *One or Two Chinese Models?* China Analysis (European Council on Foreign Relations, 2011), 1–16.
30. Lanxing Xiang, "The Bo Xilai Affair and China's Future," *Survival* 54, no. 3 (2012): 59–68, https://doi.org/10.1080/00396338.2012.690979.
31. Alice Miller, "The Bo Xilai Affair in Central Leadership Politics," *China Leadership Monitor*, no. 38 (Summer 2012).

32. Joseph Fewsmith, "Bo Xilai and Reform: What Will Be the Impact of His Removal?" *China Leadership Monitor*, no. 38 (Summer 2012); Andreas Mulvad, "Competing Hegemonic Projects within China's Variegated Capitalism: 'Liberal' Guangdong vs. 'Statist' Chongqing," *New Political Economy* 20, no. 2 (2015): 199–227, https://doi.org/10.1080/13563467.2014.914160; Bingchun Meng, "Political Scandal at the End of Ideology? The Mediatized Politics of the Bo Xilai Case," *Media, Culture & Society* 38, no. 6 (2016): 811–826, https://doi.org/10.1177/0163443716635858; Yueran Zhang, "The Chongqing Model One Decade On," *Made in China Journal*, no. 3 (2020): 31–39, https://madeinchinajournal.com/2021/01/11/the-chongqing-model-one-decade-on/; Tony Saich, *From Rebel to Ruler: One Hundred Years of the Chinese Communist Party* (Harvard University Press, 2021), 386–466.
33. Yuezhi Zhao, "The Struggle for Socialism in China: The Bo Xilai Saga and Beyond," *Monthly Review* 64, no. 5 (2012): 1–17; Cheng Li, *Chinese Politics in the Xi Jinping Era: Reassessing Collective Leadership* (Brookings Institution Press, 2016), 249–300.
34. Gueorguiev and Schuler, "Keeping Your Head Down," 87–116.
35. Victor Shih, "Contentious Elites in China: New Evidence and Approaches," *Journal of East Asian Studies* 16, no. 1 (2016): 1–15, https://doi.org/10.1017/jea.2015.2.
36. Zhengxu Wang and Anastas Vangeli, "The Rules and Norms of Leadership Succession in China: From Deng Xiaoping to Xi Jinping and Beyond," *The China Journal* 76 (2016): 24–40, https://doi.org/10.1086/686141.
37. Miller, "The Bo Xilai Affair"; Fewsmith, "Bo Xilai and Reform."
38. Junyan Jiang et al., "In the Shadows of Great Men: Retired Leaders and Informal Power Constraints in Autocracies," *British Journal of Political Science* 54, no. 4 (2024): 1088–1114, https://doi.org/10.1017/S0007123424000012; Andrew Leber et al., "When Can Dictators Go It Alone? Personalization and Oversight in Authoritarian Regimes," *Politics & Society* 51, no. 1 (2023): 66–107, https://doi.org/10.1177/00323292221078661.
39. Alfred L. Chan, *Xi Jinping: Political Career, Governance, and Leadership, 1953–2018* (Oxford University Press, 2022), 161–168; David Shambaugh, *China's Leaders: From Mao to Now* (Polity, 2021), 224.
40. Willy Wo-Lap Lam, "The Maoist Revival and the Conservative Turn in Chinese Politics," *China Perspectives*, no. 2 (2012): 5–15, https://doi.org/10.4000/chinaperspectives.5851; Willy Wo-Lap Lam, *Chinese Politics in the Era of Xi Jinping: Renaissance, Reform, or Retrogression?* (Routledge, 2015), 3–74; Susan Shirk, *Overreach: How China Derailed Its Peaceful Rise* (Oxford University Press, 2022), 55–118; Chen and Dickson, "Coping with growth in China," 197–222.

41. Ho and Huang, *Zhongguo quangui*, 339, 357; Fewsmith, *Rethinking Chinese Politics*, 157–184.
42. Garnaut, *The Rise and Fall*, 32, 64, 78; Ho and Huang, *Zhongguo quangui*, 392.
43. Garnaut, *The Rise and Fall*, 45–46, 77, 114–115, 118–119; Ho and Huang, *Zhongguo quangui*, 339; Desmond Shum, *Red Roulette: An Insider's Story of Wealth, Power, Corruption, and Vengeance in Today's China* (Scribner, 2021), 239–263.
44. Li, *Chinese Politics in the Xi Jinping Era*, 249–300.
45. Garnaut, *The Rise and Fall*, 31, 45–46, 52.
46. Victor Shih, Wei Shan, and Mingxing Liu, "Gauging the Elite Political Equilibrium in the CCP: A Quantitative Approach Using Biographical Data," *The China Quarterly* 201 (2010): 79–103, https://doi.org/10.1017/S0305741009991081; Franziska Barbara Keller, "Moving Beyond Factions: Using Social Network Analysis to Uncover Patronage Networks among Chinese Elites," *Journal of East Asian Studies* 16, no. 1 (2016): 17–41, https://doi.org/10.1017/jea.2015.3; Shih, "Contentious Elites in China."
47. Zhiyue Bo, "Factional Politics in the Party-State Apparatus," in *Routledge Handbook of the Chinese Communist Party*, ed. Willy Wo-Lap Lam (Routledge, 2018), 122–134, https://doi.org/10.4324/9781315543918-8; Alice Miller, "The Trouble with Factions," *China Leadership Monitor*, no. 46 (Summer 2015).
48. Ho and Huang, *Zhongguo quangui*, 25.
49. Garnaut, *The Rise and Fall*, 47–49, 53, 124.
50. Garnaut, *The Rise and Fall*, 49, 57.
51. Garnaut, *The Rise and Fall*, 6–7.
52. Geremie R. Barmé, "Red Allure and the Crimson Blindfold," *China Perspectives*, no. 2 (2012): 29–40; Kerry Brown and Simone van Nieuwenhuizen, *China and the New Maoists* (Zed Books, 2016).
53. Ian Johnson, "China's Falling Star," *The New York Review of Books*, April 26, 2012, https://www.nybooks.com/articles/2012/04/26/chinas-falling-star/.
54. Johnson, "China's Falling Star"; Zhang, "The Chongqing Model"; Zhao, "The Struggle for Socialism"; Fewsmith, "Bo Xilai and Reform"; Miller, "The Bo Xilai Affair"; Anderlini, "Bo Xilai"; Zhun Xu, "The Chongqing Event and Its Implications," *Economic and Political Weekly* 47, no. 16 (2012): 12–14; Chan, *Xi Jinping*, 175–220.
55. Garnaut, *The Rise and Fall*, 5, 29.
56. The phrase in original Chinese language is *bu zai yi ge cengci*. See Song Yafei, ed., *Bo Xilai tingshen shilu* [The Bo Xilai Trial Transcript] (Xin shijie chuanmei, 2013), 384.

57. Garnaut, *The Rise and Fall*, 115.
58. Li, "The Bo Xilai Crisis"; Frederick C. Teiwes, "The Study of Elite Political Conflict in the PRC: Politics Inside the 'Black Box,'" in *Handbook of the Politics of China*, ed. David S. G. Goodman (Edward Elgar Publishing, 2015), 21–41.
59. Ho and Huang, *Zhongguo quangui*, 30–85; Garnaut, *The Rise and Fall*, 80–104.
60. Garnaut, *The Rise and Fall*, 9.
61. Ho and Huang, *Zhongguo quangui*, 7–8, 36.
62. Ho and Huang, *Zhongguo quangui*, 182.
63. Ho and Huang, *Zhongguo quangui*, 324–326.
64. Jude Blanchette, *China's New Red Guards: The Return of Radicalism and the Rebirth of Mao Zedong* (Oxford University Press, 2019); Joseph Y. S. Cheng, "The 'Chongqing Model': What It Means to China Today," *Journal of Comparative Asian Development* 12, no. 3 (2013): 411–442, https://doi.org/10.1080/15339114.2013.862919.
65. Le, "Chinese Politics since Hu Jintao"; Le, *China's Conservative Turn*.
66. Jisheng Yang, *Zhongguo gaige niandai de zhengzhi douzheng* [The Political Struggles during China's Reform Era] (Tiandi tushu youxian gonsi, 2010); Julian Gewirtz, *Never Turn Back: China and the Forbidden History of the 1980s* (Harvard University Press, 2022).
67. Lam, "The Maoist Revival."
68. Huang Shudong, "Gongping yu zhongguo de mingyun" [Fairness and China's Destiny], *Hongqi Wengao*, no. 24 (2012): 4–7.
69. Ho and Huang, *Zhongguo quangui*, 170.
70. Part of this section is adapted from the theoretical discussion in Le, "Chinese Politics since Hu Jintao."
71. Bryn Rosenfeld and Jeremy Wallace, "Information Politics and Propaganda in Authoritarian Societies," *Annual Review of Political Science* 27 (2024): 263–281, https://doi.org/10.1146/annurev-polisci-041322-035951; Martin K. Dimitrov, *Dictatorship and Information: Authoritarian Regime Resilience in Communist Europe and China* (Oxford University Press, 2023).
72. Alexander Dukalskis, *The Authoritarian Public Sphere: Legitimation and Autocratic Power in North Korea, Burma, and China* (Routledge, 2017); Gary King et al., "How the Chinese Government Fabricates Social Media Posts for Strategic Distraction, Not Engaged Argument," *American Political Science Review* 111, no. 3 (2017): 484–501, ttps://doi.org/10.1017/S0003055417000144; Erin Baggott Carter and Brett L. Carter, *Propaganda in Autocracies: Institutions, Information, and the Politics of Belief* (Cambridge University Press, 2023).

73. Gary King et al., "How Censorship in China Allows Government Criticism but Silences Collective Expression," *American Political Science Review* 107, no. 2 (2013): 326–343, https://doi.org/10.1017/S0003055413000014; Margaret E. Roberts, *Censored: Distraction and Diversion Inside China's Great Firewall* (Princeton University Press, 2018).
74. Beatriz Magaloni, *Voting for Autocracy: Hegemonic Party Survival and Its Demise in Mexico* (Cambridge University Press, 2006); Andreas Schedler and Bert Hoffmann, "Communicating Authoritarian Elite Cohesion," *Democratization* 23, no. 1 (2016): 93–117, https://doi.org/10.1080/13510347.2015.1095181; Andreas Schedler, *The Politics of Uncertainty: Sustaining and Subverting Electoral Authoritarianism* (Oxford University Press, 2013).
75. Haifeng Huang, "Propaganda as Signaling," *Comparative Politics* 47, no. 4 (2015): 419–444, https://doi.org/10.5129/001041515816103220.
76. Timur Kuran, "Now Out of Never: The Element of Surprise in the East European Revolution of 1989," *World Politics* 44, no. 1 (1991): 7–48, https://doi.org/10.2307/2010422.
77. Wedeen, Lisa. *Ambiguities of Domination: Politics, Rhetoric, and Symbols in Contemporary Syria.* University of Chicago Press, 1999; Michael Suk-Young Chwe, *Rational Ritual: Culture, Coordination, and Common Knowledge* (Princeton University Press, 2001).
78. Peter Lorentzen, "China's Strategic Censorship," *American Journal of Political Science* 58, no. 2 (2014): 402–414, https://doi.org/10.1111/ajps.12065; Peter Lorentzen, "Designing Contentious Politics in Post-1989 China," *Modern China* 43, no. 5 (2017): 459–493, https://doi.org/10.1177/0097700416688895; Barbara Geddes et al., *How Dictatorships Work: Power, Personalization, and Collapse* (Cambridge University Press, 2018).
79. Ronald Wintrobe, *The Political Economy of Dictatorship* (Cambridge University Press, 1998).
80. For instance, the widely known "selectorate theory" assumes that "the leader acts as an individual" and explicitly avoids addressing "the internal politics of that group." See Bruce Bueno de Mesquita et al., *The Logic of Political Survival* (MIT Press, 2003), 74. By assuming a homogeneous leadership, the theory effectively "assumes away politics itself." See Mary E. Gallagher and Jonathan K. Hanson, "Power Tool or Dull Blade? Selectorate Theory for Autocracies," *Annual Review of Political Science* 18 (2015): 378, https://doi.org/10.1146/annurev-polisci-071213-041224.

81. Anne Meng et al., "Authoritarian Power Sharing: Concepts, Mechanisms, and Strategies," *Annual Review of Political Science* 26 (2023): 153–173, https://doi.org/10.1146/annurev-polisci-052121-020406.
82. Roger B. Myerson, "The Autocrat's Credibility Problem and Foundations of the Constitutional State," *American Political Science Review* 102, no. 1 (2008): 125–139, https://doi.org/10.1017/S0003055408080076.
83. Milan W. Svolik, *The Politics of Authoritarian Rule* (Cambridge University Press, 2012).
84. Jason Brownlee, Authoritarianism in an Age of Democratization (Cambridge University Press, 2007); Jennifer Gandhi, *Political Institutions under Dictatorship* (Cambridge University Press, 2008).
85. Carles Boix and Milan W. Svolik, "The Foundations of Limited Authoritarian Government: Institutions, Commitment, and Power-Sharing in Dictatorships," *The Journal of Politics* 75, no. 2 (2013): 300–316, https://doi.org/10.1017/S0022381613000029.
86. There must be a credible threat of removing the dictator. In practice, this usually requires coordinated collective action by a unified coalition of ruling elites—a difficult feat given persistent factionalism, dictators' divide-and-rule tactics, and the general tendency toward risk aversion under conditions of uncertainty. See Boix and Svolik, "The Foundations of Limited Authoritarian Government"; Geddes et al., *How dictatorships work*; Svolik, *The Politics of Authoritarian Rule*; Meng et al., "Authoritarian Power Sharing"; Anne Meng, *Constraining Dictatorship: From Personalized Rule to Institutionalized Regimes* (Cambridge University Press, 2020); Beatriz Magaloni, "Credible Power-Sharing and the Longevity of Authoritarian Rule," *Comparative Political Studies* 41, nos. 4–5 (2008): 715–741, https://doi.org/10.1177/0010414007313124.
87. This analytical blind spot likely stems from the conventional assumption that autocrats seek to avoid any publicity that might reveal internal disunity.
88. Olivia Cheung's theory of "factional model-making" similarly observes that politics in authoritarian regimes often takes the form of ideological debates, and that such ideological or political contestation requires the production of tangible effects and the shaping of public opinion. However, her theory has two major limitations. First, by employing the framework of authoritarian resilience, her functionalist explanation tends to downplay the power struggle underlying ideological debates. Second, the theoretical scope is narrow, focusing on one particular form of political communication, rather than the broader political use of information under authoritarianism. See Olivia Cheung, *Factional-Ideological Conflicts in Chinese Politics: To the Left or to the Right?* (Amsterdam University Press, 2023).

89. Alice L. Miller, "Valedictory: Analyzing the Chinese Leadership in an Era of Sex, Money, and Power," *China Leadership Monitor*, no. 57 (Fall 2018).
90. Adam Przeworski, Democracy and the Market: Political and Economic Reforms in Eastern Europe and Latin America (Cambridge University Press, 1991); Barbara Geddes, "Why Parties and Elections in Authoritarian Regimes?" paper presented at the annual meeting of the American Political Science Association, Philadelphia, PA, August 31–September 3, 2006; Beatriz Magaloni and Ruth Kricheli, "Political Order and One-Party Rule," *Annual Review of Political Science* 13 (2010): 123–143, https://doi.org/10.1146/annurev.polisci.031908.220529.
91. Eva Bellin, "Reconsidering the Robustness of Authoritarianism in the Middle East: Lessons from the Arab Spring," *Comparative Politics* 44, no. 2 (2012): 127–149, https://doi.org/10.5129/001041512798838021; Jason Brownlee et al., *The Arab Spring: Pathways of Repression and Reform* (Oxford University Press, 2015).
92. This is why securing mass support and obedience is extremely important to the dictator. That being said, under certain circumstances, mass unrest can increase elite cohesion because a common threat from below can force the elites to prioritize the regime survival over their self-interested internal struggle. See Dan Slater, *Ordering Power: Contentious Politics and Authoritarian Leviathans in Southeast Asia* (Cambridge University Press, 2010); James R. Hollyer et al., "Why Do Autocrats Disclose? Economic Transparency and Inter-Elite Politics in the Shadow of Mass Unrest," *Journal of Conflict Resolution* 63, no. 6 (2019): 1488–1516, https://doi.org/10.1177/0022002718792602.
93. Brett Allen Casper and Scott A. Tyson, "Popular Protest and Elite Coordination in a Coup d'État," *The Journal of Politics* 76, no. 2 (2014): 548–564, https://doi.org/10.1017/S0022381613001485.
94. Geddes et al., *How dictatorships work*.
95. In the other direction, the degree of elite unity/disunity may influence the probability of the masses taking collective action, because intra-elite struggle influences the people's perception and assessment of the regime survivability. From a perspective of contentious politics, elite split, elite defection, and political realignment of the leadership constitute favorable opportunity structures for mass collective activism. That is why keeping the public from "perceiving" such opportunities through construction and manipulation of perception is crucial for maintaining autocratic rule. See Doug McAdam, Sidney Tarrow, and Charles Tilly, *Dynamics of Contention* (Cambridge University Press, 2001); Sidney G. Tarrow, *Power in Movement: Social Movements and Contentious Politics*, 3rd ed. (Cambridge University Press, 2011).

96. Grzegorz Ekiert and Elizabeth J. Perry, "State-Mobilized Movements: A Research Agenda," in *Ruling by Other Means: State-Mobilized Movements*, ed. Grzegorz Ekiert, Elizabeth J. Perry, and Yan Xiaojun (Cambridge University Press, 2020), 1–23.
97. This section is adapted from Le, *China's Conservative Turn*, 16–19.
98. Gongyang, ed., *Si chao: Zhongguo "xin zuo pai" ji qi yingxiang* [Trends of Thought: China's "New Left" and Its Influence] (Zhongguo shehui kexue chubanshe, 2003); He Li, *Political Thought and China's Transformation: Ideas Shaping Reform in Post-Mao China* (Springer, 2015).
99. Cas Mudde, "The Populist Zeitgeist," *Government and Opposition* 39, no. 4 (2004): 541–564, https://doi.org/10.1111/j.1477-7053.2004.00135.x; Cas Mudde, "Populism: An Ideational Approach," in *The Oxford Handbook of Populism*, ed. Cristóbal Rovira Kaltwasser et al. (Oxford University Press, 2017), 27–47.
100. Kurt Weyland, "Clarifying a Contested Concept: Populism in the Study of Latin American Politics," *Comparative Politics* 34, no. 1 (2001): 1–22, https://doi.org/10.2307/422412; Kurt Weyland, "Populism: A Political-Strategic Approach," in *The Oxford Handbook of Populism*, ed. Cristóbal Rovira Kaltwasser et al. (Oxford University Press, 2017), 48–72.
101. Pierre Ostiguy, "Populism: A Socio-Cultural Approach," in *The Oxford Handbook of Populism*, ed. Cristóbal Rovira Kaltwasser et al. (Oxford University Press, 2017), 73–97.
102. While anti-elite is more commonly referred to as a defining feature of populism elsewhere, anti-establishment or anti-regime is considered more appropriate a focus in the case of authoritarianism, where the society maintains a minimal level of independence vis-à-vis the state and where state elite and non-state elite often overlap significantly and are closely intertwined.
103. Conceptual stretching has been a major problem in scholarly efforts to define populism. See Benjamín Arditi, *Is There Such a Thing as Populism?: 3 Provocations and 5 1/2 Proposals* (Routledge, 2024), 13; David Art, "The Myth of Global Populism," *Perspectives on Politics* 20, no. 3 (2022): 999–1011, https://doi.org/10.1017/S1537592720003552; Andrew Arato and Jean L. Cohen, *Populism and Civil Society: The Challenge to Constitutional Democracy* (Oxford University Press, 2022), 2–4. A related issue in this regard is how to distinguish populism from routine democratic mobilization and politics in general. All politicians appeal to the people. Political mobilization is part and parcel of democratic politics, legitimizing active participation and interest-driven contention. Anti-elite and anti-establishment rhetoric are commonplace features of political dis-

sent, as is an us-versus-them logic. These elements may be present in any genuine democratization revolution or uprising.

104. Dongsheng Zang, "Rise of Political Populism and the Trouble with the Legal Profession in China," *Harvard China Review* 6 (2010): 79–99, https://digitalcommons.law.uw.edu/faculty-articles/830; Sida Liu, Lily Liang, and Terence C. Halliday, "The Trial of Li Zhuang: Chinese Lawyers' Collective Action against Populism," *Asian Journal of Law and Society* 1, no. 1 (2014): 79–97, https://doi.org/10.1017/als.2013.9; Benjamin L. Liebman, "A Return to Populist Legality? Historical Legacies and Legal Reform," in *Mao's Invisible Hand: The Political Foundations of Adaptive Governance in China*, ed. Sebastian Heilmann and Elizabeth J. Perry (Harvard University Press, 2011), 165–200; Michelle Miao, "Capital Punishment in China: A Populist Instrument of Social Governance," *Theoretical Criminology* 17, no. 2 (2013): 233–250, https://doi.org/10.1177/1362480613476788.
105. Khalid Nadiri, "China's Peasant Populism: A Look Inland," *SAIS Review* 27, no. 1 (Winter–Spring 2007): 125–126, https://doi.org/10.1353/sais.2007.0017.
106. Jane Duckett and Ana Inés Langer, "Populism versus Neoliberalism: Diversity and Ideology in the Chinese Media's Narratives of Health Care Reform," *Modern China* 39, no. 6 (2013): 653–680, https://doi.org/10.1177/0097700413492602.
107. Wenfang Tang, *Populist Authoritarianism: Chinese Political Culture and Regime Sustainability* (Oxford University Press, 2016)
108. Ben Xu, "Chinese Populist Nationalism: Its Intellectual Politics and Moral Dilemma," *Representations* 76, no. 1 (2001): 120–140, https://doi.org/10.1525/rep.2001.76.1.120; Chenchen Zhang, "Right-Wing Populism with Chinese Characteristics? Identity, Otherness and Global Imaginaries in Debating World Politics Online," *European Journal of International Relations* 26, no. 1 (2020): 88–115, https://doi.org/10.1177/1354066119850253; Ralph Schroeder, "Political Power and the Globalizing Spread of Populist Politics," *Journal of Political Power* 13, no. 1 (2020): 22–40, https://doi.org/10.1080/2158379X.2020.1720101; He Li, "Populism in China," in *The Routledge Handbook of Chinese Studies*, ed. Chris Shei and Weixiao Wei (Routledge, 2021), 376–388.
109. Some even propose that populism in China has two subtypes. One is pro-system, in response to threats to the Chinese nation, and the other is anti-system, driven by discontent with social problems. See Sarah Eaton and Armin Müller, "Varieties of Chinese Populism: Mapping the Mindsets of Pro- and Anti-System Populists," in *Three Faces of Populism in Asia: Populism as a Multifaceted Political Practice*, ed. Shiru Wang (Routledge,

2024), 44–64. The question is how this binary classification adds to our existing knowledge by referring to populism.

110. Yaoyao Dai and Zijie Shao, "Populism and Authoritarian Survival in China: Concept and Measurement," *Comparative Politics Newsletter* 26, no. 2 (2016): 31–39; Xiang Gao, "Patriotic Songs and Populism in Chinese Politics," in *The Routledge Handbook of Populism in the Asia Pacific*, ed. D. B. Subedi, Howard Brasted, Karin von Strokirch, and Alan Scott (Routledge, 2024), 330–342.
111. Ying Miao, "Can China Be Populist? Grassroot Populist Narratives in the Chinese Cyberspace," *Contemporary Politics* 26, no. 3 (2020): 268–287, https://doi.org/10.1080/13569775.2020.1727398; B. Guy Peters and Jon Pierre, "A Typology of Populism: Understanding the Different Forms of Populism and Their Implications," *Democratization* 27, no. 6 (2020): 928–946, https://doi.org/10.1080/13510347.2020.1751615 .
112. Similarly, if populism merely refers to certain political tactics, situations, or phenomena under authoritarianism—such as attempts to disrupt the political order or modes of negotiating elite power struggles—without anchoring it to its defining elements, then what value is added by using the term populism? For example, see Mark Chou, Benjamin Moffitt, and Octavia Bryant, *Political Meritocracy and Populism: Cure or Curse?* (Routledge, 2020), 62.
113. Zixue Tai, "Networked Resistance: Digital Populism, Online Activism, and Mass Dissent in China," *Popular Communication* 13, no. 2 (2015): 120–131, https://doi.org/10.1080/15405702.2015.1021469; Tianru Guan and Yilu Yang, "Rights-Oriented or Responsibility-Oriented? Two Subtypes of Populism in Contemporary China," *International Political Science Review* 42, no. 5 (2021): 672–689, https://doi.org/10.1177/0192512120925555; Kun He, Scott A. Eldridge II, and Marcel Broersma, "Conceptualizing Populism: A Comparative Study between China and Liberal Democratic Countries," *International Journal of Communication* 15 (2021): 3006–3024; Li, "Populism in China."
114. Kun He, Scott A. Eldridge II, and Marcel Broersma, "Who Are the People? Populists' Articulation of 'the People' in Contemporary China," *Chinese Journal of Communication* 16, no. 3 (2023): 267–284, https://doi.org/10.1080/17544750.2023.2183970.
115. Maurice Meisner, "Leninism and Maoism: Some Populist Perspectives in Marxism-Leninism in China," *The China Quarterly* 45 (1971): 2–36, https://doi.org/10.1017/S0305741000010407; James R. Townsend, "Chinese Populism and the Legacy of Mao Tse-Tung," *Asian Survey* 17, no. 11 (1977): 1003–1015, https://doi.org/10.2307/2643349.

116. Li, "Populism in China"; Miao, "Can China be Populist"; Tang, *Populist Authoritarianism*.
117. One exception is Andrew Junker, "Left Populism in a Communist Civil Sphere: The Lesson of Bo Xilai," in *Populism in the Civil Sphere*, ed. Jeffrey C. Alexander et al. (Polity Press, 2020), 232–250.
118. To be sure, even those who view populism as threatening still consider it an integral part of democratic politics: populism is a slippery slope toward autocracy, but it falls short of being authoritarian. See Jan-Werner Müller, *What Is Populism?* (University of Pennsylvania Press, 2016); Nadia Urbinati, "Political Theory of Populism," *Annual Review of Political Science* 22 (2019): 111–127, https://doi.org/10.1146/annurev-polisci-050317-070753; Takis S. Pappas, *Populism and Liberal Democracy: A Comparative and Theoretical Analysis* (Oxford University Press, 2019). The crux here seems to be a question of whether politics of *representation* is relevant under autocracy. While populism indeed centers on claims to represent "the people," this does not require democratic *institutions*. Rather, popular sovereignty also operates as a powerful political *imaginary*. Its normative force extends even to totalitarian regimes, as illustrated by the self-designation of North Korea as a "Democratic People's Republic." Thus, populism can emerge wherever the language of popular sovereignty retains legitimacy, regardless of institutional context.
119. Cas Mudde and Cristóbal Rovira Kaltwasser, eds., *Populism in Europe and the Americas: Threat or Corrective for Democracy?* (Cambridge University Press, 2012); Cristóbal Rovira Kaltwasser, "The Ambivalence of Populism: Threat and Corrective for Democracy," *Democratization* 19, no. 2 (2012): 184–208, https://doi.org/10.1080/13510347.2011.572619.
120. For example, the idea of "democracy" held by many Chinese students who participated in 1989 Tiananmen movement was actually very populist, i.e., they alone represent the truth and the people. See Elizabeth J. Perry, "Challenging the Mandate of Heaven: Popular Protest in Modern China," *Critical Asian Studies* 33, no. 2 (2001): 163–180, https://doi.org/10.1080/14672710122544.

CHAPTER 2

A Reformist Start

Bo Xilai initially began his tenure in Chongqing as a local leader aspiring to be a reformer. However, in response to shifts in China's elite politics, he later adopted a conservative mantle as the political wind turned to the left.

2.1 Opening Up

Echoing the rhetoric of the Seventeenth Party Congress report, Bo called for continuing Dengist reform and opening up at the beginning of his tenure in Chongqing. "For Chongqing to accelerate its development, it must possess a powerful driving force, and that force is the reform and opening up that created China's economic miracle," Bo stressed. "Only in an environment of greater openness can we discover more opportunities in larger markets and set higher goals through competition at a higher level."[1] The reformist path was described as the "fundamental way out," and Chongqing, Bo argued, must "have the courage to place itself at the forefront of openness."[2]

Being reformist at the time also meant closely adhering to the central guidelines laid out for Chongqing's development. As Bo stated, "After I arrived in Chongqing, the foremost task was to work together with everyone to implement the '3–14 Overall Arrangement' (*314 zongti bushu*) proposed by the General Secretary [Hu Jintao]," which "defined Chongqing's position and objectives, pointed out the tasks for our development in the new period, and serves as the overarching guideline for

L. Le, *Revival of Maoism in Reform-Era China*,
https://doi.org/10.1007/978-981-92-4606-9_2

Chongqing's development both now and in the future."[3] The "3–14 Overall Arrangement" referred to a set of development goals laid out by Hu Jintao in March 2007, before Bo had been appointed as party secretary of Chongqing. Reflecting the broader political climate at the time, the "3–14 Overall Arrangement" was thematically reformist and included the following objectives.[4]

Three Major Roles:

- An important growth pole in western China
- The economic center of the upper Yangtze River region
- A centrally administered municipality pioneering coordinated urban–rural development

One Overarching Goal:

- To take the lead in western China in achieving the goal of building a moderately prosperous society in all respects

Four Major Tasks:

- To intensify efforts to promote agriculture through industry and to support rural areas through urban development, thereby steadily advancing the construction of a New Socialist Countryside
- To effectively transform the mode of economic growth and accelerate the restructuring and reform of the old industrial base
- To place greater emphasis on addressing people's livelihood issues and actively build a socialist Harmonious Society
- To comprehensively strengthen urban construction and improve the level of urban governance and management

To be sure, pro-poor policies were included as part of the blueprint—namely, promoting balanced urban–rural development, advancing rural development, and addressing issues related to people's livelihoods. At this stage, however, these policies remained means to an end and, more importantly, represented a reformist response to growing leftist criticism of China's unbalanced growth. Chongqing was relatively underdeveloped compared with China's coastal regions, and economic inequality was particularly pronounced. Reducing the economic gap was therefore an integral part of the broader plan to stimulate overall economic development and build a "Socialist Harmonious Society." Later, as China's conservative forces continued to gain momentum, these pro-poor policies became increasingly politicized and were elevated to a higher level of socialist fundamentalism, aimed at challenging Dengist reformism.

For the moment, however, Bo Xilai remained on a reformist track. Dengist reform took priority over pro-poor policies. According to Bo, five major tasks were identified for 2008:[5]

1. Further opening up
2. Coordinated urban–rural development
3. Resettlement of migrants from the Three Gorges Reservoir area
4. Urban planning and development
5. People's livelihoods

Here, "opening up" referred to an ambitious plan to modernize Chongqing. At the core of this blueprint, however, was a familiar formula that had powered China's economic miracle over the previous three decades: investment-driven growth and export-oriented manufacturing. What was new this time was the idea of "domestic flying geese"—namely, that Chongqing should "actively undertake the transfer of processing trade from the eastern regions."[6] According to Bo, "[Chongqing] must broaden its horizons and seize the opportunity created by the world's and China's Fortune 500 companies that have been increasingly attaching importance to [China's] domestic market and accelerating their strategic layout, and must identify suitable areas of cooperation and make better use of both foreign and domestic capital." Opening up was not merely about attracting investment; more importantly, it was about "[gaining access to] technology, markets, and talent, and participating in a broader division of industrial labor."[7] Shortly afterward, as large inflows of foreign direct investment arrived and many major companies relocated their production lines to Chongqing, Bo boasted of having established a new model of processing trade known as "one end overseas, multiple ends at home" (*yi tou zai wai, duo tou zai nei*),[8] as opposed to the traditional arrangement described as "both ends overseas" (*liang tou zai wai*).[9]

When Chongqing convened the Third Plenum of the Third Chongqing Party Committee in July 2008—explicitly dedicated to the task of "expanding the scope of opening up" (*kuoda kaifang*)—Bo Xilai presented himself as a disciple of Deng Xiaoping, adopting a reformist approach to local development. "Today's Chongqing must expand its scope of opening up," Bo further elaborated, "and actively plunge into the tide of marketization and internationalization, pooling together all resources that can serve our development, such as capital, technology, talent, management, and other factors, so that every seed of innovation, creativity, and entrepreneurship can take root and flourish in Chongqing." The ultimate goal of opening up was to turn Chongqing into "an inland high ground of opening up" (*neilu kaifang gaodi*).[10]

Chongqing's initial reformist ambition received generous support from the central government. In early 2008, China's State Council began considering the establishment of a special economic zone in Chongqing, which would make it the third municipality to host a national-level "New Area" (*guojia ji xinqu*), following Shanghai's Pudong and Tianjin's Binhai. Chongqing submitted a detailed proposal in April 2009, and it was officially approved in May 2010.[11] Liangjiang New Area was subsequently established. The State Council directive highlighted three key missions that Chongqing was expected to pursue: reform, opening up, and innovation. The reformist tone could hardly have been more explicit. Tasked with making effective use of the economic zone to "propel the development of western China," Chongqing was placed alongside Shenzhen, Shanghai, and Tianjin—cities described as representing four "landmark events" in China's 30 years of reform. Liangjiang New Area was said to symbolize that "China's strategy of development and opening up, once concentrated along the coast, had now advanced into the western inland heartland."[12] (Unfortunately, by the time Liangjiang New Area was officially established in 2010, Chongqing under Bo had already been steadily moving in a leftist direction, and the initial reformist agenda had been effectively marginalized.)

2.2 Mind Emancipation

Shortly after the Seventeenth Party Congress, Wang Yang, the provincial leader of Guangdong, launched a high-profile campaign of "Mind Emancipation" (*jiefang sixiang*). The term carries strong political symbolism, evoking the progressiveness and reformist legacy associated with Deng Xiaoping, who advanced economic reform by overcoming leftist resistance. In official party historiography, two major waves of Mind Emancipation are generally recognized. The first refers to the "Truth Criteria Controversy" (*zhenli biaozhun taolun*) of 1978. The political struggle conducted in the name of Mind Emancipation at that time primarily sought to discredit the lingering Maoist influence over economic planning in post-Mao China. The second refers to Deng Xiaoping's "Southern Tour" (*nan xun*) in 1992. This episode marked the beginning of accelerated market-oriented reform in post-Tiananmen China, as Deng relied on his political authority to prevail over conservative opposition.[13]

Wang Yang urged party cadres to be entrepreneurial in advancing local development, arguing that they should emulate the reformist pioneers of the early Dengist reform era, who embodied a spirit of "carving out a bloody path forward" (*sha kai yi tiao xue lu*).[14] Other provinces soon followed suit, launching "Mind Emancipation" campaigns modeled on Guangdong's initiative. Among them, Hunan's party secretary at the time, Zhang Chunxian, made perhaps the boldest statement during the campaign: "The first two waves of Mind Emancipation mainly emphasized returning benefits to the people (*huan li yu min*), whereas this round of Mind Emancipation, while continuing to emphasize returning benefits to the people, places even greater emphasis on returning power to the people (*huan quan yu min*)."[15] By explicitly invoking the language of political reform, the reformist orientation of this "Third Wave" of Mind Emancipation was unmistakable.

Bo Xilai also joined the reformist chorus. In March 2008, a Mind Emancipation campaign was officially launched in Chongqing. The campaign had three specific objectives:

1. To make local cadres aware that Chongqing was lagging behind
2. To instill in cadres a sense of urgency and motivation to close this gap
3. To encourage cadres to enhance their capabilities and become better equipped to carry out these tasks

According to the official statement, the campaign aimed "to cultivate an open mindset, strengthen the capacity for opening up, expand the scope of openness, participate with greater courage in both domestic and international competition, and make full use of both domestic and international resources and markets." The tasks awaiting Chongqing's cadres were clearly embedded in the Dengist logic of market-oriented reform: "Only in an open environment can the soil for economic development, especially the development of the private economy, be better cultivated," the rhetoric went on, "only then can more market factors from home and abroad be brought together, enabling participation in a broader division of industrial labor and allowing development to be pursued at a higher level and across wider fields."[16] There is little doubt that when the campaign was in full swing, it was still Bo the Reformer who was in charge.

First, Bo Xilai urged local cadres to "open [their] eyes wide to observe both China and the world," that is, to recognize the gap between Chongqing and more developed regions. "Daring to compare and daring to think," Bo argued, "is the prerequisite for development." To drive home this message, Bo introduced the metaphor of the "three rulers" (*san ba chizi*).[17]

- The "vertical" ruler: measuring Chongqing against its own past—the progress the city had made since becoming a centrally administered municipality a decade earlier
- The "horizontal" ruler: measuring Chongqing against other provinces—more developed regions that served as a mirror reflecting the city's relative backwardness
- The "national" ruler: measuring Chongqing against the developmental objectives set by the Party center—Hu Jintao's "3–14 Overall Arrangement"

Months later, as the campaign was winding down, Bo noted with satisfaction that a tangible change had taken place in the work style of Chongqing's cadres: at meetings, there was now more discussion of shortcomings than of achievements.[18]

Second, only from an awareness of backwardness can the motivation for progress emerge. When an article titled "Chongqing People Lack a Bit of Drive When It Comes to Economic Development" went viral online at the time, Bo ordered every local cadre to read it and take notes.[19] A *Chongqing Daily* editorial remarked that "development requires motivation" and that "our ideational motivation comes from a clear self-assessment." To overcome the attitudinal tendencies that predisposed them to be "content with modest prosperity" and "follow well-trodden paths,"[20] Chongqing cadres were urged to "cultivate a perspective attuned to the times and to the world, and to face squarely the gap between Chongqing and more developed regions and countries."[21] The campaign thus aimed to help party cadres "gain a clear understanding of the situation, identify existing gaps, and place greater pressure on themselves." Through the "Mind Emancipation" discussions, cadres were expected to "strengthen their sense of responsibility to the Party center, to the people of Chongqing, and to Chongqing's future, thinking more about problems, identifying more problems, and devising better solutions." Ultimately, they were to "locate the pain points, the difficult points, the focal points, and new points of growth for development."[22]

Just as Bo had relentlessly sought to spur local cadres to work harder during his early days in Chongqing, his rationale was not difficult to discern: he needed a group of local officials who were both willing to carry out his directives and capable of matching the scale of his political ambitions. From the outset, Bo repeatedly stressed to Chongqing cadres the importance of emulating more advanced regions and striving for greater ambition, rather than remaining complacent with past achievements.[23]

Third, once party cadres had become sufficiently motivated (*xiang gan shi*) and willing to work hard (*ken gan shi*), the next issue concerned their capabilities—namely, whether they knew how to get things done (*hui gan shi*) and could actually deliver results (*gan cheng shi*).[24] It was reported that when visiting some rural areas of Chongqing, Bo Xilai discovered that many local cadres possessed only limited knowledge of modern economics. This prompted him to organize a training program for more than 140 Chongqing leaders in March 2008. Amusingly, Bo himself, together with the then deputy mayor Huang Qifan, personally delivered lectures during the program. In a surprisingly candid tone, Chongqing's state media acknowledged the technocratic shortcomings of local cadres: "Some comrades indeed suffer from rather serious deficiencies in their knowledge structure and capability; the most prominent problem is their lack of modern economic knowledge—they do not fully or genuinely understand the economy."[25] Therefore, "the knowledge structure of leading cadres at all levels must undergo a revolutionary transformation."[26] To this end, the Chongqing Party School was later tasked with putting all cadres above the county level through a training program in economics.[27] In this official rhetoric, an "open economy" was essentially equated with a mature market economy. Accordingly, "open-minded cadres" were defined as officials who "possess knowledge of the market economy, have experience operating within it, and are capable of managing and navigating market-economic processes."[28]

Bo sought to instill a strong sense of urgency among Chongqing cadres—"[we] can't afford to lose, can't sit still, and can't wait" (*shu bu qi, zuo bu zhu, deng bu ji*).[29] In doing so, Bo aimed to mobilize, discipline, and exert control over the local bureaucracy, preparing a cadre corps capable of carrying out his directives and ultimately advancing his political ambitions.

Bo's ambition appeared to be as large as the gap separating Chongqing from China's leading cities. To catch up, Chongqing would need to find "a path of extraordinary development" (*chao changgui fazhan*). From the very beginning, Bo aspired to turn Chongqing into the next milestone in China's reform and national development. "Shanghai and Shenzhen have provided the country with many valuable experiences in reform and opening up. Now that Chongqing has become a centrally administered municipality, do we have the capability to do the same?" Bo continued, "Without emancipating our mind, we will not be able to generate new experiences." Foreshadowing the upcoming debate over the Chongqing Model, Bo's initial goal was to elevate Chongqing into "an important platform for discussing China's major and pressing issues, contributing insights and providing experience for national development."[30]

2.3 Reformist Flamboyance

Before arriving in Chongqing, the media-savvy Bo Xilai was already known for his flamboyant work style—an approach that would soon capture national attention when he mobilized the entire city to sing revolutionary songs and launched a high-profile anti-organized-crime campaign.

But flamboyance can go with any ideological project; it is essentially a value-neutral amplifier. During the Mind Emancipation campaign, Bo's flair for political theatrics was on full display as he sought to cultivate the image of a reform-minded party leader guiding Chongqing toward modernization.

First and foremost, Bo understood that simply following conventional practices would not make Chongqing's initiative stand out from similar campaigns underway elsewhere. To attract public attention, Bo recognized that something new had to be introduced—something that would necessarily depart from routine practices. Whereas party-led campaigns are often carried out largely through propaganda—declared successful simply by being proclaimed as such—Bo sought to make the campaign "come alive" by pushing local cadres onto the front stage and encouraging them to speak and act in public.

The initial plan was drafted using the traditional template of the Party's post-Mao rectification campaigns, probably not by Bo himself.[31] It also relied on conventional propaganda methods, with a focus on "creating a favorable atmosphere."[32]

Bo overhauled the plan one month later, emphasizing that this wave of the Mind Emancipation campaign should be fundamentally different from the traditional ones aimed at cadre rectification.[33] Responding directly to criticisms that such party-led campaigns were nothing more than "empty showmanship" and that Chongqing under Bo was merely "following the trend," Bo insisted that "[we] must introduce some concrete and substantive measures, and must not allow this campaign to degenerate into formalism." Adopting a nontraditional approach, the campaign was instructed to avoid placing excessive emphasis on "shaping public opinion" through formulaic propaganda. Instead, it should "highlight the intrinsic appeal and persuasive power of the activities themselves, thereby increasing audience attention and expanding their influence." As Bo put it, the key was that "we ourselves should speak less and do more." From the specific tasks he assigned to Chongqing cadres,[34] one can detect a whiff of Western-style political openness and accountability. Bo required every county-level party leader to deliver a public lecture on the campaign's central theme and allow ordinary citizens to evaluate his or her proposals.

Several other tasks were designed specifically to attract high-profile media coverage and public attention. In April 2008, Bo Xilai and the then mayor of Chongqing, Wang Hongju, led two groups of party cadres on study tours to the Yangtze River Delta region (i.e., Shanghai, Jiangsu, and Zhejiang) and to Guangdong Province, respectively. The trip was officially described as a "going-out" mission, the largest of its kind ever organized by Chongqing policymakers since the beginning of the reform era.[35] Dubbed a "self-motivation tour" (*zhui ci gu zhi lü*),[36] the tour was intended to encourage cadres to learn from their counterparts in more economically developed regions, in line with Bo's exhortation that Chongqing officials should recognize the development gap, become motivated, and work harder. The tour also resulted in the signing of numerous investment agreements between Chongqing and these regions, where labor-intensive manufacturing had played a major role in their economic takeoff. In this sense, Bo Xilai was actively promoting industrial relocation, a strategy known as the "domestic flying geese" model.[37]

A more eye-catching event took place in June 2008. Chongqing's local cadres were asked to form teams and participate in a televised debate competition. Claimed to be the "first of its kind" both in Chongqing and nationwide, the competition was "not designed to determine winners and losers." Instead, its purpose was "to use debate to stimulate broader discussion, making the discussions more lively and engaging, ensuring that they resonate with people's minds and hearts, and providing the ideological and public-opinion foundation for emancipating the mind and expanding the scope of opening up."[38] The competition thus served both as "a renewed mobilization for the citywide grand discussion" and as "a major public display of Chongqing's cadre corps."[39] Chongqing's state media quickly pointed to the novelty of this high-profile public spectacle. "The debate competition captured the point of convergence between issues that concern leading cadres and those that matter to the general public," the propaganda noted. "By leveraging the guiding and amplifying functions of mass media, it represents a useful attempt to innovate the methods of propaganda and ideological work."[40]

Bo Xilai's apparent reformist stance at the time was clearly reflected in the main theme of the debate competition. His remarks, delivered during a debate in which he served as a referee, further testified to his pro-reform thinking in the early days of his tenure. At one semi-final match, participants debated whether Chongqing's economic development should prioritize "quality" (*hao*) or "speed" (*kuai*). In a brief post-debate comment, Bo presented arguments both for and against the positions assigned to each side.[41] Supporting the view that developmental speed should take priority, Bo argued that "developing at a faster pace does not necessarily mean sacrificing 'quality.'" According to Bo, China's economic growth at an average rate of around 10 percent during the reform era "was in fact very 'good' in quality," particularly in the case of some coastal provinces. More importantly, Bo underlined the necessity of maintaining rapid growth: "Given China's specific circumstances, without a certain level of growth speed it is impossible to resolve the employment problem," he reasoned. "The issue of employment and the absorption of labor is the largest, indeed the most fundamental, problem in China's economic and social development." In hindsight, it is noteworthy that Bo would soon abandon this line of argument and adopt the opposite stance.

More indicative of the contrast between the early and the later Bo was *how* he himself defended the view that the quality of economic growth should take precedence over speed. As Bo argued, "only with balanced economic development can a region achieve faster growth." What he meant by imbalance here referred to the uneven distribution of infrastructure and energy resources across the country. While Bo stressed that "quality" formed the basis of "speed," he was referring to the idea that a larger share of the international market could be secured only if the quality of traded products was high. By contrast, for the later Bo, who moved closer to the Chinese Left, the crux of China's economic imbalance lay in the excesses of the unrestrained market economy and the widening of socioeconomic inequality.

Another high-profile event was the "Open Forum" (*kaifang luntan*) of 2008, jointly organized as part of the Mind Emancipation campaign by the Chongqing government, the *People's Daily*, and China's Ministry of Commerce, where Bo had worked before his appointment in Chongqing. Numerous central-level officials, as well as scholars and entrepreneurs, were invited to share their views and proposals on Chongqing's development.

The forum was nominally presented as a platform for gathering expert advice, but in reality it functioned largely as a public-relations event to promote Bo's reformist image. It was proposed that the forum would be held annually thereafter. The ultimate goal was to elevate Chongqing's status—transforming it into a "platform" for discussing major national issues in China. In doing so, it aimed "to enhance Chongqing's soft power and gradually cultivate a distinctive cultural brand."[42] However, as Bo later shifted toward a leftist stance, the forum was never convened again. His political ambitions were instead expressed through other channels.

The forum was reformist not only in theme but also in substance. Its agenda was unmistakably developmental, focusing on three subtopics: (1) Chongqing as an open inland economy; (2) coordinated urban–rural development and rural reform; and (3) economic development for cities in western China. Responding to prospective investors' concerns about local "hidden rules" (*qian guize*),[43] Chongqing officials pledged to eliminate certain traditional "bad habits" in governance and to welcome entrepreneurs with a more open and transparent attitude. Anti-corruption was also emphasized as an important measure for reducing the "business costs" and "interpersonal costs" associated with investing in Chongqing.[44] Even more politically symbolic was the presence of Gao Shangquan, a well-known liberal reformer. In his speech, Gao reviewed the "glorious" history of Dengist reform, spoke about the need to constrain state power, and warned against the resurgence of conservative ideologies.[45] Echoing this reformist keynote address, liberal advocacy also appeared in Chongqing's official media outlets around the same time, calling for further political reform and for breaking the grip of vested interests.[46] These progressive voices, however, would soon be replaced by more conservative ones as Bo gradually shifted toward the left.

2.4 "Sing Red": Spiritual Motivation

The Sing Red (*chang hong*), or "sing revolutionary songs," movement—later closely associated with Bo's Maoist image—actually began as part of his reformist flamboyance in the early days of his tenure in Chongqing. Initially, the campaign was framed as a way to raise the morale of both cadres and ordinary citizens, inspire their aspirations, and motivate them to contribute actively to Chongqing's development.

According to Chongqing's state media at the time, red songs could contribute to people's physical and psychological well-being, while also nurturing Chongqing's "spirit and vitality" (*jing qi shen*).[47] High-spirited citizens, in turn, would work harder. The goals of the "3–14 Overall Arrangement" would thus be achieved more quickly with the help of such spiritual motivation.[48] As Chongqing stood at a critical stage of its development, red songs were expected to play a key role in helping citizens "gather energy and raise morale," stimulating their "entrepreneurial enthusiasm," and encouraging them to "embrace challenges."[49] When "reading classics" (*du jingdian*) was later added to the Sing Red program in late 2008, official sources explained that this initiative originated from Chongqing leaders' effort to encourage more self-motivated learning among cadres, with the aim of making their knowledge structure more comprehensive.[50] This rationale was consistent with Bo's earlier expectation in the Mind Emancipation campaign that Chongqing cadres should improve their technocratic capabilities.

It seems inevitable that any discussion of red songs would touch upon the Party's revolutionary legacy. In these early days, however, references to the revolutionary past were intended primarily to underscore the need to push forward Dengist reform. Just as red songs were said to "express the passion of the years of struggle" and "bear witness to the growth and rise of New China," they were also described as part of the "new-era panorama of reform and opening-up."[51] With much of their substantive historical context stripped away, what was emphasized above all was the motivation for *making progress*. "The classic red songs embody that spirit of the past—a certain drive, a revolutionary will, and a fighting determination," the narrative continued. "Today, reform, opening-up, and modernization still require this same spirit."[52] However, because this type of political framing is inherently selective in determining which elements to foreground, it is hardly surprising that the conservative and revolutionary aspects of "redness" were later accentuated as Bo gradually moved toward the leftist camp.

Despite its initial reformist aura, there were signs that Bo was positioning the Sing Red movement for a different purpose—that is, a discourse that reframed red songs as a source of ideological strength.

The ostensible origin of the movement was widely publicized. Shortly before Children's Day (June 1), Bo Xilai paid a visit to a local elementary school and discovered that the students did not even know how to sing the popular red song "Ode to My Homeland" (*gechang zuguo*). This episode was later presented in official narratives as the moment when Bo conceived the idea of promoting red songs. As Bo remarked, red songs "can awaken noble sentiments in people's hearts, purify the soul, and encourage children from an early age to cultivate patriotic and uplifting aspirations." Indeed, Bo's statement here presented a markedly different framing from the earlier one aimed at reformist galvanization. At the same time, Bo explicitly invoked Mao's famous metaphor likening young people to the "morning sun" (*ba jiu dian zhong de taiyang*).[53]

Deviation from the reformist line was even more evident elsewhere. In a *Chongqing Daily* article, the red songs were described as a symbol of "mainstream culture" (*zhuliu wenhua*). The key message was a call to safeguard China's cultural independence: "For any nation, while upholding cultural and artistic diversity, it must also preserve respect for and continuity with its traditions, which is the core that enables the nation to remain cohesive."[54] Around the same time, the Mind Emancipation debate competition appeared to echo the subtle shift taking place. Whereas all the previous debate topics had focused on economic development, the question posed in the final match asked whether non-economic "soft power" (*ruan shili*) might be more important than economic "hard" power.[55] In a somewhat discordant tone, an ideologically driven interpretation of soft power also surfaced at the Open Forum of 2008 held in Chongqing, which had otherwise been dedicated to an explicitly reformist agenda. When addressing the theme of "city spirit," one speaker digressed at length, arguing that Chongqing's development required "wisdom," which was said to derive from the "social sciences and philosophy." In the Party's political jargon, these fields of academic study were regarded as essentially ideological in nature. Soft power was therefore deemed crucial to the survival of a political regime. As an illustration, the speaker pointed to ideological erosion as the ultimate cause of the Soviet Union's collapse—a classic interpretation commonly advanced by Chinese leftists.[56]

All these early signs of moving away from reformism echoed the official agenda on cultural development laid out in the Seventeenth Party Congress report. Under the theme of "making socialist culture develop and prosper" (*shehui zhuyi wenhua da fazhan da fanrong*), the report emphasized the importance of "soft power" and "national culture," and more ominously, the "Socialist Core Value System" (*shehui zhuyi hexin jiazhi tixi*), a program largely aimed at promoting ideological loyalty to Marxism and socialism. It was therefore no coincidence that "making socialist culture develop and prosper" became the official theme of Chongqing's Fifth Party Plenum. Later, the Sing Red movement was explicitly linked to the promotion of socialist values once Bo decided to align himself with the leftist camp.

Nevertheless, Bo's leftist transformation had not yet become explicitly visible until the Fourth Plenum of the Chongqing Party Committee, held in late 2008. Prior to that, the overall political atmosphere in Chongqing still appeared reformist. To deflect potential public suspicion and criticism, Chongqing's state media moved quickly to emphasize that Chongqing neither took the lead nor acted alone in organizing people to sing revolutionary songs. Similar activities, they noted, had also taken place in other provinces.[57]

It appears that by mid-2008 Bo may already have sensed something on the horizon, though he had not yet made up his mind to take a left turn. Aligning himself with China's conservatives was not an easy choice when Dengist reform still remained the hegemonic political framework. At the same time, Bo would hardly have wanted to miss any opportunity that might advance his political career. If betting on the strong was his overarching strategy, then initiating the Sing Red movement seemed to be a clever straddling tactic: the red songs could be framed either way, depending on which side—the reformers or the conservatives—Bo ultimately judged to hold the political upper hand.

This was not unlike what Bo intended when he mobilized the entire city to plant trees. As Bo once proudly claimed, "one can never go wrong with planting trees" (*zhongshu yongyuan bu hui fancuo*).[58] Making Chongqing greener could be advertised as part of the city's modernization effort, appealing to a reformist audience. Alternatively, following a more conservative script, it could also be promoted as a manifestation of Chongqing leaders' "new attitude toward political achievements" (*xinxing zhengji guan*),[59] a concept introduced under Hu Jintao as an implicit leftist critique of China's GDP-oriented development model. In short, as a seasoned Chinese politician, Bo knew how to play it safe while always leaving some wiggle room for adjustment.

Notes

1. Bo Xilai, "Zai shi san jie ren da yi ci huiyi shang de jianghua" [The Speech at the First Session of Chongqing's Third People's Congress], *Chongqing ribao*, January 27, 2008.
2. "Zhan zai kaifang qianyan shixian xin de kuayue" [Standing at the Forefront of Openness, Achieving a New Leap Forward], *Jinri Chongqing*, no. 1 (2008): 15.
3. "Zhan zai kaifang qianyan," 14; Mou Fengjing, Liu Changfa, and Luo Jingwen, "Quanmian luoshi '314' you hao you kuai cu fazhan" [Fully Implementing the "3–14" Overall Arrangements, Promoting Development in a High-Quality and Rapid Manner], *Chongqing ribao*, December 26, 2007.
4. Hu Jintao, "Zai shi jie quan guo ren da wu ci huiyi Chongqing daibiao tuan de zhongyao jianghua (zhaiyao)" [An Important Speech Delivered to the Chongqing Delegation at the Fifth Session of the Tenth National People's Congress (Excerpt)], in *Kexue fazhan de Chongqing shijian daxing jishi wenxian* [A Comprehensive Documentary on Chongqing's Practice of Scientific Development] (Zhongyang wenxian chubanshe, 2011), 2–4.
5. Liu Changfa and Zhang Xuefeng, "Guanche 'lianghui jingshen' zhua hao wu jian dashi" [Implementing the "Two Sessions Spirit" and Focusing on Five Major Tasks], *Chongqing ribao*, March 23, 2008; "Jin nian zhongdian zhua hao wu jian dashi" [Focusing on Five Major Tasks This Year], *Jinri Chongqing*, no. 4 (2008): 14–15.
6. It suggests that Chongqing's local practice began two years before this domestic industrial transfer policy was formally elevated to a national development strategy in 2010. See Yuen Yuen Ang, "Domestic Flying Geese: Industrial Transfer and Delayed Policy Diffusion in China," *The China Quarterly* 234 (2018): 420–443, https://doi.org/10.1017/S0305741018000516.
7. "Zhan zai kaifang qianyan," 15; Mou, Liu and Luo, "Quanmian luoshi '314.'"
8. It means that the market lies overseas while raw materials and components are provisioned and produced locally.
9. It means that both the production and supply of raw materials and components, and the market, are located outside of China.
10. Tao Weihong and Liu Changfa, "Zai kuoda kaifang zhong shixian you hao you kuai fazhan" [Realizing High-Quality and Rapid Development by Expanding the Scope of Opening-Up], *Chongqing ribao*, July 21, 2008.
11. Yang Bing, "Shi zhengfu zhaokai Liangjiang xin qu chengli xinwen fabu hui" [The Chongqing Municipal Government Held a Press Conference on

the Establishment of Liangjiang New Area], *Chongqing ribao*, June 19, 2010.

12. "Da jizhe wen shilu" [Transcript of Answers to Reporters' Questions], *Chongqing ribao*, June 19, 2010.
13. Zhou Ruijin, "'Di san ci sixiang jiefang' yao jiejue liu da wenti" ["The Third Wave of Mind Emancipation" Needs to Address Six Major Questions], *Xin jing bao*, March 17, 2008, http://www.chinanews.com.cn/gn/news/2008/03-17/1193735.shtml.
14. Wang Chu and Liu Taishan, "Wang Yang: Zheng dang shijian kexue fazhan guan de paituobing" [Wang Yang: Striving to Be the Vanguard in Practicing the Scientific Outlook on Development], *Renmin ribao*, December 29, 2007.
15. Other localities that launched the Mind Emancipation campaigns include Shanghai, Jilin and Qinghai. See Ma Guochuan, *Zou chu weiwen niandai: 2008–2013 Zhongguo shehui sixiang jiaofeng* [Moving Beyond the Age of Stability Maintenance: Clashing Social Thoughts in China, 2008–2013] (Hong Kong Zhonghe chuban, 2013), 73–74.
16. "Guanyu kaizhan 'jiefang sixiang, kuoda kaifang' da taolun de yijian" [Opinions on Launching a Major Discussion on "Emancipating the Mind and Expanding the Scope of Opening-Up"], *Chongqing ribao*, March 31, 2008.
17. Tao Weihong and Zhang Xuefeng, "Jiefang sixiang, kuoda kaifang, ba '314' zongti bushu luo dao shichu" [Emancipating the Mind, Expanding the Scope of Opening-Up, and Fully Implementing the "3–14" Overall Arrangements], *Chongqing ribao*, March 28, 2008.
18. "Jiefang sixiang tuidong Chongqing da kaifang" [Emancipating the Mind to Promote Greater Opening-Up in Chongqing], *Jinri Chongqing*, no. 9 (2008): 12–15.
19. External Propaganda Office of the Chongqing Party Committee (EPOCPC) and Chongqing Center for Internet News Research (CCINR), *Yu lun 2008* [Public Opinion in Chongqing 2008] (self-published, 2009), 34.
20. "Yi sixiang da jiefang, cu da kaifang da fazhan" [Promoting Greater Opening-Up and Development through Mind Emancipation], *Chongqing ribao*, March 28, 2008.
21. Theoretical Research Team of the Propaganda Department of Chongqing Party Committee, "Jiefang sixiang shi guanche luoshi '314' zongti bushu de fabao" [Mind Emancipation Is the Magic Weapon for Ensuring the Implementation of the "3–14" Overall Arrangements], *Chongqing ribao*, March 8, 2008.
22. Tao and Zhang, "Jiefang sixiang, kuoda kaifang."

23. Mou Fengjing and Shang Yu, "Qu xian gongzuo da you ke wei" [District and County Work Holds Great Promise], *Chongqing ribao*, December 27, 2007.
24. Mou Fengjing and Tao Weihong, "Zai fazhan chanye zhong zengjia jiuye gaishan minsheng" [Increasing Employment and Improving People's Livelihoods through Industrial Development], *Chongqing ribao*, January 8, 2008; "Zai kuoda kaifang zhong shixian you hao you kuai fazhan" [Realizing High-Quality and Rapid Development through Expanding the Scope of Opening-Up], *Jinri Chongqing*, no. 8 (2008): 15.
25. Theoretical Research Team of the Propaganda Department of Chongqing Party Committee, "Jiefang sixiang shi guanche luoshi."
26. "Jiefang sixiang zhao chaju, qinzheng lianzheng qiu fazhan" [Identifying Gaps through Mind Emancipation and Pursuing Development through Diligent and Clean Governance], *Chongqing ribao*, February 22, 2008.
27. "Kuoda kaifang, re ci dianji" [Expanding the Scope of Opening-Up: Buzzwords in Focus], *Chongqing ribao*, July 22, 2008.
28. Chongqing Research Center for Sinicized Marxism, "Kuoda kaifang zhongdian yao dazao kaifang xing ganbu duiwu" [The Key to Expanding the Scope of Opening-Up Is Building a Team of Opening-Oriented Cadres], *Chongqing ribao*, October 15, 2008.
29. Liu Changfa, "Zhonggong Chongqing shi wei san jie san ci quanwei hui shengli bimu" [The Third Plenum of the Third Chongqing Party Committee Successfully Concluded], *Chongqing ribao*, July 22, 2008.
30. Chongqing Association for Social Sciences, *Chongqing shi "jiefang sixiang, kuoda kaifang" da taolun da xing wenji* [A Complete Anthology of Chongqing's Grand Discussion on "Emancipating the Mind and Expanding Opening-Up"] (Sichuan chuban jituan/Sichuan kexue jishu chubanshe, 2009), 14–18.
31. According to this template, a typical post-Mao rectification campaign targeting party cadres goes through the following phases: studying party documents, reflection (usually during discussion and meetings), and correction (usually by making some adjustment in current policies or improving public service).
32. "Guanyu kaizhan 'jiefang sixiang, kuoda kaifang.'"
33. Chongqing Association for Social Sciences, *Chongqing shi "jiefang sixiang, kuoda kaifang,"* 14–18.
34. The initial plan laid out six main tasks, only three of which remained on Bo Xilai's list of nine.
35. "Nanwang de xingcheng, xuexi de geming" [An Unforgettable Journey and a Revolution in Learning], *Jinri Chongqing*, no. 5 (2008): 15.
36. "'Zhui ci gu zhi lü' ling ren zhenhan" ["A Journey of Self-Motivation" Is Striking], *Jinri Chongqing*, no. 5 (2008): 23.

37. "Hezuo zhi hua nu fang zai si yue de chun guang li" [The Flower of Cooperation Blooms in the Spring Light of April], *Jinri Chongqing*, no. 5 (2008): 21.
38. Propaganda Department of Chongqing Party Committee (PDCPC), *Shan cheng lun jian: "jiefang sixiang, kuoda kaifang" dianshi bianlun sai shilu* [A Contest at the City of Hills: A Documentary of the TV Debate on "Emancipating the Mind and Expanding Opening-Up"] (Chongqing chubanshe, 2008), 1.
39. PDCPC, *Shan cheng lun jian*, 2.
40. PDCPC, *Shan cheng lun jian*, 6.
41. PDCPC, *Shan cheng lun jian*, 197–198.
42. Xiong Yi, "Kaifang de luntan, sixiang de shengyan" [An Open Forum and a Feast of Ideas], *Jinri Chongqing*, no. 8 (2008): 16.
43. EPOCPC and CCINR, *Yu lun 2008*, 107.
44. EPOCPC and CCINR, *Yu lun 2008*, 40.
45. Propaganda Department of Chongqing Party Committee (PDCPC), *Kaifang luntan yanjiang ji* [A Collection of Speeches at the 2008 Open Forum] (Chongqing chubanshe, 2008), 65–67.
46. Deng Quanlun, "Jiefang sixiang zui zhuyao de shi yao gaige" [The Key to Mind Emancipation Is Reform], *Chongqing ribao*, July 28, 2008.
47. Tao and Liu, "Zai kuoda kaifang zhong shixian"; "Zai kuoda kaifang zhong shixian," 15.
48. Shang Yu, "Chuan chang hongse gequ, shufa shidai haoqing" [Singing Red Songs and Writing the Heroic Spirit of the Era], *Chongqing ribao*, June 18, 2008.
49. Zhang Xuefeng, "'Hong ge' dianran Chongqing jiqing" ["Red Songs" Ignite Chongqing's Passion], *Chongqing ribao*, July 11, 2008.
50. "Chongqing xian ge" [String Songs of Chongqing], *Jinri Chongqing*, no. 5 (2009), preface.
51. "Hong ge jiyi: na xie nanwang de suiyue" [Memories of Red Songs: Those Unforgettable Years], *Jinri Chongqing*, no. 9 (2008): 72.
52. Yu Ting, "You shi zhi jiguan ge yong hui xiang dao de" [Reflections Inspired by the Singing Contest of Municipal Government Departments], *Chongqing ribao*, July 21, 2008.
53. Tao Weihong and Zhang Xuefeng, "Yao peiyang haizi men angyang jiankang de jing qi shen" [We Must Cultivate in Children a Vigorous and Healthy Spirit], *Chongqing ribao*, May 31, 2008.
54. Zhang, "'Hong ge' dianran."
55. PDCPC, *Shan cheng lun jian.*
56. PDCPC, *Kaifang luntan yanjiang ji*, 124–130.
57. Other localities mentioned include Jiangxi, Hebei, Anhui provinces, and Donglan county in Guangxi province. See Zhu Chuhua, "Hong ge chuan-

chang, tizhen Chongqing jing qi shen" [Singing Red Songs and Raising Chongqing's Spirit], *Chongqing ribao*, November 13, 2008.

58. Liu Changfa and Zhang Xuefeng, "Guanche 'lianghui' jingshen qidong si xiang gongzuo" [Implementing the Spirit of the "Two Sessions" and Initiating Work in Four Areas], *Chongqing ribao*, March 18, 2010.
59. EPOCPC and CCINR, *Yu lun 2008*, 18.

CHAPTER 3

Embracing Leftism

Bo Xilai's leftist transformation began with a reorientation of the Sing Red movement. Toward the end of 2008, a major shift in discourse had become increasingly palpable: red songs were now associated with the transmission and indoctrination of socialist values, rather than simply serving as apolitical and non-ideological motivators for developmental progress. Red songs still played a role in providing motivation and inspiration, but they now did so by transforming the people themselves. The source of strength was no longer the desire to emulate revolutionary forefathers who had persevered and triumphed in the old days, but rather the ideological superiority of socialism.

3.1 "Sing Red": Socialist Values

At the Fourth Plenum of the Chongqing Party Committee, held in November 2008 and nominally dedicated to discussing reform and development in rural areas, Bo Xilai made an incongruous digression to address the Sing Red movement. He presented it in a new, leftist framing that was both ideological and politicized.[1] China's future, he argued, now hinged not only on the hardworking spirit of the younger generation but also on whether they had internalized the "[socialist] core values" and "[communist] ideals and convictions" (*lixiang xinnian*). Consolidating this ideological foundation was seen as especially imperative given that various non-socialist ideas had already permeated society, posing a threat to the

L. Le, *Revival of Maoism in Reform-Era China*,
https://doi.org/10.1007/978-981-92-4606-9_3

Party's guiding ideology. Bo further emphasized that the ongoing financial crisis in the West testified to the correctness of the "Chinese path." To ensure that China would continue to "proceed in the right direction," Bo advocated "using language and forms that the masses readily understand and enjoy to explain the Socialist Core Value System, and integrating it into national education and the process of building socialist spiritual civilization."

Hence the importance and usefulness of the Sing Red movement. It could serve as "an important vehicle for ideological work and for cultivating advanced culture."[2] Moreover, at the plenum Bo also linked the singing of red songs to the task of addressing China's perceived crisis of social morality. "When a country or a nation lacks ideals and convictions and has no core values, it will inevitably suffer from spiritual malaise, moral decline, and cultural backwardness," Bo argued. "Even if it temporarily develops rapidly and accumulates strong economic power, social cohesion will erode, and it will fail to develop lasting competitiveness." In this rhetoric, spiritual well-being took precedence over material achievements. Bo was clearly echoing the widely circulating leftist critique of Dengist reform at the time. According to this view, China's capitalist approach to reform, driven largely by the logic of market economy, had exacted a significant cost: a profound crisis of moral degeneration in society. Red songs, therefore, were presented as "a dose of good medicine."[3]

This ideologization and politicization of the Sing Red movement paved the way for the elevation of "culture" as the central theme of Chongqing's Fifth Party Plenum, held in June 2009. The theme was a call for "making culture develop and prosper." It was identical to the title of Section 7 of the Seventeenth Party Congress report, which addressed China's cultural policies. According to the official statement,[4] the ultimate goal of Chongqing's cultural development from that point onward was "to firmly establish the Socialist Core Value System and provide strong spiritual motivation for implementing the 3–14 Overall Arrangement." The motivational element was still clearly emphasized: the power of "advanced thought and culture" could arouse "the *determination* not to fall behind, the *courage* to catch up, and the *ambition* to surpass others" (emphasis added), thus enabling Chongqing to "transcend itself" and accomplish the tasks assigned by the Party center.

However, the role of "culture," or red songs in particular, as an embodiment of socialist values, had come to be treated as an important end in itself, rather than merely a stimulus or a mobilizing instrument. Spiritual strength was now regarded as a major variable in the equation rather than simply a coefficient that amplified the effects of other factors. Culture was said to exert a direct influence on economic development. More importantly, it was portrayed as the foundation upon which other contributing factors depended for their effectiveness. "Culture is the lifeblood and soul of a nation," the resolution of Chongqing's Fifth Plenum wrote. "Advanced culture is the backbone, the spirit, and the engine of economic development and social progress for a country or region."

Bo Xilai was straightforward regarding the politicized and ideological significance of *culture*.[5] At the plenum, he underscored the close relationship between culture, "soft power," and "national competitiveness," noting that "the deeper contest between nations is ultimately a contest of ideas and will." This framing carried a strong, somewhat anachronistic bellicosity reminiscent of the anti-capitalist struggles of China's Mao era. Bo called for "promoting the main melody" (*zhu xuanlü*) and "building a mainstream culture," arguing that this was necessary because "socialism with Chinese characteristics is suited to China and superior to the various 'isms' found in other countries." Alluding to leftist criticisms of China's market-oriented reform—criticisms that were implicitly embedded in Hu Jintao's concept of Scientific Outlook on Development—Bo stressed that culture exerted a decisive influence on the "direction and goals of development." Since certain values and beliefs lie at the core of culture, he concluded that "taking cultural work seriously is tantamount to steering the [political] course competently."

In short, the significance of Chongqing's Sing Red movement was now framed as essentially concerning how the Party center's political and ideological agenda could be, and indeed had been, materialized on the ground at the local level. First, although the movement had still been largely about reformist motivation only months earlier, its focus had unmistakably shifted. As the official account put it, "The promotion of red songs is a process of exploring how to use the Socialist Core Value System to guide social trends of thought and to enhance the appeal and cohesion of socialist ideology."[6] Second, the Sing Red campaign provided a convenient instrument for ideological indoctrination. Red songs were described as "an important vehicle for transforming the Socialist Core Value System from 'abstraction' to 'concreteness.'"[7]

This rhetoric portraying the Sing Red movement as a facilitator of socialist indoctrination soon received high-level political endorsement. In late 2009, during a visit to Chongqing, Liu Yunshan, the incumbent director of the Party's Central Propaganda Department, lavished praise on the movement. After attending a revolutionary song concert in person, Liu described the experience as one that "made people's hearts pound and their blood boil," adding that the way Chongqing had been promoting red culture was "worthy of nationwide promotion."[8] Liu further remarked that the Party's revolutionary history provided "a vivid illustration" of the Socialist Core Value System and served as "the best textbook" for its dissemination.[9] About a year later, in August 2010, Li Changchun, then a Politburo Standing Committee member in charge of ideological work, also visited Chongqing. After affirming the Sing Red movement as an effective method for propagating socialist values, Li urged Chongqing to further explore mechanisms that could ensure "long-term effectiveness" (*changxiao jizhi*). Likewise, Li called on the Central Propaganda Department to "summarize the experience and promote it nationwide,"[10] endorsing what Chongqing itself had been advocating—namely, to make the red culture movement "go deeper, last longer, and become more effective," and to render it "normalized" (*changtai hua*).[11]

By the end of 2010, Bo Xilai's conservative turn had been completed. Not long before, Chongqing's state media had still been reporting that Chongqing's Sing Red initiative was not unique, attempting to avoid portraying Chongqing as the mastermind that had taken the lead. Now, however, Chongqing presented itself as a pioneer implementing the Party center's ideological agenda in an innovative way. The contrast could hardly have been starker. Previously employed as a flamboyant means toward a reformist end, the Sing Red movement had now been transformed into an ideological symbol and a tool for safeguarding the Party's political supremacy: "[singing red songs] can strengthen ideals and convictions, forge political consensus, and ensure that the revolutionary cause is passed on from generation to generation."[12] Accordingly, Bo's defense of Sing Red became increasingly political. "Nowadays some people deliberately avoid red culture, as if promoting the [Chinese] Communist Party's theories and doctrines makes one appear 'leftist' or 'outdated,'" Bo remarked. "In fact, Marxism–Leninism, Mao Zedong Thought, and Deng Xiaoping Theory are all scientific."[13] Indeed, what loomed in the background was the lingering specter of the Party's Mao-era political mindset that placed ideological conviction above everything else. As Bo put it, "in carrying out reform and opening up, we have never meant to abandon our original ideals and convictions." At this point—just before Chongqing's Eighth

Party Plenum—Bo the Leftist stood only one step away from becoming Maoist and further "revolutionized."

3.2 "City Spirit"

With the rhetoric of the Sing Red movement shifting to the left, the discourse surrounding Bo Xilai's urban planning project also changed its course accordingly.

One possible ideational origin of Bo Xilai's red culture movement can arguably be traced to a city-building project that sought to forge a "city spirit" (*chengshi jingshen*) for Chongqing. The project was actually initiated in early 2006—well before Bo arrived in Chongqing—by his predecessor, Wang Yang. According to official records,[14] Wang was the first to call for "summarizing, distilling, cultivating, and promoting Chongqing's humanistic spirit (*renwen jingshen*)." The project was a largely non-ideological cultural initiative aimed at promoting development. At its core lay the commercial logic of city branding. As the official explanation put it, "Just as the kindness of Shandong people, the forthrightness of Northeasterners, and the shrewdness of Shanghainese have come to serve as city brands, Chongqing's humanistic spirit should likewise become the city's brand—a moral norm for its residents and a defining cultural characteristic of the city."

As soon as he assumed office in Chongqing, Bo Xilai reframed Wang Yang's "humanistic spirit" project under the theme of "city spirit," though in essence it was little more than a continuation of Wang Yang's earlier agenda. On May 23, 2008—just a week before his well-known visit to an elementary school where he taught children to sing a red song and called for a citywide Sing Red campaign—Bo paid a visit to the Chongqing Propaganda Department. During the visit, Bo urged party cadres to make full use of local cultural resources in constructing Chongqing's city spirit. "Chongqing is a city endowed with a deep cultural heritage, as well as rich and distinctive resources in culture, art, and ideology," he noted. These resources included "Hongyan spirit," the culture of "wartime provisional capital" (*pei du*), and the spirit of "the Three Gorges migrants" (*sanxia yimin*). It is worth noting that, at this point, the cultural references extended beyond the legacy of communist revolution to include those associated with China's Republican and reform eras as well. This diversity would later stand in sharp contrast to the overwhelming emphasis placed on the Party's revolutionary heritage. Acting on Bo's directive, a research team was established and assigned a project titled "Research on the Cultivation of Chongqing's City Spirit." The project was later placed on the agenda of Chongqing's Fifth Party Plenum.

Consistent with Bo's reformist policy orientation in his early days in Chongqing, part of the City Spirit project focused on the technical aspects of urban planning. Taking a comparative approach, the project team examined how Chongqing might learn from the experience of other major cities, including Shanghai, Tokyo, Paris, and London, all of which were said to have developed distinctive city spirits in the course of their development.[15] What Chongqing aimed for here was anything but political. Chongqing's revolutionary past, or its "red history," which was treated here as a kind of cultural and economic resource, was juxtaposed with Beijing's "royal grandeur" and Shanghai's "fusion of East and West."[16] Speaking in a reformist tone, a Chongqing official highlighted that city spirit primarily concerned "public morality," "civic spirit," and "the spirit of the times."[17] In addition, probably modeled on Shanghai's city PR slogan—"Be receptive to diversity and pursue excellence" (*hai na bai chuan, zhui qiu zhuo yue*)—the eight-character summary of Chongqing's city spirit, "reach high and far, persevere and strengthen oneself under burden" (*deng gao she yuan, fu zhong zi qiang*), clearly resonated with the theme of reformist self-motivation. On the flip side, cautionary tales were also told: Chongqing might fall far behind due to its perceived cultural barrenness and the supposed indolence of citizens who indulged in playing mahjong and rarely read.[18] This intended technocratic construction of city spirit was consistent with, and fit well within, Chongqing's official rhetoric at the time that "soft power" was necessary for the city's social and economic progress.[19]

When the City Spirit project officially came to a conclusion around mid-2009, the political wind had already shifted. It is difficult to determine precisely *to what extent* the project was initially intended as a technical and developmental effort in urban planning, and, if so, whether it was only later derailed after Bo made an about-face and adopted a more leftist political stance.

That being said, what we can see clearly is that the construction of the city spirit became closely bound up with the red culture movement. A politicized tone was firmly established: "spirit is something that belongs to the realm of ideology."[20] Cultivating a city spirit was thus framed as part of a defensive effort against ideological threats. "In an era of diverse ideologies and choices, the mainstream value system is being penetrated and divided from all angles by [the forces of] Westernization." This logic was used to explain why the promotion of the Sing Red movement had to be "elevated to a strategic level," which was said to demonstrate "the political wisdom and clairvoyance of the city's policymaker [i.e., Bo Xilai]."[21]

In particular, the red culture movement aimed to "mould the soul" (*su hun*) of Chongqing by "spreading mainstream values, enriching mass culture, cultivating the spirit of the city, and enhancing the civic capacity of its residents."[22] The material goals of urban development, it was argued, could only be achieved through spiritual means. As the rhetoric put it, "the city spirit is an inexhaustible wellspring of motivation that leads a city to greatness."[23] Red culture was said not only to "shape the city's external image and brand," but also to "consolidate its inner vitality and collective spirit."[24] More importantly, what had begun as a reformist project of city culture was now reduced to a manifestation of the Party's preoccupation with ideological security. Red culture could shape the soul of the city not least because it helped consolidate and propagate the Socialist Core Value System.[25]

The politicization of the Sing Red movement not only derailed the search for Chongqing's city spirit, but also reshaped the rhetorical framing of the municipality's urban development more broadly. The city's initial reformist agenda gradually drifted away from its original technocratic orientation.

Bo Xilai was well known for his urban planning achievements in Dalian, which he helped transform into a "garden city." In recognition of these efforts, the United Nations awarded him the Habitat Scroll of Honour in 1999. It is therefore hardly surprising that during his early days in Chongqing, or what might be described as a brief period of reformist flamboyance, Bo attempted to emulate his earlier approach in a similarly reformist vein. First, Bo stressed the economic logic behind taking city building seriously. "Cities are the locomotive driving economic and social development, and in modern economic life, the center of gravity lies in cities," Bo argued. "A survey of human history shows that the development of markets has always been closely linked to the growth of cities." Accordingly, he noted that "major cities across China are now paying close attention to improving the urban environment, and such improvements directly strengthen a city's ability to attract various economic resources, enhance its cohesion, and, most importantly, draw talented people."[26] Second, Bo emphasized that city planning had to be conducted professionally. "A city may encounter an opportunity for large-scale expansion or reconstruction only once in fifty years," Bo said. "Once the pattern is set, it becomes difficult to change for the next thirty or fifty years." Sound design, in this view, would contribute to a city's economic development for decades to come. As Bo put it, "the image of a city is also its calling card, or its advertisement, and it can generate benefits in many different ways."[27]

The concrete policy framework that emerged from Bo's advocacy was the so-called Five Chongqings (*wu ge Chongqing*). It consisted of five policy programs aimed at improving Chongqing's urban environment, infrastructure, and public services.

1. "Hospitable Chongqing" (*yiju Chongqing*): an initiative to improve housing conditions and urban infrastructure
2. "Connected Chongqing" (*changtong Chongqing*): a program intended to ease traffic congestion and expand the transportation network
3. "Forested Chongqing" (*senlin Chongqing*): an effort to increase urban green coverage and develop forest-related agricultural industries
4. "Safe Chongqing" (*ping'an Chongqing*): a program aimed at improving public safety more broadly (later closely associated with the anti-organized-crime campaign)
5. "Healthy Chongqing" (*jiankang Chongqing*): an initiative to expand access to medical services and promote public fitness activities

It is worth noting that, at the outset, the Five Chongqings, as a city-building initiative, was explicitly intended to foster Chongqing's reform-oriented development. Bo Xilai stated clearly at the Third Plenum of the Chongqing Party Committee in July 2008 that "providing an environment with both sound 'software' and 'hardware' is the foundation for expanding the scope of opening-up." More specifically, this referred to creating a business environment in which "enterprises feel secure and receive supportive services" (*an shang zhu shang*).[28] This initial positioning was highly consistent with Bo Xilai's early reformist policy orientation and with the aforementioned logic that city building ultimately functioned as a marketing tool for developing the market economy.

However, just as Bo made the fateful decision to turn left by politicizing the Sing Red movement, his city-building project was likewise ideologically reoriented. "Culture" now replaced economics as the primary driver of development. It was claimed that Chongqing "has been searching for a new frontier of development" and that a major "breakthrough" had finally been achieved—namely, the strategy of "strengthening the city through culture" (*wenhua qiang shi*). Specifically, this meant that, with "advanced culture occupying the battleground of ideology and culture," the red culture movement could "accumulate powerful force to propel Chongqing's socioeconomic development forward."[29]

When it came to the Five Chongqings program, an additional component was introduced: "Culturally edified Chongqing" (*renwen Chongqing*). The framework was thus recast as "a 5+1 model of Chongqing's scientific development."[30] Whereas the original five policy areas focused primarily on the development of "hardware," culture was intended to address the dimension of "soft power." Previously, singing red songs had been linked to the Five Chongqings through the notion of "mental well-being," which fell under the fifth policy category of "Healthy Chongqing."[31] Now, however, the red culture movement was elevated into something far more encompassing. According to the official elaboration, "for any country or region, it is insufficient to develop hard power alone; there must also be strong support from soft power, including *advanced* development concepts as well as the ideas and culture that represent the direction of future progress [emphasis added]."[32]

The key question here is how the term "advanced" was understood. According to the propaganda materials, a soft-power approach to development and growth was considered superior because it could help avoid the "commonsensical pitfalls" associated with a "one-sided focus on economic growth."[33] Once again, this formulation implicitly echoed the leftist critique of China's market-oriented reforms, a critique that had been subtly embedded in Hu Jintao's concept of Scientific Development.

More importantly, the supposed superiority of a culture-driven model of development was said to rest on the ideological strength inherent in *socialism*. From this point onward, the rhetoric became increasingly political. There was still talk of culture as a source of self-motivation—for example, the claim that "a region's economic backwardness in itself is not fatal, but what must not lag behind is its mindset."[34] Yet, as discussed above, what had initially been presented as an apolitical instrument for developmental purposes was now recast as the fundamental source of the Party's ideological power and political legitimacy. In this context, "advanced thought" became synonymous with "revolutionary aspiration" (*geming lixiang*).[35]

It was claimed that the revolutionary spirit embodied in the Party's red culture could first unite and mobilize the people and then enable them to accomplish missions that had once seemed impossible. "The strength of a political party does not lie in the number of its members," according to the rhetoric. "If it grasps advanced ideas and the entire party acts with one heart and mind…then spirit can be transformed into material force, making success, progress, and development possible."[36] In the case of Chongqing, the propaganda further asserted that "we must use advanced ideas and culture to concentrate morale and energy, use scientific concepts of development to cultivate a firm guiding core, and use forward-looking soft power to build the engine of development, the ultimate goal being to generate a powerful acceleration." In this way, Chongqing would be able to "overtake others on a bend" (*wandao chaoche*).[37]

Furthermore, ideological correctness—namely, adherence to the socialist path under the Party's leadership—was said to determine not only success or failure in development but also something deeper and more fundamental: the survival of the regime itself. "If a decision concerning an economic project proves mistaken, the resulting losses are limited and measurable," the propaganda warned, "but if the direction of thought and theory goes astray, the losses will be systemic and immeasurable." Accordingly, when it comes to ideology, "either nothing goes wrong, or, if something does go wrong, it becomes a major and irreversible matter."[38]

Once fully politicized, cultural policy became equated with the political control of people's minds. Culture was elevated to the "top priority" on the agenda of ideological work, with the Socialist Core Value System serving as the concrete policy framework.[39] In this context, cultural development came to be framed as a matter of life and death. As one assertion put it, "Our struggle with various hostile forces in the ideological sphere is, in essence, a contest between the socialist value system and the capitalist value system—a struggle over leadership in the realm of thought and culture."[40]

3.3 People's Livelihoods

In addition to this general ideologization, the conservative turn in Bo Xilai's city-building project—the Five Chongqings—also had an economic dimension. Urban upgrading and development were no longer framed as part of Chongqing's effort to achieve modernization through the market economy. Instead, they were redefined as serving the overarching goal of improving "people's livelihoods" (*min sheng*). According to official discourse, "All the related investments [in the Five Chongqings] are part of a project aimed at improving people's livelihoods."[41]

To be sure, this shift in attention toward social welfare did not originate with Bo Xilai. Rather, improving people's livelihoods was regarded as the core of the so-called Hu–Wen New Deal. State media highlighted that the party-state's emphasis on "improving people's livelihoods" was "unprecedented," noting that four full pages of the 2008 Government Work Report were devoted to the issue.[42]

In fact, improving people's livelihoods had already been part of Chongqing's developmental agenda long before Bo Xilai arrived. The generous allocation of Chongqing's state budget to social welfare projects—something Bo later frequently highlighted—had already been put into practice under his predecessor, Wang Yang. According to official sources,[43] 30 percent of Chongqing's fiscal revenue was spent on projects related to people's livelihoods in 2003; by 2007, the figure had risen to more than 50 percent. The rationale behind this policy shift was broadly consistent with the policy environment under Hu Jintao, which featured a distinctly pro-poor policy orientation. It was reported that whereas the approach to social welfare during the early reform period had focused on concentrating limited resources on the poorest segments of society, due to the government's "limited fiscal strength," the newer approach—channeling a larger share of state revenue into social welfare—was justified by China's "increased national strength." In addition, it is worth noting that Chongqing's people's livelihoods policy under Wang Yang still bore a clear, if implicit, imprint of reformism. It was not merely about the transfer of financial resources; it also aimed to help the disadvantaged and the poor to stand on their own feet. In other words, the relevant policies sought to "nurture and improve the social environment in which members of society would be assisted and guided to exercise their own agency and achieve self-reliance." According to *A Compilation of Chongqing's Policies Benefiting the People 2005–2007*, published by the Chongqing municipal government, these social welfare policies were intended to "energize society, improve public services, and create conditions for various productive factors to circulate more actively."

Hence, there was clear policy continuity from Wang Yang to Bo Xilai. As noted earlier, improving people's livelihoods had already been part of

Chongqing's developmental agenda in Bo's early days, although it had not yet been elevated to the position of top priority. Moreover, the onset of the 2008 global financial crisis may well have further heightened the salience of the social welfare agenda under Hu Jintao. The Chongqing Economic Work Conference held in December 2008 was devoted to discussing how the city could weather the financial crisis, at a time when China's manufacturing sector was widely expected to bear the brunt of the global economic downturn.

However, in tandem with the politicization of the red culture movement, Bo Xilai's paternalistic reorientation of economic policy proved to be more than a merely technical response to immediate economic pressures. What Bo was attempting to accomplish was the substitution of an alternative logic of development for the reformist paradigm centered on the market economy—that is, the Dengist program of reform and opening-up. The theory Bo advanced can be seen as an effort to corroborate and extend the leftist critique of China's market-oriented reforms, a critique that had circulated widely since the mid-2000s under the banner of Hu Jintao's Scientific Outlook on Development. The key move was to supplement the initial *negative* accusation—namely, the claim that the prevailing Dengist, market-oriented approach was flawed—with a *positive* and constructive logic explaining what the alternative solution should be and how it would work.

Bo's new theory of development, the "Chongqing path of people's-livelihoods-oriented economic development" (*min sheng wei daoxiang de Chongqing fazhan jingji zhi lu*), was officially announced at the Seventh Plenum of the Chongqing Party Committee in June 2010. "People's livelihoods constitute domestic demand and generate consumption," the official narrative stated. "Effectively improving people's livelihoods not only does not hold back economic growth, but it can also powerfully and sustainably drive it forward."[44] The essence of the argument was to reconcile economic growth with social welfare and redistribution by asserting that the two were not necessarily in tension. On the contrary, the latter could serve as the driving force of the former. Bo presented his reasoning as follows: according to the traditional development model, priority was given to economic growth, while improvements in people's livelihoods were postponed until the country became wealthy. By contrast, Bo argued that there was no inherent contradiction between economic development and the improvement of social welfare, because "the process of improving people's livelihoods is itself the process of developing the economy."[45]

Far from being merely a policy response to the contingencies of the global economic crisis, Bo's new theory embodied "a major shift in [China's] development outlook," as Chongqing's state media proudly claimed.[46] This qualitative change was said to lie not only in identifying a people-centered driver of growth, but also in introducing a new, non-material criterion for measuring success—namely, "happiness" (*xingfu*).[47] This new conception of development was presented as originating with a critique and rejection of the flawed GDP-oriented model of growth. According to the official narrative, "During the early reform period, it was necessary to use GDP as a comprehensive indicator for evaluation purposes, particularly when expanding the overall size of the national economy was the priority." However, "with the development of society and the economy, the GDP-centered evaluation mechanism has generated serious problems, especially widening disparities between urban and rural areas and between the rich and the poor." In response, "some countries and cities have begun using the 'happiness index' to measure developmental achievements, with the weight of GDP in evaluation systems gradually declining." Therefore, "especially in today's context, when human-centered Scientific Development is being advocated, there is an urgent need to change the prevailing tendency to worship GDP."

Now, as pro-poor economic policies moved to the forefront, the earlier reformist call for further opening-up largely disappeared from the discourse. The justification was that "a higher level of happiness is possible even when per capita GDP and total GDP remain relatively low."[48] Hence, Chongqing's strategy of catching up was framed in largely non-material, or "spiritual," terms. "Chongqing's total economic output and per capita income are relatively low and lag far behind those of more developed cities," Bo asserted, "yet if we attach great importance to improving people's livelihoods and carry out our work effectively, the happiness index of Chongqing's residents could very well rise to the top within a relatively short period of time."

Taking the issue to a more explicitly political level, Bo further argued that "reform and opening-up are powerful driving forces, but equity and justice are equally powerful driving forces of development."[49] At the core, he suggested, was the question of how to "motivate the entire society to become more proactive." Implicitly alluding to market incentives as a counterpart, Bo stressed that social justice and equity were equally important sources of motivation. "Nowadays some economists speak only of economic laws, but it is people who put those laws into practice," Bo questioned. "If people become disheartened, what can possibly be accomplished?" In other words, pro-poor social policies would contribute to economic growth by "consolidating public support." This narrative explicitly echoed the shifting discourse at the central level, which revolved around whether "efficiency" (*xiaolü*) should continue to take precedence over "equity" (*gongping*). Since Deng Xiaoping's 1992 Southern Tour, the principle of "giving priority to efficiency while giving due consideration to equity" (*xiaolü youxian, jiangu gongping*) had served as the guiding principle of redistribution enshrined in top-level Party documents until the mid-2000s.[50] At the Fourth Plenum of the Sixteenth Central Committee in 2004, however, "social equity" (*shehui gongping*) effectively replaced the earlier pro-efficiency guideline. Both the Seventeenth Party Congress report and the Fifth Plenum of the Seventeenth Central Committee resolution subsequently emphasized the need to "appropriately balance efficiency and equity in both primary distribution and redistribution, while paying greater attention to equity in the latter process."

As Bo realigned Chongqing's policies with this broader conservative trend, the transition from developmentalism to economic leftism was effectively completed. Economic development in China has never been a purely economic task; it has always been closely tied to the Party's performance-based legitimacy as well as to the political advancement of Party leaders. However, when Bo claimed that improving people's livelihoods "has consistently been a central goal of the [Chinese] Communist Party's struggle,"[51] the socioeconomic issue was further politicized and transformed into something fundamentally different. Bo was no longer simply operating within the existing framework; rather, he was beginning to challenge the prevailing reformist political orthodoxy. As he put it, "development makes no sense (*mei daoli*) if it fails to improve people's livelihoods." Political insiders in China would readily recognize that this statement amounted to a direct challenge to Deng Xiaoping's well-known developmental maxim: "development is the absolute principle (*ying daoli*)." While Bo still presented himself as a loyal follower at the time—signaling his alignment with the conservative Party line through policy reorientation—he would soon assume the mantle of a leftist vanguard, advocating a more radical return to Maoist ideas.

3.4 The Mass Line

When Bo Xilai asserted that "whatever is done for the people is rightly done" and that "all the money spent for the people is rightly spent,"[52] his remarks implied an underlying assumption about the Party's obligation toward the people. They suggested that Chongqing's leftist policy reorientation under Bo's leadership aimed not only at the pro-poor redistribution of material resources, thereby subtly invoking Marxist egalitarian ideals, but also carried a deeper political implication. Beyond the policy dimension, it also concerned the political attitude of party cadres toward ordinary people, that is, the relationship between the Party and the people.

Party cadres are expected to "serve" the people wholeheartedly and altruistically. This requirement reflects the Party's self-proclaimed mission of leading and assisting the proletariat in becoming masters of their own destiny by overthrowing their oppressors. Furthermore, Party cadres are urged to maintain close contact with the people, or "the masses" (*qunzhong*). In doing so, cadres are expected, on the one hand, to learn firsthand about the masses' real needs and aspirations and, on the other, after processing this grassroots information through the lens of Marxist theory, to instill a higher level of political consciousness among the people and guide their political actions. In theory, this style of work is known as the "Mass Line" (*qunzhong luxian*), first articulated by Mao Zedong and later enshrined as a core component of Mao Zedong Thought.

The revival of the Mass Line spirit in Chongqing appeared to follow the same logic as Bo Xilai's leftist realignment in other policy domains—that is, Bo seemed to perceive the rising tide of leftism and decided to stake his political career on what he regarded as the most likely ascendant faction. At the central level, the Party's Fourth Plenum of the Seventeenth Central Committee was held in September 2009 and was devoted to "strengthening and improving party building under new circumstances." Shortly thereafter, this agenda of party building became the central theme of Chongqing's Sixth Party Plenum, convened in December 2009.

The most notable shift in discourse accompanying the resurgence of the Mass Line in Chongqing centered on the type of ideal party cadre Bo Xilai sought to cultivate among the municipality's local officials. During the "Mind Emancipation" campaign in 2008, when Bo was still broadly following a reformist Party line, he urged Chongqing cadres to improve themselves in three respects: capability, perseverance, and motivation. To illustrate this point, Bo introduced the metaphor of the "three rulers" when mobilizing local officials to be proactive and encouraging them to work hard so that Chongqing could catch up with more developed regions. By 2009, however, this technocratic emphasis had begun to fade. A fourth "ruler" was added to the original three—the "people's ruler" (*min chi*).[53] Literally, the term suggests that cadres should be evaluated according to how well they serve the people. By the time Chongqing's Sixth Party Plenum convened at the end of 2009, revolutionary faith and the spirit of the Mass Line had taken precedence over technocratic expertise and reformist aspiration. According to Bo, party cadres should strive to meet four criteria:[54]

1. Remain loyal to the Party's [socialist] cause. Stand firmly on the Party's side on major political questions of right and wrong and withstand political tests.
2. Maintain integrity and incorruptibility.
3. Care for the people and maintain close ties with the masses.
4. Leverage one's strengths and expertise. Contribute to areas such as scientific planning, modern governance, deepening reform, and expanding opening-up.

At the Sixth Plenum, Bo reiterated the *political* requirements for Party cadres.[55] "As a [Chinese] Communist Party member, it does not matter if one's level of education is low," Bo exhorted. "As long as one constantly thinks about serving the people and genuinely works to do things for them, one can be considered basically a qualified Communist." Conversely, Bo continued, "no matter how highly educated one may be, if one departs from this fundamental purpose, one cannot be regarded as a true Communist." Spiritual commitment was portrayed as the decisive factor in governance. It is worth noting that while the central-level party documents framed the approach to party building in somewhat ambiguous terms, containing both reformist and leftist elements, Bo Xilai clearly leaned toward one side. In contrast to the reformist emphasis on cadres' technocratic competence, Bo followed the leftist line, foregrounding revolutionary willpower and an altruistic ethos as the ultimate source of effective governance.

The theme of being "good communists" constituted another prong of the leftists' veiled criticism of Dengist reform. According to this line of argument, the reform era had produced two major socioeconomic problems in China: first, rising inequality, and second, corruption. Bo Xilai explicitly urged cadres, on the one hand, to "remain vigilant against the danger of rich–poor polarization" and, on the other, to "maintain integrity, fight corruption, and guard against degeneration."[56] The two problems were seen as closely intertwined. In this context, the Mass Line functioned less as a policy instrument for addressing structural economic imbalances than as a leftist prescription for correcting cadre behavior, although poverty reduction and the provision of public services were also conventionally listed as key responsibilities for politically reliable cadres.

Leftist discourse on corruption typically attributed the problem to collusion between rent-seeking party officials and profit-seeking capitalists, while remaining largely silent about the institutional root of the problem—namely, the Party's unchecked power. Accordingly, leftist critics often spoke in a peculiar register, presenting themselves as the "true" Communists who represented the ever-righteous Party, while calling on other cadres to correct their attitudes, recognize their proper position vis-à-vis the masses, and rectify their work styles. As Bo Xilai stated at the plenum, "The Chinese Communist Party is great, glorious, and correct not because it seized power, but because it serves the interests of the broad masses of the people." What, then, was to be done? "There may be thousands of revolutionary principles, but they all boil down to one: serving the people wholeheartedly." This was because, in Bo's words, "the people are the masters of society, while party cadres are the servants of the people."[57] Accordingly, cadres were urged to "maintain the flesh-and-blood ties between the Party and the people" and to "truly place the masses at the center of their thinking, remain emotionally close to them, rely on them in their work, and resolutely address the problem of becoming detached from the masses."[58]

In terms of concrete actions on the ground, some mass-oriented policies had already been implemented before they were retrospectively framed under the overarching theme of the Mass Line. In mid-2009, Bo Xilai decided to send Chongqing's party cadres into rural villages. The first campaign was called the "Cadres Visiting the People" movement (*ganbu da zoufang*). Cadres were required to reach out to local residents, inquire about their situations, difficulties, and grievances, and ultimately seek solutions for them. The campaign was also known as the "Downward Petitioning" movement (*da xia fang*), a term deliberately coined as a counterpart to "upward petitioning" (*shang fang*). When ordinary citizens felt wronged and local officials failed to respond, they often attempted to bring their cases to higher-level authorities or even directly to Beijing.

Under Hu Jintao, this particular state–society tension at the local level was regarded as a major threat to political stability in China. Petitioning became so widespread that it was closely associated with mass protests (*qunti xing shijian*) and with the state's strategy of repression and control known as "stability maintenance" (*wei wen*). In this context, the rhetorical maneuver employed by Bo becomes clear: framed as a manifestation of the Mass Line, party cadres were now to go down to the people, symbolically reversing the problematic direction of cadre–people relations in practice. Initially, the "Downward Petitioning" campaign was described in state media as an effort to clear petition backlogs, address popular grievances, and "maintain stability." The explicit Mass Line framing emerged only later, following the Party's Fourth Plenum and Chongqing's Sixth Party Plenum.

The second campaign went a step further. Cadres were asked to "enter the grassroots, villages, and rural households" and to "eat, live, and work together with peasants." Officially, the initiative was called the "Three Enters and Three Togethers" program (*san jin san tong*). The idea was said to have originated from a Chongqing-based establishment intellectual, who proposed a week-long practical training program for party cadres titled "Let Me Serve as the Party's Village Branch Secretary."

A third campaign grew out of the second and was launched in early 2010, demanding even greater commitment from party cadres. Under this initiative, all officials were required to be paired with several rural households. Cadres were tasked with helping these households improve their livelihoods and addressing their practical needs. State media described the initiative with the slogan "Form ties with poor relatives, assist them, and visit them regularly" (*jie qiong qin, bang qiong qin, zou qiong qin*). These three campaigns were later collectively referred to as the "Three Activities" (*san xiang huodong*).

Accompanying these campaigns, which both mobilized and tested Party cadres, were complementary regulations and evaluation mechanisms. One such initiative was the "Three Rules" (*san xiang zhidu*), whose origins can be traced back to October 2008. The Three Rules stipulated that (1) party secretaries of all party units must receive members of the public under their jurisdiction once every week; (2) each member of a party unit must visit members of the public twice every year; and (3) the requests of the masses must be handled and responded to on a regular basis. In addition, beginning in early 2009, cadres were required to undergo a mass-involved assessment known as the "Three-Dimensional

Evaluation" (*sanwei kaohe*). Beyond reporting their policy achievements themselves, party leaders were now subject to "democratic assessment" (*minzhu ceping*). Party colleagues, service recipients, and ordinary citizens were asked to evaluate cadres' performance and to participate in public opinion surveys. Independent polling firms were also hired to collect public feedback on the quality of governance.

A fourth campaign, launched in late 2008, dispatched not only party cadres but also recent university graduates and professionals to rural areas. It was known as the "Three Ten-Thousands Plan" (*san wan jihua*), referring to three groups of personnel deployed in batches: (1) 10,000 college graduates appointed as village officials (*cun guan*); (2) 10,000 professionals sent to provide assistance in agriculture, education, and healthcare (*zhi nong zhi jiao zhi yi*); and (3) 10,000 cadres stationed in villages (*zhu cun*).[59]

Judging from the timeline of these campaigns, they can plausibly be interpreted as Chongqing's immediate policy response to a party-wide rectification campaign launched at the central level.[60] This campaign, named after Hu Jintao's signature Party line—"Studying and Practicing the Scientific Outlook on Development" (*xuexi shijian kexue fazhan guan*)—was officially launched in September 2008 and concluded in April 2010. Although both the Mass Line and Mind Emancipation were listed among the "fundamental principles" of this central-level rectification campaign,[61] the former effectively became its de facto guiding principle, giving the campaign a populist orientation, while the latter was relegated to a more marginal position.

As noted above, Bo had already been leaning toward a leftist course and politicized the red culture movement when Chongqing convened its Fourth Party Plenum in late 2008. Accordingly, by mid-2009, when Bo began sending local cadres into villages, Chongqing's party-building campaigns can be understood as deliberately staged to project a leftist orientation and to evoke the spirit of the Mass Line. In this sense, they anticipated the subsequent formal elevation of the Mass Line as a major political task at the upcoming plenums at both the central and local levels—the Fourth Plenum of the Party's Seventeenth Central Committee and Chongqing's Sixth Party Plenum.

Shortly afterward, Chongqing's state media began portraying the Sing Red campaign and the leftist party-building agenda as mutually reinforcing. Just as red songs were rooted in the Party's socialist ideology and were said to matter for the Party's vitality and survival, they were also presented as a natural expression of the Mass Line spirit. Given that "the fundamental principle of our party is to serve the people" and that "the essence of the Scientific Outlook on Development is to be people-centered," it followed that red songs were inherently meant to "praise and energize" the people.[62] At the same time, red culture was portrayed as central to the project of building "learning-oriented party organizations" (*xuexi xing dang zuzhi*). Cadres were urged both to study socialist values and to learn from the masses.[63] In this sense, singing red songs was presented as an effective antidote to the malaise of GDP-centered development, which was said to cause political "disorientation" and ultimately lead to "corruption."[64]

Finally, it is worth noting that the boundary between leftist and non-leftist party-building activities does not appear clearly demarcated, at least at first glance, in the context of Chinese politics. Even when a reformist agenda is in place, it is not uncommon to see party cadres urged to act as "good Communists." After all, the Party claims to represent the people, who are regarded as the ultimate holders of sovereignty; in theory, the former is supposed to act on behalf of the latter.

During his early days in Chongqing, Bo also exhorted local cadres to serve the people as he sought to galvanize party officials to work hard toward a reformist agenda. He urged cadres to "be accountable to the people within their jurisdiction" and to "exercise the power in their hands responsibly," so that they might prove worthy of the title of "parent-official" (*fu mu guan*), a traditional term referring to officials who cared for people's livelihoods as if they were their own parents.[65] Furthermore, Bo stressed that this self-motivated sense of accountability to the people was rooted in the Party's revolutionary tradition. As he put it, "Every Party member is a banner and must strengthen himself or herself ideologically while carrying forward the Party's glorious revolutionary traditions."[66] Party-building rhetoric, therefore, was not necessarily incompatible with a reformist developmental agenda. Just as red songs were initially promoted by Bo as a purely motivational tool, the Party's revolutionary legacies were framed in a similar way. In early 2008, the Chongqing Party Committee issued a directive instructing cadres to learn from revolutionary heroes. They were exhorted to overcome problems such as inaction, laziness, empty talk, and buck-passing. In short, a revolutionary lexicon was utilized in the service of technocratic goals.[67]

However, despite the rhetorical similarities, it is not difficult to distinguish a non-leftist discourse of "serving the masses" from a leftist one. Whereas the former is essentially a standard element derived from the general political culture, the latter is more overtly politicized. First, context matters. In the case of Chongqing, as noted above, Bo began his tenure with a reformist agenda, and the Mind Emancipation campaign stood as the clearest indication of his political stance at the time. By contrast, the later politicization of the Mass Line campaigns occurred alongside Bo's broader leftist reorientation in both ideological and economic terms. Second, the leftist framing of party building was accompanied by political mobilization on the ground. A large-scale campaign that sent cadres into villages, both ceremonially pompous and politically symbolic, would have been unnecessary if the objective had been purely technical or policy-oriented.

3.5 "Strike Black"

Chongqing's anti-organized-crime efforts, known as the Strike Black movement (*da hei*), was arguably the most eye-catching event of 2009. On the one hand, sensational as it was, the dramatic crackdown appeared to be the least overtly *political* among the measures Bo Xilai used to signal his leftist identity and allegiance to the conservative cause. Each of the other major policy initiatives carried a clear ideological agenda that directly challenged the dominant Dengist or reformist paradigm of development. By contrast, the Strike Black campaign seemed at first glance to be largely a pompous show that propelled Bo into the political spotlight, with its deeper political significance becoming apparent only when interpreted within other ideological frames. Specifically, the Sing Red movement promoted socialist values at the ideological level; the "People's Livelihoods" agenda represented an economic effort to appeal to Marxist egalitarian ideals; and the Mass Line campaigns served to remind citizens of the Party's revolutionary social contract with the proletarian masses. In comparison, Strike Black appeared to lack an independent theoretical basis for politicization; rather, its meaning can largely be understood through its connections to these other initiatives.

On the other hand, it may well have been precisely this sensationalism that rendered the Strike Black campaign political in another sense. The Manichean imagery of the campaign—black versus white, or good versus evil—effectively invoked popular memories of stylized historical episodes, such as proletarian revolution against oppression or the uprising of the exploited masses against a corrupt bureaucratic class. The latter image, in particular, reflected a utopian interpretation of Mao's Cultural Revolution that circulated widely among China's leftists, especially its radical wing. It was precisely in this regard that Chinese liberals found the Strike Black campaign troubling and unsettling. From their perspective, the campaign paid inappropriate homage to the Maoist past, a period in which "the rule of man" (*ren zhi*) ran rampant without the constraints of "the rule of law." For leftists, however, Bo's anti-organized-crime campaign represented a powerful and timely manifestation of proletarian justice, suggesting what should, and could, be done in communist China, which, ironically, they believed had strayed too far along the path of capitalism.

During Bo Xilai's early reformist phase, the "Safe Chongqing" program was promoted as part of a broader effort to facilitate Chongqing's market-oriented development. Public safety was regarded as an integral component of the investment-friendly environment that the municipality sought to build. According to the official rhetoric, "development depends on the environment, and the development environment itself constitutes competitiveness." In particular, "a just, efficient, safe, and orderly environment governed by the rule of law plays an important role in attracting various economic factors and fostering a modern market."[68] Hence, echoing the reformist agenda Bo articulated at Chongqing's Third Party Plenum, the goal was "to turn 'Safe Chongqing' program into a hallmark of Chongqing's opening-up and to transform the city into a secure and reassuring destination for outside investors."[69] At the time, the anti-organized-crime initiative was not even included among the program's main tasks, which instead focused on issues such as fire safety, the handling of public petitions, and counterterrorism.[70] "Safe Chongqing" thus initially functioned as an umbrella concept encompassing a wide range of technical concerns related to governance.

Although the Strike Black campaign officially began in mid-2009, Wang Lijun, who would later be tasked with leading the anti-organized-crime crackdown, had already been transferred from Liaoning to Chongqing in June 2008. The timing suggests that Bo Xilai had placed anti-organized-crime efforts on his agenda early on. Wang had earned a reputation in Liaoning—the province where Bo began his political career—for his high-profile successes in combating organized crime.

However, available records suggest that what Bo initially had in mind was probably a rather straightforward script of Batman-style heroism combined with a high-profile display of paternalistic benevolence toward the people—an approach that aligned well with his flamboyant style of governance.[71] The arrival of Wang Lijun was soon followed by a large-scale,

80-day policing campaign known as the "Comprehensive Public Security Operation." It was claimed that during the summer of 2008, some 92 criminal organizations were dismantled. According to Bo, the campaign "has not only made the city's residents feel safer, but has also reassured outside investors and strengthened their confidence," emphasizing that social stability must be ensured alongside economic development. Responding to accusations that the campaign amounted to mere "showmanship," Bo framed it instead as an effort to restore justice. "Taking a hard line against criminal and evil forces," he declared, "means using righteousness to suppress wrongdoing and eliminating threats to the people." Moreover, as his leftist ideological reorientation began to unfold alongside ongoing populist-style cadre rectification campaigns, Bo argued that this policing campaign complemented the "Downward Petitioning" movement, since both initiatives helped resolve many long-standing grievances at once. "Echoing the earlier citywide 'Downward Petitioning' campaign," Bo noted, "it resolved a large number of cases that had long remained unsettled and removed many burdens weighing on the hearts of ordinary people."

According to official sources, the strike staged by Chongqing taxi drivers in November 2008, protesting rising business costs, was identified as the immediate trigger for the Strike Black campaign. Reportedly, the strike was orchestrated by "gangsters seeking to monopolize the transportation industry," who were said to have manipulated the protest from behind the scenes in order to exert pressure on the local government.[72] As Bo further argued, the incident revealed a deeper systemic social problem that required thorough rectification. In addition to the so-called "internal contradictions among the people," another factor explaining the persistence of mass protests in Chongqing was said to be the presence of "black hands" operating behind the scenes, "stirring up tensions and putting pressure on the Party and the government." From this perspective, many incidents of collective petitioning were allegedly driven by coercion from organized crime groups, which prevented ordinary citizens from freely voicing their grievances.[73]

The Strike Black campaign officially began in mid-2009 and entered a "trial phase" in October. Criticism from Chinese liberal intellectuals focused primarily on Chongqing's alleged abuse of public power in the name of law enforcement. Unsurprisingly, the crackdown appeared selective; individuals who enjoyed protection from powerful patrons were largely left untouched. For instance, Weng Zhengjie, reportedly connected to China's military-industrial establishment as well as to the family of Jiang Zemin, was spared.[74] Drawing on the historical precedent of the Party's campaign-style approach to social policing, Bo's critics derisively labeled the campaign "Black Strike" (i.e., *hei da*), a sarcastic term created by reversing the order of the two Chinese characters in the original phrase "Strike Black" (i.e., *da hei*), to suggest that the campaign itself had essentially been a "black," lawless crackdown.

As for Bo's true intentions behind the Strike Black campaign, at least two plausible interpretations can be proposed. First, Bo may have been responding primarily to noncompliance and resistance from local bureaucrats toward his policy agenda. The most suggestive evidence lies in the taxi drivers' strike, which was officially portrayed as having been orchestrated by local forces seeking to pressure the Chongqing government. Moreover, Wen Qiang, the former director of Chongqing's Public Security Bureau, had been removed from his post three months before the launch of Strike Black. He was subsequently arrested and eventually charged with serving as a "protective umbrella" (*baohu san*) for organized crime groups. With Wen cast as the principal villain and brought down, Chongqing's police force underwent a sweeping purge and internal cleansing. Further lending credence to this interpretation was the curious episode in which Chongqing's then mayor, Wang Hongju, voluntarily resigned from his position at the end of 2009. According to official sources, Wang offered three explanations for his departure. First, "I am getting older, and this is simply the law of nature." Second, "Chongqing's economy has begun to recover from the financial crisis, so the timing is appropriate." Third, "there are capable and energetic younger cadres in Chongqing, who should be given more opportunities."[75] Yet the real motivation may have been Wang's recognition of the potential danger of being implicated, as the Strike Black campaign was increasingly targeting the political patrons who had allegedly protected the arrested gangsters. As a Chongqing native, Wang was presumably deeply embedded in the city's local political networks. In his own words, perhaps with a hint of irony, the anti-organized-crime campaign "will inevitably bring up the sludge when the carrot is pulled out" (*ba chu luobo dai chu wuni*),[76] implying that exposing criminal elements would also reveal the corrupt networks behind them.

Second, Bo's intention may also have been instrumental in achieving certain financial objectives. Many private-sector entrepreneurs in Chongqing were identified as leaders of organized crime groups and stripped of their personal assets. It is therefore plausible that the Strike

Black campaign functioned, at least in part, as a disguised effort to siphon resources from the private sector in order to fund Bo's pro-poor policies.

To be sure, the *responsive* and *instrumental* rationales are not mutually exclusive. Both could be readily incorporated into the crackdown, which was visibly staged as a high-profile demonstration of restoring social justice.

As the most intense phase of the Strike Black campaign came to a close, a "mid-term assessment and commendation conference" was held in March 2010. On that occasion, Bo Xilai's defense of the campaign was largely nonpolitical; it neither articulated a leftist ideological vision nor advanced a broader challenge to the status quo of reformism. Rather, Bo's rebuttals consisted mainly of direct responses to the criticisms raised by reformist commentators.

- Speaking of the campaign's overarching theme, Bo framed it as a heroic struggle in which the forces of justice defeated evildoers in the name of the people's interests. As he put it, the campaign "brought down a number of criminal and evil forces and their 'protective umbrellas,' demonstrated the authority of the rule of law, responded to the will of the people, and upheld justice."[77]
- Regarding the campaign's origins, Bo offered a twofold justification. First, he argued that the campaign enjoyed broad popular support rather than being a purely top-down initiative. The masses, he claimed, actively participated by providing clues and information to the police. Second, the problem of organized crime had long been a persistent issue in Chongqing, commonly associated with the city's so-called Pao Ge culture, a reference to local secret-society traditions.[78] This framing also allowed the Strike Black campaign to be juxtaposed with the Sing Red movement. According to Bo's narrative, the two initiatives worked in tandem to purify the social and moral atmosphere by eradicating gangster culture. As Bo put it, "Sing Red" and "Strike Black" reinforced each other in the shared goal of "supporting the righteous and eliminating the evil" (*fu zheng qu xie*).[79]
- To dispel the notion that the Strike Black campaign was merely his whimsical decision, Bo emphasized that anti-organized-crime campaigns of this kind had long been routine operations. Chongqing's campaign was certainly not the first, nor would it be the last. First and foremost, Bo stressed that such campaigns were a "stipulated

action" (*guiding dongzuo*)—that is, a task mandated and approved by the Party center—rather than an "invention" of the Chongqing leadership.[80] Moreover, Bo went out of his way to credit his predecessors. To underscore this continuity, he likened Chongqing's anti-organized-crime campaign to a relay race. Chongqing's state media quickly supplied historical examples of similar campaigns launched elsewhere, emphasizing that Chongqing could learn from the experience of other provinces.[81]

- In response to criticism that the Strike Black campaign amounted to a lawless abuse of power, Bo stressed that all actions taken by the Chongqing police were conducted strictly according to legal procedures and were free from improper arbitrariness. In Bo's words, "cases were handled in accordance with the law: the scope of the crackdown was neither narrowed nor expanded, and the characterization of offenses was neither downgraded nor exaggerated."[82]
- While critics accused the campaign of effectively expropriating private entrepreneurs, Bo instead underscored the pro-development effects of the anti-organized-crime campaign. "A city that seeks to develop must uphold righteousness," Bo stressed. "The campaign against organized crime not only had no negative impact on economic growth, but also opened up broader prospects for further development."[83] Elsewhere, a more detailed defense claimed that "after the gangster groups that had been manipulating enterprises from behind the scenes were eliminated, the [Chongqing] government temporarily placed the companies under trusteeship, helping them continue operating legally and preventing economic losses."[84]

Around the same time, a symposium devoted to the discussion of "gangster-related crimes and theories of legal control" was held in Chongqing. Party-affiliated intellectuals were invited to attend and, unsurprisingly, offered strong endorsements of the campaign. At the same time, they appeared to be tasked with developing a framework that would give the Strike Black campaign an enhanced *political* meaning—that is, elevating the crackdown beyond the straightforward narrative of combating criminals. One idea that emerged was that anti-organized-crime efforts should proceed in tandem with anti-corruption measures within officialdom. The reason was that "without the backing of government officials behind the scenes (*cheng yao*), criminal and evil forces could not have grown so powerful."[85] Indeed, this argument foreshadowed developments that would soon follow, as Bo Xilai became increasingly swept up in the rising tide of leftist discourse toward the end of Hu Jintao's second term.

Notes

1. "Jiaodian shizheng" [Current Political Focus], *Jinri Chongqing*, no. 12 (2008): 22; Mou Fengjing and Zhang Xuefeng, "Zai xin de qidian shang tuijin nongcun gaige fazhan" [Advancing Rural Reform and Development from a New Starting Point], *Chongqing ribao*, November 27, 2008.
2. Yu Xuan Wen, "Hong ge: rang Chongqing ninghun juqi" [Red Songs: Uniting Chongqing's Spirit and Energy], *Chongqing ribao*, November 19, 2008.
3. Yu Xuan Wen, "Hong ge."
4. Mou Fengjing and Liu Changfa, "Shiwei zhaokai san jie wu ci quanwei huiyi" [The Municipal Party Committee Convenes the Fifth Plenum of the Third Committee], *Chongqing ribao*, June 19, 2009.
5. "Chang xiang zhu xuanlü, ningju jing qi shen" [Singing the Main Melody and Consolidating the Spirit], *Chongqing ribao*, June 23, 2009.
6. Zhang Qin, "Chang xiang zhu xuanlü, ningju jingqishen" [Singing the Main Melody and Consolidating the Spirit], *Chongqing ribao*, July 13, 2009.
7. Zhou Yanyong, "'Chang du jiang chuan': hongyang shehui zhuyi hexin jiazhi tixi yiyi" ["Sing, Read, Speak, and Spread": The Significance of Promoting the Socialist Core Value System], *Chongqing ribao*, July 15, 2009.
8. Shang Yu, "Rang zhuliu wenhua ru nao ru xin, yinling chaoliu" [Let Mainstream Culture Take Root in Minds and Hearts and Lead the Trend], *Chongqing ribao*, November 14, 2009.
9. "Yue du: 2009 nian 11 yue–12 yue" [Monthly Review: November–December 2009], *Jinri Chongqing*, no. 12 (2009): 4.
10. Xiao Zhu, "Xiwang dajia ba 'chang du jiang chuan' gao de geng hao" [Hoping Everyone Can Better Carry Out "Sing, Read, Speak, and Spread"], *Chongqing ribao*, September 1, 2010; Xiao Zhu, "Li Changchun zai Chongqing kaocha diaoyan" [Li Changchun on an Inspection and Research Tour in Chongqing], *Jinri Chongqing*, no. 9 (2010): 14–17.
11. Dai Juan and Liu Shuang, "Rang 'chang du jiang chuan' huodong gengjia shenru chijiu youxiao" [Making "Sing, Read, Speak, and Spread" Activities More In-Depth, Sustained, and Effective], *Chongqing ribao*, July 24, 2009; Kuang Lina, "Nuli ba chang hong ge du jingdian jiang gushi dazao cheng Chongqing wenhua pinpai" [Striving to Turn Singing Red Songs, Reading Classics, and Telling Stories into a Cultural Brand of Chongqing], *Chongqing ribao*, April 1, 2009.

12. Wang Heqing, "Chongqing 'chang du jiang chuan' huodong de liangdian yu tedian" [Highlights and Features of Chongqing's "Sing, Read, Speak, and Spread" Activities], *Chongqing ribao*, September 20, 2010.
13. Xiao Zhu, "Tiyan zai shan cheng, changtan zai Chongqing" [Experiencing the Mountain City and Engaging in Lively Conversations in Chongqing], *Chongqing ribao*, August 8, 2010.
14. Propaganda Department of Chongqing Party Committee (PDCPC), *Chengshi hangbiao: Chongqing chengshi jingshen tanxun* [Beacons for Urban Development: Searching for Chongqing's City Spirit] (Xinan shifan daxue chubanshe, 2010), preface.
15. PDCPC, *Chengshi hangbiao*, 221.
16. "Hongse zhi cheng: ba yu dadi de hengjiu meili" [The Red City: The Enduring Charm of the Bayu Region], *Chongqing ribao*, July 19, 2008.
17. PDCPC, *Chengshi hangbiao*, 223.
18. PDCPC, *Chengshi hangbiao*, 228.
19. PDCPC, *Chengshi hangbiao*, 69.
20. PDCPC, *Chengshi hangbiao*, 73.
21. PDCPC, *Chengshi hangbiao*, 233.
22. PDCPC, *Chengshi hangbiao*, 228.
23. PDCPC, *Chengshi hangbiao*, 221.
24. PDCPC, *Chengshi hangbiao*, 230.
25. Deng Quanlun, "Chongqing, rang wenhua wei chengshi su hun" [Chongqing: Let Culture Shape the Soul of the City], *Chongqing ribao*, April 14, 2009.
26. Mou Fengjing, Liu Changfa, and Luo Jingwen, "Quanmian luoshi '314' you hao you kuai cu fazhan" [Fully Implementing the "3–14" Overall Arrangements, Promoting Development in a High-Quality and Rapid Manner], *Chongqing ribao*, December 26, 2007.
27. Tao Weihong, "Ji yao zhua fazhan, ye yao zhua fengqi" [Focusing Not Only on Development but Also on Conduct and Work Style], *Chongqing ribao*, April 5, 2008.
28. Tao Weihong and Liu Changfa, "Zai kuoda kaifang zhong shixian you hao you kuai fazhan" [Realizing High-Quality and Rapid Development by Expanding the Scope of Opening-Up], *Chongqing ribao*, July 21, 2008.
29. Chongqing Daily Commentator, "Wenhua qiang shi: Chongqing fazhan de xin jingjie" [Strengthening the City through Culture: A New Stage of Chongqing's Development], *Chongqing ribao*, June 23, 2009; Ye Xiaoyong, "Zhongguo hong, hong le Chongqing" [The Chinese Red Makes Chongqing Red], *Jinri Chongqing*, no. 2–3 (2010): 77.
30. Propaganda Department of Chongqing Party Committee (PDCPC), *Kexue fazhan xin zhuiqiu* [The New Pursuits of Scientific Development] (Chongqing chubanshe, 2009), 85.

31. Tao and Liu, "Zai kuoda kaifang zhong shixian"; "Zhan zai kaifang qianyan shixian xin de kuayue" [Standing at the Forefront of Openness, Achieving a New Leap Forward], *Jinri Chongqing*, no. 1 (2008): 15.
32. PDCPC, *Kexue fazhan xin zhuiqiu*, 88.
33. PDCPC, *Kexue fazhan xin zhuiqiu*, 103.
34. PDCPC, *Kexue fazhan xin zhuiqiu*, 103.
35. PDCPC, *Kexue fazhan xin zhuiqiu*, 89.
36. PDCPC, *Kexue fazhan xin zhuiqiu*, 91
37. PDCPC, *Kexue fazhan xin zhuiqiu*, 103.
38. PDCPC, *Kexue fazhan xin zhuiqiu*, 91.
39. PDCPC, *Kexue fazhan xin zhuiqiu*, 91.
40. PDCPC, *Kexue fazhan xin zhuiqiu*, 91–92.
41. "Zhong wai meiti jujiao Chongqing" [Chinese and Foreign Media Focus on Chongqing], *Chongqing ribao*, March 11, 2009.
42. Tao Weihong and Zhang Xuefeng, "Yi kexue fazhan guan zhidao luoshi '314' zongti bushu" [Guiding the Implementation of the "3–14" Overall Arrangements with the Scientific Outlook on Development], *Chongqing ribao*, March 7, 2008.
43. Luo Jingwen, "Baixing ganshou huimin zhengce: cong 'doudi' dao puhui" [The Public's Experience of Pro-People Policies: From "Safety-Net Protection" to Universal Benefits], *Chongqing ribao*, February 19, 2008.
44. Chongqing Daily Commentator, "Zhu minsheng bu hui che jingji de houtui" [Focusing on People's Livelihoods Will Not Hold Back Economic Development], *Chongqing ribao*, July 8, 2010.
45. Xiao Zhu, "Tiyan zai shan cheng."
46. Xiao Zhu, "Tiyan zai shan cheng."
47. Chongqing Daily Commentator, "Xingfu zhishu bu jiandan qujue yu GDP" [The Happiness Index Does Not Simply Depend on GDP], *Chongqing ribao*, July 6, 2010.
48. Chongqing Daily Commentator, "Xingfu zhishu."
49. Xiao Zhu, "Fahui quwei youshi, zhengqu geng da zuowei" [Leveraging Geographical Advantages and Striving for Greater Achievements], *Chongqing ribao*, September 2, 2010.
50. See party congress reports and party plenum resolutions.
51. Xiao Zhu, "Zhuahao 10 jian dashi, qieshi gaishan minsheng" [Focusing on Ten Major Tasks and Effectively Improving People's Livelihoods], *Chongqing ribao*, June 28, 2010.
52. Xiao Zhu, "Zhuahao 10 jian da shi."
53. External Propaganda Office of the Chongqing Party Committee (EPOCPC) and Chongqing Center for Internet News Research (CCINR), *Yu lun 2008* [Public Opinion in Chongqing 2008] (self-published, 2009), 24

54. Mou Fengjing and Liu Changfa, "Qu xian shi duanlian nianqing ganbu de da ketang" [Districts and Counties Are a Major Training Ground for Young Cadres], *Chongqing ribao*, August 7, 2009.
55. Mou Fengjing, Pan Yong, and Zhang Xuefeng, "Hangshi dang jian jichu, tuidong Chongqing fazhan" [Strengthening the Foundations of Party Building and Promoting Chongqing's Development], *Chongqing ribao*, December 3, 2009.
56. Zhang Xuefeng, "Zhashi tuijin xin xingshi xia dang de jianshe" [Steadily Advancing Party Building under New Circumstances], *Chongqing ribao*, September 24, 2009.
57. Mou, Pan and Zhang, "Hangshi dang jian jichu."
58. Theoretical Research Team of the Propaganda Department of Chongqing Party Committee, "Chongwen 'wei renmin fuwu' miqie dang qun guanxi" [Revisiting the Principle of "Serve the People" and Strengthening Party–Mass Relations], *Chongqing ribao*, December 18, 2009.
59. Propaganda Department of Chongqing Party Committee (PDCPC), *Chongqing zhuiqiu* [Chongqing's Pursuit] (Chongqing chubanshe, 2012), 194–195.
60. The so-called "village officials" project was initiated by the Party center, with Chongqing merely implementing it locally, as did other provinces. See "Hu Jintao zhongyao pishi zai daxuesheng 'cun guan' zhong yinqi qianglie fanxiang" [Hu Jintao's Important Directive Sparks Strong Response among University Student "Village Officials"], *Xinhua*, December 23, 2008, http://www.gov.cn/ldhd/2008-12/23/content_1185163.htm.
61. The other two principles concerned campaign methods. See "Zhonggong zhongyang guanyu zai quan dang kaizhan shenru xuexi shijian kexue fazhan guan huodong de yijian" [Opinions of the Central Committee of the Chinese Communist Party on Carrying Out In-Depth Study and Practice of the Scientific Outlook on Development throughout the Party], September 14, 2008, in *Shi qi da yi lai zhongyao wenxian xuan bian* [Selected Important Documents since the Seventeenth Party Congress, i.e., *SID17PC*], vol. 1 (Zhongyang wenxian chubanshe, 2009), 554–565.
62. Luo Jingwen, "Hong ge de xingzhi jiu shi gechang renmin, zanmei renmin, guwu renmin" [The Nature of Red Songs Is to Sing about the People, Praise the People, and Inspire the People], *Chongqing ribao*, April 23, 2010.
63. "Zhonggong Chongqing shi wei guanyu guanche 'Zhonggong zhongyang guanyu jiaqiang he gaijin xin xingshi xia dang de jianshe ruogan zhongda wenti de jueding' de yijian" [Opinions of Chongqing Party Committee on Implementing "The Decision of the Central Committee of the Chinese Communist Party on Several Major Issues Concerning

Strengthening and Improving Party Building under New Circumstances"]. *Chongqing ribao*, December 25, 2009.

64. Liu Changfa and Zhang Xuefeng, "Guanche 'liang hui' jingshen qidong si xiang gongzuo" [Implementing the Spirit of the "Two Sessions" and Initiating Work in Four Areas], *Chongqing ribao*, March 18, 2010; Liu Changfa and Zhang Xuefeng, "Chongqing qidong si jian da shi" [Chongqing Initiates Four Major Tasks], *Jinri Chongqing*, no. 4 (2010): 11.
65. Tao Weihong and Zhang Xuefeng, "Fengqi zheng, shouxian shi yongren fengqi yao zheng" [A Sound Political Climate Begins with Proper Personnel Selection], *Chongqing ribao*, March 29, 2008.
66. Mou Fengjing and Tao Weihong, "Jianchi kexue fazhan, zaofu kuqu baixing" [Adhering to Scientific Development and Benefiting the People in the Reservoir Area], *Chongqing ribao*, January 10, 2008.
67. Dai Juan and Zhou Xu, "Jianding lixiang xinnian, lizhi gan shi chuangye" [Strengthening Ideals and Beliefs, Committing to Work and Entrepreneurship], *Chongqing ribao*, February 20, 2008; Theoretical Research Team of the Propaganda Department of Chongqing Party Committee, "Yangmu xianxian fengfan, yangyu haoran zhengqi" [Admiring the Virtues of the Sages and Cultivating a Righteous Spirit], *Chongqing ribao*, February 28, 2008.
68. Tao Weihong and Zhang Xuefeng, "Wei kaifang yu fazhan chuangzao lianghao de fazhi huanjing" [Creating a Favorable Legal Environment for Opening-Up and Development], *Chongqing ribao*, January 16, 2008.
69. "Zhonggong Chongqing shi wei guanyu jin yi bu kuoda kaifang de jueding" [Decision of the Chongqing Party Committee on Further Expanding the Scope of Opening-Up], *Chongqing ribao*, July 21, 2008; Chen Huankui, "Yi kexue fazhan guan wei zhidao nuli dazao 'ping'an Chongqing'" [Guided by the Scientific Outlook on Development, Striving to Build a "Safe Chongqing"], *Chongqing ribao*, October 20, 2008.
70. Liu Guanglei, "Tuijin qi xiang zhongdian gongzuo yingzao lianghao fazhi huanjing" [Advancing Seven Key Tasks and Creating a Favorable Legal Environment], *Chongqing ribao*, September 22, 2008.
71. Liu Changfa, "Daji fanzui, wei min chuhai" [Fighting Crime and Eliminating Harm for the People], *Chongqing ribao*, November 3, 2008.
72. PDCPC, *Chongqing zhuiqiu*, 163.
73. Pan Yong and Zhang Xuefeng, "Yi fa ban an, shi shi qiu shi, bu wang bu zong" [Handling Cases in Accordance with the Law, Seeking Truth from Facts, and Allowing Neither Wrongful Conviction nor Undue Leniency], *Chongqing ribao*, October 29, 2009.
74. John Garnaut, *The Rise and Fall of the House of Bo* (Penguin, 2012), 62.

75. He Qingping, "Zhizheng Chongqing qijian zuo chu zhongyao gongxian" [Significant Contributions Made during the Governance of Chongqing], *Chongqing ribao*, December 7, 2009.
76. Luo Jingwen, "Da hei chu e, biran yao 'bachu luobo dai chu wuni'" [Cracking Down on Organized Crime and Eliminating Evil Necessarily "Brings Out the Mud When Pulling Up the Carrot"], *Chongqing ribao*, November 7, 2009.
77. Zhang Xuefeng, "Shan cheng renmin bu hui wangji nimen de yingxiong yeji" [The People of Chongqing Will Not Forget Your Heroic Achievements], *Chongqing ribao*, March 1, 2010.
78. Wen Feng and Liu Yang, "Chongqing wei daji shehei xingzhi fanzui chuangzao baogui jingyan" [Chongqing Has Created Valuable Experience in Combating Organized Crime], *Chongqing ribao*, April 29, 2010.
79. Tao Weihong, Huang Huo, and Zhang Xuefeng, "Chang hong da hei, fu zheng qu xie" [Singing Red and Striking Black, Upholding the Right and Eliminating Evil], *Chongqing ribao*, January 18, 2010.
80. Pan and Zhang, "Yi fa ban an."
81. Yu Hu, Liu Yang, and Li Xing, "Da hei chu e, li jie bu chuo" [Cracking Down on Organized Crime and Eliminating Evil: A Task Continuously Pursued across Successive Administrations], *Chongqing ribao*, October 30, 2009.
82. Zhang, "Shan cheng renmin bu hui wangji."
83. Zhang, "Shan cheng renmin bu hui wangji."
84. Wen and Liu, "Chongqing wei daji she hei xingzhi fanzui."
85. Wen and Liu, "Chongqing wei daji she hei xingzhi fanzui."

CHAPTER 4

Vanguard of Maoism

By the time Chongqing's Eighth Party Plenum convened in late 2010, Bo Xilai was poised to expand his political program and take another significant step to the left.[1] This moment marked the official debut of Bo's "Common Prosperity" agenda (*gongtong fuyu*). Whereas in the previous phase Bo had largely acted as a loyal *follower*, operating under the central mandate of improving "people's livelihoods," he now positioned himself as a Maoist *vanguard*, advancing a paradigm-shifting program that was arguably too bold to be openly championed by the conservative forces within the party leadership.

A clear indication of Bo's vanguardist escalation of his political campaign was the shift in the focus of Chongqing's broader propaganda efforts. *Yu Lun* (Chongqing's Public Opinion), a book series published as an internal reference for local cadres on propaganda strategies,[2] was assigned different political communication tasks at different times, reflecting Bo's evolving political orientation.

At Bo's behest, the book series was initially issued to promote his public profile as a reform-minded official endowed with administrative ingenuity. In this early phase, *Yu Lun* was said to serve the purpose of "guiding public opinion" and "constructing mainstream culture" in the new age of the internet,[3] where political participation increasingly took place online and where China's "civil society" and "civic spirit" were said to flourish through "mind emancipation."[4] In keeping with Bo's flamboyant style, Chongqing was praised as a pioneer in developing "internet-based

L. Le, *Revival of Maoism in Reform-Era China*,
https://doi.org/10.1007/978-981-92-4606-9_4

governance" in China. While Hu Jintao's online exchange with Chinese netizens in June 2008 was widely described as marking the beginning of China's "internet democracy" (*wangluo minzhu*), its prototype was claimed to have first emerged in Chongqing.[5]

As Bo gradually moved away from reformism and leaned further to the left, *Yu Lun* likewise shifted its focus. It came to assume the role of an "eye" through which the public could observe how Bo was developing a distinctive "Chongqing Model."[6] Eventually, *Yu Lun* adopted an increasingly militant tone, as Bo positioned himself to spearhead a conservative challenge to China's political status quo. In this new phase, Chongqing's propaganda apparatus was expected not merely to reflect or record public opinion, but to actively *influence* and *shape* it. The task was described in explicitly combative terms: "it is like two armies facing each other, with swords drawn and bows bent, sand flying and stones rolling, and drums and horns sounding."[7] It was further asserted that "in the age of the internet, the voice that wins the hearts of the people becomes the mainstream voice."[8] As this statement suggests, the very meaning of the "mainstream" was open to redefinition, indicating that, in Bo's view, the ideological landscape remained contested and that a new order could potentially emerge.

4.1 Common Prosperity

While still paying lip service to the discourse of reform and opening-up at Chongqing's Eighth Party Plenum, Bo Xilai formally announced that "the purpose of this plenary session is to unify our ideological understanding, and [we] must place common prosperity at the top of our priorities."[9] First and foremost, this represented an explicit departure from the central agenda. The local party plenum was expected to follow the line set by the Fifth Plenum of the Seventeenth Central Committee. Devoted to the formulation of the Twelfth Five-Year Plan, the central plenum focused on the theme of "transforming the mode of economic development" (*zhuanbian jingji fazhan fangshi*). Improving "people's livelihoods" was included as one component of the plan and was accompanied by a decorative statement that "[we must] unswervingly advance along the path of common prosperity." However, this notion was not intended to serve as the central principle guiding all other policy objectives.

Second, by demonstrating such conspicuous noncompliance, Bo was in effect seeking to redirect China's Dengist development paradigm onto a leftist track strongly reminiscent of Maoist utopianism. This intention was explicitly reflected in the way he manipulated the party line laid down at the Party's Fifth Plenum. Commenting on the mandate of "transforming the mode of economic development," Bo noted that there were "competing views" about "how the transformation should proceed and what exactly should be transformed" (*ruhe zhuan, zhuan shenme*). He further argued that most prevailing approaches were merely "technically oriented," while very few "touched upon the more fundamental questions of developmental outlook and the [economic] system itself."[10]

To be sure, the concept of "common prosperity" has never disappeared from top-level party documents, particularly the reports of major party congresses. In practice, however, it has largely remained a rhetorical ornament. It has consistently been framed as an ultimate goal to be realized in the distant future promised by Communism. In reality, party leaders understand that China must continue to follow Dengist pragmatism, which holds that "some people should be allowed to get rich first" under a market-oriented economy.

Bo was now attempting to transform the notion of common prosperity into a substantive policy project. At Chongqing's Ninth Party Plenum in July 2011, where common prosperity was formally enshrined as the central theme, Bo made this point explicit. "Nowadays, some people regard common prosperity merely as the starting point (*qidian*) and ultimate destination (*guisu*) of development—in my view, this is far from sufficient," he remarked. "Rather, common prosperity should serve as the driving force and source of vitality for the agenda of Scientific Development, and it ought to run through the entire process of development (*guanchuan fazhan quan guocheng*)."[11]

The core logic of Bo's anti-reform agenda had already been foreshadowed in his earlier rhetoric on "people's livelihoods–oriented economic development," formally proposed at Chongqing's Sixth Party Plenum. Echoing the leftist critique that market-oriented reforms had produced severe socioeconomic inequality, the key message was that truly sustainable growth must be grounded in economic equity and social justice. In Marxist terms, it was argued that "because the relations of production exert a powerful active influence on the productive forces, properly adjusting the former can greatly promote the development of the latter."[12] Hence, "getting income distribution right essentially means promoting the development of productive forces by adjusting the relations of production." This line of reasoning downplayed the role of the market in economic development and instead foregrounded human agency, evoking the Maoist notion that material feasibility is ultimately a function of political and spiritual mobilization. "Marxism holds that among all productive forces, human beings constitute the most dynamic and powerful factor," Bo noted. It follows that "only when people themselves are motivated to work and produce can productive forces be powerfully driven to grow and advance."

A short while earlier, socioeconomic equity and Dengist reform and opening-up had still been treated as two parallel and equally legitimate sources of growth. Now, by contrast, the latter was said to be predicated on the former. As Bo put it, "when we say that reform and opening-up is a driving force, we mean that it is a force capable of motivating and energizing the masses to take initiative, since the ultimate productive force lies with the masses." In policy terms, redistribution was justified on the grounds that it was fundamentally pro-development. According to Bo, "the more vigorously we invest in people's livelihoods and the more money we spend on them, the more vibrant economic life becomes and the more financially capable the government grows—this is a virtuous process of development."[13]

4.1.1 The Metaphor of Cake

To better appeal to popular sentiment, Bo illustrated the core logic of his Common Prosperity program with a "cake" metaphor. According to this narrative, it was misguided for the government to focus solely on "making the cake bigger" (*zuo da dangao*) while making little effort to "divide the cake fairly" (*fen hao dangao*). Instead, the two tasks were presented as equally important. Bo observed that "some comrades hold the view that only after the cake has grown big can it be fairly divided." By contrast, he argued that "it is impossible to make the cake big if it is not fairly divided," because "the people responsible for making the cake will lack the motivation to do so." In this reasoning, only when it is widely understood that the cake is, and will be, shared fairly can it continue to grow larger and larger.[14]

Bo's use of the cake metaphor anticipated a broader debate over "efficiency versus equity" that attracted considerable public attention in mid-2011. Challenging Bo's leftist agenda head-on, Guangdong's then party secretary Wang Yang argued that market-oriented reform and opening-up should remain the top priority. Employing similar metaphorical language, Wang stressed that "making the cake bigger still depends primarily on taking economic development as the central task"—that is, the priority should be making the cake rather than dividing it.[15] As noted earlier, Wang had been Bo's reformist predecessor, launching the Mind Emancipation campaign in Guangdong shortly after the Seventeenth Party Congress. Many provinces subsequently followed suit, including Chongqing during Bo's own reformist phase in his early tenure.

The original use of the cake metaphor was intended to emphasize the importance of addressing inequality while maintaining priority on the development of China's market economy—an idea that reflected the broader political climate under Hu Jintao, who promoted the concepts of Scientific Development and Harmonious Society. According to a propaganda booklet published by the Chongqing Propaganda Department in 2006, when Wang Yang was still in charge, the initial framing of the cake metaphor was unmistakably reformist.[16] Chapter 2 of the booklet was titled "Making the 'Cake' Bigger—Building a Prosperous Chongqing (*fuyu Chongqing*)." Under the overarching theme of building a "Harmonious" Chongqing, the need to better manage economic redistribution was acknowledged. In this discourse, helping the people become prosperous meant not only making the economic "cake" bigger and better, but also dividing it fairly.[17]

However, economic growth remained the overriding priority. According to the booklet, "to build a Harmonious Chongqing, [we] must first build a Prosperous Chongqing." The latter referred to "consistently taking economic development as the central task…so that the economy continues to grow, economic strength steadily increases, and social wealth accumulates."[18] Accordingly, the narrative surrounding common prosperity followed the typical reform-era framing: it was treated as a long-term objective rather than a concrete policy agenda—"the realization of common prosperity is both the starting point and the ultimate destination of the Prosperous Chongqing project." Furthermore, the booklet emphasized that common prosperity could not be achieved without realizing economic development in the first place. "[We] must focus on development as the foremost task for enriching the people and revitalizing Chongqing (*fu min xing yu*), and address the conflicts and problems that arise in the process of achieving common prosperity through development."[19]

Complementing this reformist narrative on common prosperity, Chapter 3 of the booklet sought to temper the egalitarian fervor that often accompanied calls for equity and social justice. The "Fair and Just Chongqing" project (*gongzheng Chongqing*) was never intended to revive the outdated notion of "equal distribution of wealth" (*jun pin fu*).[20] The aim of reducing inequality, the booklet explained, "is not, and cannot be, the complete elimination of income disparities." Rather, it is about "keeping income disparities within a reasonable range by improving market mechanisms and strengthening redistributive institutions."[21] A larger "cake," in this logic, would provide the "material foundation" for building a Fair and Just Chongqing. Conversely, the booklet cautioned that "[we must] avoid placing excessive emphasis on fairness lest it impede economic development" and "[must] avoid equating fairness with absolute egalitarianism." Equity, it concluded, should be understood as a form of fairness that "acknowledges differences and values efficiency."[22]

It is worth noting that Bo occasionally qualified his program by emphasizing that dividing the cake more fairly did not imply "a return to the old path of egalitarianism."[23] Rather than advocating "robbing the rich to help the poor" (*jie fu ji pin*), Bo sought to clarify that common prosperity was about "achieving fairness in distribution and caring for those in need,"[24] and that it must be pursued "within the framework of a market economy."[25] However, when situated in its broader context—the themes of party plenums, shifting political discourses, and policy developments on the ground—it becomes possible to distinguish substantive political signaling and alignment from the strategic ambiguity of rhetorically adhering to the central line whenever necessary. After all, despite abundant evidence of his leftist reorientation, Bo continued to invoke the language of reform and opening-up, even as his actions cast doubt on the sincerity of that commitment.

The immediate precursor to Bo's Common Prosperity program appears to have been a public speech delivered by Chinese Premier Wen Jiabao in February 2010 on the dual tasks of making the "cake" bigger while also dividing it fairly.[26] Wen did not specify which of the two should take priority. The solutions he proposed, however, were largely technical in nature, consistent with his reformist orientation. At the same time, a leftist narrative surrounding common prosperity, and, unsurprisingly, the use of the cake metaphor, had already begun circulating as early as 2008.[27] As later developments made clear, Bo actively promoted and championed a distinctly leftist interpretation of common prosperity. One major hallmark of Chinese leftism was the belief that state-owned enterprises constituted the principal instrument for addressing socioeconomic inequality. The underlying logic held that public ownership was inherently conducive to fairer income distribution, whereas capitalism was structurally deficient in this regard.[28] In ideological terms, the pursuit of common prosperity was understood as embodying the very "nature" of socialism, rather than merely serving as a technical adjustment aimed at achieving balanced growth.

4.1.2 *Bo's Ambition*

In early 2010, Bo began to adopt a more overtly politicized rhetoric, preparing the ground for what was to come. The image he sought to project was one in which true communists stood with the poor against the rich, evoking a stark, almost Manichean opposition. Bo warned that "although attracting investment and developing the economy are part of our work, we must not favor the rich over the poor, spending all our time revolving around the wealthy while forgetting the Party's principles and distancing ourselves from the masses in need."[29] Months later, Bo reiterated the Party's populist tradition: "While some people consider it fashionable to befriend the rich, we should carry forward the Party's old tradition, making friends with the masses, including workers and peasants, and forming close ties with those who are poor and in need."[30] More importantly, Bo expressed his determination to realize what had long been framed as a communist "ideal." Referring to Chongqing's poverty reduction efforts, he asserted that "this has been a dream shared by successive municipal Party committees and governments, and we, the current generation of cadres, must not pass this problem on to those who come after us."[31] Projecting his ambition more explicitly through state media, Bo announced in March 2011—four months before Chongqing's Ninth Party Plenum—that "from now on, we will undertake an even greater task: realizing common prosperity."[32]

With Chongqing's leftist vanguardism now embodied in the Common Prosperity blueprint, the normative relationship between local initiatives and major central mandates began to shift or, more precisely, reversed. Under normal circumstances, local officials are expected to follow central guidelines when implementing policies at the local level, while exercising limited discretion to adapt and experiment within the boundaries of political authorization—that is, engaging primarily in technical operations under political mandate. In case of Chongqing under Bo, however, this pattern began to change. Bo was effectively competing for the authority to define the next guiding political program. As Table 4.1 shows, before Bo's tenure, Chongqing's local party congresses were convened primarily for two purposes: either (1) to reiterate and disseminate the agenda set by central-level party conferences or (2) to formulate concrete plans for implementing local policies closely aligned with the main themes established by the party center. Under Bo, although the first function of local party plenums was largely retained, local party meetings after mid-2009 increasingly became a discretionary instrument through which Bo advanced novel policy agendas and projected his image as a political pioneer with far-reaching vision.

More significantly, in Bo's narrative common prosperity was framed as a political vision, or even a long-standing intra-elite consensus, toward which the policy frameworks and guiding principles of the Jiang Zemin and Hu Jintao eras had always been oriented. According to Bo, all Chongqing-specific policy directives issued by the party center could be subsumed under the framework of common prosperity. "Since Chongqing became a municipality directly under the central government, both the 'Four Major Tasks' assigned by the party center and the '3–14 Overall Arrangement' have required the realization of common prosperity," Bo remarked.[33] Moreover, the same logic was extended to the signature ideological formulations of China's top leaders. Hu Jintao's Scientific Development concept, Bo argued, "necessarily requires narrowing the Three Gaps (*san ge chaju*),[34] and realizing common prosperity."[35] As for Jiang Zemin's Three Represents, "each of the three 'Represents' is closely connected with the idea of common prosperity."[36] In a similar vein, perhaps to demonstrate his own prescience, Bo retrospectively claimed that everything he had done since assuming leadership in Chongqing had been oriented toward the goal of achieving common prosperity. All of Chongqing's party plenums, he asserted, were "closely related to the overarching theme of common prosperity" and were "paving the way for its realization." Bo further elaborated on the "logic" guiding his work: "after a series of initial measures began to show results, this plenum explicitly established common prosperity as the central theme, as Chongqing prepares to launch a final push to conquer this fortress."[37] In short, by emphasizing this sense of continuity, Bo was effectively claiming credit for articulating the Party's next guiding ideology. A privilege traditionally reserved for the Party's top leader was now being implicitly appropriated by a local official; politically attentive observers could hardly fail to grasp the message or recognize the ambition behind it.

Table 4.1 Chronicle of major party conferences in Chongqing

Chongqing Party Committee Plenum	*Plenum Theme*	*Chongqing Party Secretary*	*Central Party Committee Conference*	*Conference Theme*
			16 (November 8–14, 2002)	/
2-2 (November 19–20, 2002)	The Spirit of the Sixteenth Party Congress	Huang Zhendong		
2-3 (June 16–27, 2003)	Urbanization	Huang Zhendong		
			16-3 (October 11–14, 2003)	Socialist Market Economy
2-4 (December 15–17, 2003)	Socialist Market Economy	Huang Zhendong		
2-5 (June 16–18, 2004)	Industrialization	Huang Zhendong		
			16-4 (September 16–19, 2004)	Governing Capacity
2-6 (October 27–28, 2004)	The Party's Governing Capacity	Huang Zhendong		
2-7 (May 30–31, 2005)	Rural Development	Huang Zhendong		
			16-5 (October 8–11, 2005)	The 11th Five-Year Plan
2-8 (November 12–14, 2005)	The 11th Five-Year Plan	Huang Zhendong		
2-9 (June 18–19, 2006)	Development of the Reservoir Area	Wang Yang		
			16-6 (October 8–11, 2006)	Harmonious Society
2-10 (November 15, 2006)	Harmonious Society	Wang Yang		

(*continued*)

Table 4.1 (continued)

Chongqing Party Committee Plenum	*Plenum Theme*	*Chongqing Party Secretary*	*Central Party Committee Conference*	*Conference Theme*
2-11 (November 28, 2006)	Personnel	Wang Yang		
2-12 (April 24, 2007)	Party Representative	Wang Yang		
2-13 (May 20, 2007)	Local Party Congress Preparation	Wang Yang		
3 (May 23–27, 2007)	Integrated Urban-Rural Development	Wang Yang		
3-1 (May 27, 2007)	Personnel	Wang Yang		
			17 (October 15–21, 2007)	/
3-2 (November 14–15, 2007)	The Spirit of the Seventeenth Party Congress & Integrated Urban-Rural Development	Wang Yang		
3-3 (July 20–21, 2008)	The "3–14 Overall Arrangement" & Further Opening-up	Bo Xilai		
			17-3 (October 9–12, 2008)	Rural Development
3-4 (November 25–26, 2008)	Rural Development	Bo Xilai		
3-5 (June 16–17, 2009)	Cultural Development	Bo Xilai		
			17-4 (September 15–18, 2009)	Party Building
3-6 (December 1–2, 2009)	Party Building	Bo Xilai		

(*continued*)

Table 4.1 (continued)

Chongqing Party Committee Plenum	*Plenum Theme*	*Chongqing Party Secretary*	*Central Party Committee Conference*	*Conference Theme*
3-7 (June 24–25, 2010)	People's Livelihoods	Bo Xilai		
			17-5 (October 15–18, 2010)	The 12th Five-Year Plan
3-8 (November 16–17, 2010)	The 12th Five-Year Plan	Bo Xilai		
3-9 (July 20–21, 2011)	Common Prosperity	Bo Xilai		
			17-6 (October 15–18, 2011)	Cultural Development
3-10 (December 19–20, 2011)	Socialist Democracy and Rule of Law & Cultural Development	Bo Xilai		
3-11 (NA)	NA			
3-12 (June 15, 2012)	Local Party Congress Preparation	Zhang Dejiang		

Note: The numbers in X-X format are shorthand terms for specific party conferences. For example, "2-2" refers to the Second Plenum of Chongqing's Second Party Committee, "16" the Sixteenth Party Congress, and "16-3" the Third Plenum of the Sixteenth Party Central Committee

4.1.3 *For Socialism*

Ideologically, Bo's Common Prosperity agenda was promoted as part of a broader struggle over competing "isms." In Bo's own words, "common prosperity is a fundamental issue that concerns the very nature and direction of socialism."[38]

For Chinese leftists, rectifying what they viewed as China's de facto capitalist mode of development required a fundamental challenge to the prevailing political hegemony—namely, the reform and opening-up policy that carried the authoritative endorsement of China's paramount leader, Deng Xiaoping. Directly repudiating Deng himself, however, seemed politically unfeasible and unlikely to become a viable option in the foreseeable future. Instead, the leftist strategy was to highlight the long-neglected "socialist" dimension of Deng's legacy, particularly by promoting the idea that the "late" Deng had been deeply troubled by, and concerned about, the problem of rising inequality in China.[39] In effect, this narrative sought to undermine the political legitimacy of China's reformist camp.

Specifically, Deng's own definition of the so-called nature of socialism (*shehui zhuyi de benzhi*) became one of the most frequently cited justifications among leftists for emphasizing the need to bring China's reform, which they believed had gone astray, back onto the right track. In Deng's words, "the nature of socialism is to liberate and develop the productive forces, eliminate exploitation and extreme economic polarization, and finally achieve common prosperity."[40] Whereas reformers tended to emphasize the first half of Deng's statement, leftists increasingly called attention to the second.

Obviously, the timeline for achieving common prosperity was a major point of contention. Deng never specified what he meant by "finally," nor how long it would take to reach that stage. From a reformist perspective, the phrase functioned largely as a rhetorical gesture paying lip service to the communist ideal. Historically, reform-minded party leaders had advanced various formulations to temper and restrain the radicalism inherent in communist ideology. For instance, Zhao Ziyang introduced the concept of the "primary stage of socialism" (*shehui zhuyi chuji jieduan*) to underscore that communism would not be within reach for a very long time. Later, Jiang Zemin advanced the distinction between the "highest program" (*zuigao gangling*) and the "basic program" (*zuidi gangling*)—that is, communism as a long-term ideal versus economic development as the immediate practical task. By contrast, for Chinese conservatives around 2010–2011, Deng's "finally" had effectively arrived. The argument was that, with China surpassing Japan in 2010 to become the world's second-largest economy, the country was now in a sufficiently strong position to place common prosperity on the agenda as a substantive policy objective.

All the leftist rhetoric about socialism was articulated against a backdrop of anti-capitalism. In support of this interpretation, leftist commentators frequently invoked the words of the "late" Deng Xiaoping, recorded in *The Chronicle of Deng Xiaoping* published in 2004, as a source of endorsement and legitimacy. As Deng was quoted as saying, "If only a minority of people can become rich, then this would amount to a regression to capitalism."[41] He further warned that "without socialism as a prerequisite, reform and opening-up would lead to capitalism, manifested in extreme economic polarization."[42]

A detailed and fully articulated version of this leftist advocacy—seeking to "save" China's socialism by restoring the socialist economy and realizing "common prosperity" in the name of Deng—was presented at a symposium held in mid-2011. The symposium's central theme was "Common Prosperity and Socialism with Chinese Characteristics." An anthology compiling the participants' speeches was published several months later.[43] Most attendees were prominent party theorists known for their conservative stance.[44] This leftist gathering appeared to have been deliberately orchestrated to praise Bo Xilai's audacity and his explicit demonstration of socialist commitment. The timing of the event coincided with the ongoing "Cake Debate" and the heated discussions surrounding the Guangdong versus Chongqing Models.

Bo Xilai closely followed the leftist script. Citing Deng Xiaoping directly, he emphasized that "when economic development reaches a certain stage, common prosperity must be placed on the agenda."[45] Bo argued that the time had now arrived: "judging from the course of historical development, the moment has come to undertake the great project of common prosperity."[46] Referring to Deng's two-step blueprint—"letting some people get rich first" (*xian fu*) followed by the realization of common prosperity (*gong fu*)—Bo proclaimed that "after more than three decades [of reform], the goal set in the first half [of Deng's plan] has essentially been achieved; from now on, we must devote greater effort to the second half, in order to fulfill Xiaoping's unfinished wish."[47]

More importantly, Bo emphasized that what was ultimately at stake was the fate of socialism itself, given what he described as an ongoing competition between socialism and capitalism. "There are two major 'isms' in today's world," Bo noted. "One is capitalism, represented by the United States and Europe, and the other is Socialism with Chinese Characteristics."[48] Echoing the leftist critique of the reformist belief that China's future depended on learning from the developed Western world, Bo insisted that China must chart its own path. As he argued, Socialism with Chinese Characteristics by definition required that China's development follow a socialist path rather than a capitalist one, and that it be guided by Chinese experience rather than Western or American paradigms.[49] Bo therefore rejected convergence with the West as a desirable national goal. "It will not do for a nation of more than a billion people to always follow in others' footsteps." He then posed a rhetorical question: "As a great nation known for its thousands of years of splendid culture and remarkable creativity, what can [China] contribute to humanity today?"[50] The answer, in Bo's rhetoric, was common prosperity, which he praised as "the most fundamental superiority" of socialism.[51] Demonstrating that "socialism is superior to capitalism," he argued, required achieving socioeconomic equity, particularly given that this problem remained unresolved even in the most powerful Western country, the United States.[52]

4.1.4 *From Bo to Xi*

Many years later, Xi Jinping returned the concept of common prosperity to the center stage of Chinese politics, at a time when he was widely regarded as the most powerful Chinese leader since Mao and had effectively brought an end to the Dengist era of reform. China analysts, however, have tended to focus overwhelmingly on the instrumental motivations—namely, strengthening socialist ideology, reinforcing the Party's legitimacy, consolidating personal authority, and tightening political control over business elites—behind a campaign framed around egalitarian ideals.[53] Little attention has been paid to the earlier role of Bo Xilai. The overlooked historical linkage between Bo and Xi, in fact, points to an important political-ideological continuity: that the Xi era represents an extension of the revived conservatism that had already begun to emerge under Hu Jintao.

The existence of a fierce elite-level power struggle during Bo's tenure in Chongqing is also suggested by the fact that his Common Prosperity program translated into concrete policies and was implemented more substantively. By contrast, redistribution under Xi's Common Prosperity campaign has been limited and largely superficial.[54] At most, it has taken the form of redistribution through anti-monopoly measures, which impose little direct fiscal cost on the state.[55] Xi's rhetorical profession of faith in leftism—"now [China] has reached a historical stage in which common prosperity can be advanced in a solid manner"—appeared to serve primarily as a justification for tightening control over leading private-sector entrepreneurs. In Xi's own words, the objective was to "oppose the disorderly expansion of capital,"[56] a stance exemplified by the cancellation of Ant Group's IPO in late 2020 and subsequent regulatory restrictions and fines imposed on major technology firms.

What, then, explains the stark difference between Bo's and Xi's Common Prosperity campaigns? During periods of political struggle, concrete actions are often necessary to signal strength, demonstrate commitment, and persuade potential supporters. By contrast, when political dominance has already been secured, rhetoric alone may suffice, especially when substantive policies would entail significant costs.

4.2 The Chongqing Model

With the Maoist banner raised and the Common Prosperity agenda brought to the fore, a sustained promotional campaign for Chongqing's vanguardism was launched in late 2010, when Bo Xilai had made a decisive turn to the left. The propaganda drive centered on the so-called Chongqing Model, a term coined to showcase Bo's achievements as a coherent political program built around an egalitarian-oriented economic blueprint.

Public discourse on the Chongqing Model initially consisted of a relatively uncoordinated chorus of voices praising the purported novelty of Chongqing's policies. A qualitative shift occurred around late 2010. In line with the paradigm-challenging nature of Bo's Common Prosperity project, the Chongqing Model was subsequently promoted as a socialist pioneer, cast in a quasi-prophetic role of charting a new path for China and guiding the nation's march toward a more promising future.

Bo Xilai and Chongqing's state media largely refrained from directly promoting the Chongqing Model, apart from Bo's occasional remarks expressing unusually high expectations for the so-called Chongqing "experience" or "practice." This rhetorical distance undoubtedly provided a political buffer, allowing Bo to plausibly claim that he had little to do with the surrounding hype should it become politically compromising or turn into a liability.

Instead, most of the propaganda work was carried out through semi-official channels and by conservative party theorists and intellectuals. Viewed in a broader context, leftist discourses surrounding the Chongqing Model appeared to form part of the intensifying left–right power struggle during Hu Jintao's second term.[57] This arrangement created a mutually beneficial dynamic. The leftist camp embraced Bo Xilai as a model communist and benefited from his political maneuvering, through which many leftist ideals were translated into tangible policies on the ground. In turn, Bo relied on such factional endorsement to advance his political ambitions. Ideas that were too bold to be articulated directly by Bo or the

Chongqing government could instead be expressed more freely and explicitly through the megaphone of "non-state" public opinion.

This section focuses on the *extent* to which non-official discourses elevated the political significance of the Chongqing Model, rather than on the *diversity* of views among those who supported Bo Xilai.[58]

4.2.1 Local Experimentation

The Chongqing Model was not initially framed in explicitly political terms. The term itself is conventionally traced to an article published in *Asia Weekly* by Hong Kong–based journalist Ji Shuoming in February 2009. Titled "The Chongqing Model Creates a New Path for China's Economic Recovery," the article described how Chongqing's "innovative thinking" offered an alternative mode of development to that of China's coastal regions, which had relied heavily on labor-intensive manufacturing and investment-driven growth.[59] Against the broader backdrop of the global financial crisis, the immediate appeal of Chongqing's purported "exceptionalism" under Bo Xilai lay in its ability to sustain above-average economic growth. Hence the central question: "Why is Chongqing able to defy the trend despite facing both internal and external economic difficulties?" In Bo's own words, "I believe the key lies in knowing what we should do, how to invest, and where to direct investment…The central government firmly opposes low-level redundant investment, and given that both domestic and international markets are currently characterized by excess supply, blindly expanding production capacity is unlikely to succeed."[60] Essentially echoing the central government's long-standing emphasis on upgrading the quality of economic development, Bo's technically oriented remarks were consistent with the reformist image he sought to project in his early tenure.

More importantly, when the Chongqing Model first attracted public attention, Bo Xilai's conception of it remained confined within the framework of *local experimentation*. In response to a direct inquiry about the Chongqing Model, Bo told the media that "it was still too early" to label it a model. "Among China's many provinces, municipalities, and autonomous regions, each is showcasing its own strengths, much like the Eight Immortals crossing the sea, each using his or her unique magic," Bo commented. "Chongqing is merely one among them, and we have also drawn extensively on the experiences of our sister provinces and cities."[61] This early display of modesty likely reflected the fact that Bo was still operating within established political norms at the time: he sought to demonstrate his competence to the Party's central leadership by making Chongqing stand out in inter-provincial competition under a shared policy framework. Shortly thereafter, however, Bo began to shift his ambition toward reshaping the framework itself—that is, moving from playing by the rules to challenging them.

To be sure, the term "Chongqing Model" had already appeared frequently before Bo Xilai's arrival. In these earlier usages, the label was consistently associated with local experimentation. Whenever new practices or policies were introduced and tested, they were often described as a "Chongqing Model." For example, various "Chongqing Models" had been identified in areas such as state-owned property management,[62] technology,[63] party building,[64] agriculture,[65] infrastructure,[66] rural development,[67] and social welfare.[68]

In August 2007, a local establishment scholar affiliated with the Chongqing Academy of Social Sciences proposed that Chongqing needed a "Chongqing-ology" (*Chongqing xue*).[69] Defined as "a field of study dedicated to analyzing Chongqing's politics, economy, culture, and society," it was intended to be "a discipline that reveals the distinctive patterns of Chongqing's evolution and development." Notably, this call for "Chongqing-ology" coincided with the "City Spirit" project initiated by Wang Yang, Bo Xilai's predecessor. In essence, the project was largely propagandistic: "establishing Chongqing-ology is an integral part of a broader, systematic effort to promote Chongqing." Modeled on the branding strategies adopted by more developed cities such as Beijing and Shanghai, the notion of a "Chongqing Model" was framed as a form of rhetorical packaging aimed at enhancing the municipality's image. "Establishing Chongqing-ology is necessary for the formation of a Chongqing Model," the Chongqing scholar argued; "both the search for Chongqing's development model and the promotion of Chongqing's successful experience require the analytical support provided by Chongqing-ology."

In short, in line with the logic of local experimentation, the Chongqing Model was initially a loosely defined term used to highlight local distinctiveness, referring broadly to any successful, locally adapted implementation of central policies under conditions of local discretion.

4.2.2 *The Pilot Zone*

This narrow, inward-looking interpretation of the Chongqing Model as a particular case of local experimentation gradually evolved into something closer to its literal meaning when Chongqing was designated by the central government as a pilot site for urban–rural reform. At this point, Chongqing was officially tasked with exploring a developmental path for the nation, with the expectation that any successful experience could serve as a model for other localities to emulate. However, it soon became clear that the opportunity to make Chongqing excel in a single policy domain could not satisfy Bo Xilai. Driven by political ambition, he sought to raise the stakes in his pursuit of power during the final years of Hu Jintao's tenure.

In mid-2007, Chongqing and Chengdu were designated as a "National Experimental Zone for Comprehensive Reform of Urban–Rural Integration" (*quanguo tongchou chengxiang zonghe peitao gaige shiyan qu*). The objective was to explore solutions to the problem of uneven urban–rural development, commonly referred to as the "dual urban–rural structure" (*chengxiang er yuan jiegou*). In particular, the primary goal was to determine how to "enable rural residents and migrant workers in cities to enjoy equal rights, equitable public services, and living standards comparable to those of urban residents in all respects." On this basis, it was expected that a more balanced pattern of economic and demographic development would help China's western regions catch up with its more developed coastal areas.[70]

Chongqing was said to have been selected for its *representativeness*, which made it likely that any successful practices could be replicated and applied elsewhere. As the rhetoric put it, "Chongqing is a microcosm (*suoying*) of China's dual urban–rural structure."[71] Moreover, Chongqing's administrative structure was believed to ensure that "the experiment [in Chongqing] would be broadly replicable"—that is, "[Chongqing] is comparable in size to a medium-sized province," and "as a municipality, it operates under a three-tier administrative structure, which enhances efficiency."[72]

However, the designation of an "experimental zone" should be distinguished from the earlier concept of a "Special Economic Zone" (*jingji te qu*), a status granted to Shenzhen as a pioneer of China's export-oriented industrialization. It was explicitly emphasized that Chongqing, as an experimental site, should not be regarded as a "new special zone."[73] This distinction suggests that Chongqing's assigned task was primarily to "take the lead in adjusting underlying interest structures and institutional arrangements at a deeper level," rather than to pursue growth through "traditional preferential policies."[74]

To be sure, Chongqing and Chengdu were not the only sites selected for national-level experimentation under Hu Jintao. Shanghai and Tianjin were the first two. Shanghai was tasked with exploring how to "integrate the transformation of government functions with economic system reform and other related reforms," while Tianjin was charged with "promoting economic development in the Bohai Rim region while taking a new path of industrialization, strengthening indigenous innovation as the central priority, and advancing high-tech industries and modern service sectors." Subsequently, two additional experimental sites were established in Wuhan and Hunan Province. Their mission was to build a "two-*oriented* society" (*liang xing shehui*)—that is, a society *oriented* to "resource-conserving" and "environmentally friendly"—so as to avoid the outdated development model of "growth first, environmental protection later." According to the official narrative,[75] the chronological sequence in which these experimental zones were established signaled a shift in policy priorities, from an overriding focus on economic growth to an increasing emphasis on social harmony, reflecting the broader policy reorientation under Hu Jintao.

Given this broader political context, it is unsurprising that, during its initial phase of promotion—roughly from early 2009 to late 2010—the Chongqing Model was closely associated with the "people's livelihoods" policies rolled out by Bo Xilai, particularly in relation to the central themes of Scientific Development and Harmonious Society. At the time, the Chongqing Model referred to a diverse set of initiatives, including a self-proclaimed new mode of export-oriented manufacturing, the innovative use of state-owned assets for public services, an affordable housing program for low-income groups, an urban residency policy for rural migrants, and even Bo's highly publicized tree-planting campaign.[76]

Early public approval of the Chongqing Model appeared to be particularly gratifying to Bo, not so much because of its substantive achievements on the ground as because of the attention it generated. According to *Yu Lun*, Chongqing's official propaganda handbook, one of the city's greatest accomplishments in 2009 was precisely being labeled a "model." It was considered a model largely because of the "applause and acclaim from the arena of public opinion," which became the most significant component of the Chongqing Model.[77]

4.2.3 *The New Deal*

Further politicization reached a new level in late 2010. From that point onward, the Chongqing Model was framed as a groundbreaking blueprint for systemic and comprehensive transformation in China. It moved beyond the framework of local experimentation and was no longer merely a label for the localized implementation of centrally designed policies.

A clear sign of this shift was that Ji Shuoming, the journalist whose 2009 article had brought the Chongqing Model into the public spotlight, now advanced a new interpretation of what the model entailed. At a symposium titled "The Chongqing Practice and the New Asian Model," held in late 2010—just months before Bo Xilai announced the Common Prosperity agenda at Chongqing's Eighth Party Plenum—Ji argued that the Chongqing Model should be understood as a comprehensive project of social transformation rather than merely an innovative strategy for economic development. "Chongqing is not pursuing reform in any single domain," Ji stressed; "rather, it seeks to transform the mode of operation of society as a whole."[78] By this point, the Chongqing Model had come to be articulated as a *political* program encompassing multiple policy domains. A wide range of initiatives associated with Bo—such as the "Five Chongqings," the Sing Red movement, and the Strike Black campaign—were now incorporated and subsumed under a single overarching label.

Moreover, Ji emphasized the ideological significance of the Chongqing Model—namely, the revival of the Party's revolutionary tradition. As he noted, "what Chongqing has been doing is to revive and carry forward those values that have been abandoned or neglected by society."[79] According to Ji, Chongqing's development rested on two pillars: "the veteran cadres" (*lao tongzhi*), representing historical continuity and tradition, and "the ordinary people" (*lao baixing*), embodying the Maoist principle of "serving the people."[80] The prototype of this Maoist framing can arguably be traced back to Ji's early 2010 article, also published in *Asia Weekly*, likely as a follow-up to his 2009 piece.[81] In that article, Ji lavished praise on Chongqing's Mass Line campaigns, arguing that "Chongqing is exploring a new path toward a China model of common prosperity."

Finally, the Chongqing Model was portrayed as a challenge to the status quo and, therefore, as pathbreaking. In this framing, restoring the Party's revolutionary tradition was seen as a form of progress through a return to the past. Commenting on Bo's red culture campaign, Ji praised his willingness to go against the prevailing tide. In his words, "the governing authorities [i.e., Bo Xilai], in an era marked by the erosion of social values, seek to introduce a new set of social values by reviving red memories." Moreover, Ji juxtaposed Bo's achievements and agenda with those of Mao and Deng, invoking three distinct value paradigms: "the red political values of Mao Zedong," "the golden economic values of the early reform era," and "the Chongqing-style human-centered values."[82] In this narrative, Chongqing was elevated to a status comparable to that of Shenzhen. Whereas the latter symbolized an emphasis on "efficiency-centeredness," the former was cast as prioritizing "equity-centeredness."[83] Although Ji continued to nominally situate the Chongqing Model within Hu Jintao's framework of Scientific Development, describing it as "the Chongqing version of Scientific Development,"[84] the broader message was unmistakable: Bo, rather than the central leadership, was presented as the figure leading China into a new era.

The voices that politicized the Chongqing Model during the 2010–2011 period can largely be understood as variations on Ji Shuoming's three-pronged new framing. The Chongqing Model was celebrated through a striking array of laudatory discourse. First, it was portrayed not merely as a set of *policies* but as a comprehensive *political* program. The Chongqing Model was said to be "creating an entirely new system and establishing a new set of rules."[85] Accordingly, it should be "broadly defined," rather than narrowly understood in terms of "local development" or "problem solving." It was even characterized as Bo Xilai's "New Deal" (*xin zheng*),[86] with Chongqing's greatest advantage said to lie in its "conceptual innovation."[87]

Second, the Chongqing Model was depicted as paradigm-transcending. "Our practice has already moved far ahead of theoretical development." According to this kind of "empiricist" praise, "while there are many issues we may not fully understand in theory, we know how to make them work in practice."[88] At the same time, Bo Xilai was credited with making a great "theoretical" contribution—"Chongqing's practice has provided an answer to a question that academia has long failed to resolve, namely, the relationship between planning and the market."[89] Chongqing was thus described as the latest milestone in China's reform process: "as a pioneer of reform and opening-up, Chongqing will undoubtedly make contributions to national [development]."[90] Yet Chongqing was also portrayed as qualitatively distinct from earlier reform milestones. While "one can see Shenzhen's shadow in Pudong, and Pudong's shadow in Shenzhen," the

Chongqing Model was depicted as "entirely new," with little overlap with previous reformist model cities, and as "a region of comprehensive and strategic significance."[91] The most effusive praise, highlighting Bo's vanguardism, described Chongqing's experience as a "Thousand Days' Reform" (*qian ri wei xin*), deliberately echoing the "Hundred Days' Reform" (*bai ri wei xin*), namely the late Qing reform movement widely regarded in Chinese historiography as a progressive attempt at political transformation. Such rhetoric claimed that Bo's governance "has brought the people of Chongqing the best living conditions and the best era since the Chinese Communist Party came to power" and that the Chongqing Model "is no longer a routine local policy initiative, but a life-and-death choice bearing on the future and destiny of the party-state."[92]

Third, the Chongqing Model was celebrated as evidence of socialism's superiority over Western capitalism. It was claimed that "Chongqing has shattered many of the discursive logics of neoliberalism."[93] In highly exaggerated terms, a Renmin University research report asserted that the Chongqing Model "marks the end of a capitalism-centered developmental paradigm" and thereby "offers new hope and new possibilities for a new form of human civilization in the twenty-first century."[94] Conversely, the Chongqing Model was portrayed as a distinctly Chinese alternative to the hegemonic Western model. "The Chongqing story has deepened [the understanding of] the China Model."[95] As a concrete blueprint for the Chinese Dream grounded in common prosperity, the Chongqing Model was said to provide an antidote to the uncritical embrace of the American Dream, thereby "enhancing the discursive power (*huayu quan*) of Socialism with Chinese Characteristics in the international arena."[96] The Chongqing Model suggested that international competition was not only about economic strength, but also about "the innovation of development approaches, ideas, and models."[97] In this narrative, with the rise of Chongqing, it was claimed to have "shattered the Washington Consensus, transcended the Japanese and East Asian models, and redefined the Beijing Consensus."[98] Moreover, the Chongqing Model was expected to exert a direct impact on the global order, rather than merely serving as a non-Western alternative. Foreshadowing Xi Jinping's later formulation of "a community with a shared future for mankind" (*renlei mingyun gongtong ti*), proponents argued that once China achieved common prosperity and extended its ethos to the international community, the world would be liberated from its current Western centrism, wealth centrism, and power politics and would instead operate on a people-centered basis. "The twenty-first century will be an era in which the Chinese people make major contributions to human development."[99] The most politicized flattery of the Chongqing Model was perhaps the claim that it had become the reincarnation of the so-called Marxist sinicization. "The practice and innovation of Socialism with Chinese Characteristics in Chongqing" was described as "a creative application of the latest theories of sinicized Marxism."[100] Chongqing was thus cast as "the front line of the great practice of Socialism with Chinese Characteristics"[101] and as "a paradigmatic case of the regionalization of Marxism."[102]

In addition to what was said, *who* said it also mattered. A number of politically symbolic figures were invited to endorse the Chongqing Model. Among them was Hu Jinxing, a cousin of Hu Jintao.[103] Another was Deng Ken, a half-brother of Deng Xiaoping. To express his "admiration" for Chongqing's exploration and practice over the years, Deng Ken presented Bo with a piece of calligraphy bearing a quotation from Deng Xiaoping: "Both hands must be equally strong" (*liang shou dou yao ying*).[104] The message was implicit yet unmistakable: China's development involved not only economic growth but also the upholding of political principles, and in this regard, Bo was portrayed as having governed Chongqing effectively.

In short, the Chongqing Model was not inherently political; rather, it became unmistakably politicized as Bo Xilai shifted his political orientation. Many elements that were later framed as central to its politicized version had already been in place well before this fateful transformation.

What was poured into the new bottle was, in essence, old wine—elements with traceable origins that allow us to discern their original form prior to repackaging. A particularly illustrative case is Chongqing's statist approach to economic development.[105] The practices that Bo Xilai later promoted in Chongqing had, in fact, been developed earlier during his tenure as mayor of Dalian. Bo was known for asserting that "state-owned enterprises are state assets, and this applies even more so to cities" (*chengshi geng shi guoyou zichan*), and that "all capital ultimately belongs to the state" (*yiqie ziben gui zhengfu*). Guided by this statist logic, the Dalian municipal government sought to "manage the city as a whole as a state-owned asset." To be sure, Bo's embrace of this statist approach at the time was largely a means to an end—namely, to demonstrate his governing competence through visible achievements in urban development. In later years, however, the emphasis shifted toward lionizing statism itself into an end in its own right. A similar pattern can be observed in Chongqing Mayor Huang Qifan's efforts to expand the state sector and develop infrastructure. His measures were not novel innovations, but rather transplantation of policies he had previously implemented in Shanghai. This approach, often referred to as the "Pudong logic," involved state-owned enterprises leveraging anticipated land-value appreciation as collateral to secure bank loans. As land prices rose, partly driven by state-led investment, these enterprises would engage in successive rounds of borrowing and reinvestment, creating a self-reinforcing cycle.[106] Initially adopted as a developmental strategy, this snowballing model of financing was later promoted as generating a "third source of fiscal revenue" (*di san caizheng*), thereby enabling the Chongqing government to expand social spending and better address public needs. However, its long-term sustainability hinged on a critical question: can land and real estate prices continue to outpace wage growth indefinitely?[107]

4.3 For the People

The politicized promotion of the Chongqing Model in particular, and of Bo Xilai's governance in Chongqing more broadly, culminated in a populist revival of Mass Line rhetoric that foregrounded the Party's "fine tradition" of "serving the people." Beneath the facade of party-building discourse lay the question of political accountability. On the one hand, this rhetoric articulated a leftist accusation that certain (reformist) party cadres were responsible for the widening socioeconomic divide and pervasive corruption within China's officialdom. On the other hand, it functioned as a leftist defense of party leadership under socialism against reformist calls for political reform. It advanced an idealized vision in which the Party, when led by "true" communists imbued with a pure faith in socialism, could rectify its own shortcomings without recourse to democratic institutions or constitutional constraints.

The substantive core of Bo's populist politics lay in a form of socialist fundamentalism rooted in Maoist thought. The revival of Maoist utopian discourse marked a clear escalation of leftist critique—from an initial challenge to market-oriented development to an explicit call for a return to revolutionary orthodoxy. At the same time, the inherently populist disposition of Maoism politically empowered this leftist crusade by endowing it with mobilizational capacity, in addition to its ideological appeal to socialism.

By invoking the mythic ideal of "good" communists fighting for proletarian interests and for the sovereign people—the purported masters entitled to purge corrupt bureaucrats—Bo's populist rhetoric functioned as a strategy to claim the high ground of political legitimacy in the name of the people. With the spirit of the Mass Line serving as the central thread running through Bo's major policy initiatives, it became the overarching framework through which the Sing Red and Strike Black campaigns, as well as the Common Prosperity project, were reframed and elevated to a new level of political significance.

4.3.1 Centering the Mass Line

The Mass Line was the "soul" of the Chongqing Model,[108] claimed Su Wei, a professor at the Chongqing Party School who was closely involved in propaganda efforts promoting Bo Xilai's Chongqing "New Deal." Although neither Bo Xilai nor other local leaders in Chongqing offered an official elaboration of the Chongqing Model, Su Wei's theorization was widely regarded at the time as an authoritative interpretation presented under the guise of semi-official rhetoric.[109]

Su Wei published a book titled *The Chongqing Model* in early 2011, co-authored with two others. Its main arguments had already appeared in articles he published in August 2010.[110] The timing coincided with Ji Shuoming's revised conception of the Chongqing Model, as noted above.[111] The ideational origins of both Su's and Ji's politicized framings can arguably be traced back to Ji's second *Asia Weekly* article, published in early 2010, which praised the campaigns initiated by Bo Xilai to send party cadres into rural villages.[112]

Directly referencing Ji's article, Su Wei elevated its argument with an added populist inflection.[113] "To stay in close contact with the masses is to revive the principle of 'serving the people.'" As Su emphasized, this focus on Mass Line practice "captures the substantive essence of the Chongqing Model." At its core, the Chongqing Model aimed "to remold the soul of the party organization in Chongqing, to rebuild the image of party cadres, to restore the connection between party members and the masses, and to renew the people's trust and confidence in the party committee and the government." According to Su Wei, Mass Line campaigns were politically more significant than the Sing Red and Strike Black movements, even though the latter attracted far greater public attention.

As for policies on the ground, Chongqing's ongoing Mass Line practices (e.g., the "Three Activities"), initiated in 2009, received explicit endorsement from the Party center. Bo Xilai's Mass Line campaigns were praised as exemplary models for other localities to emulate. In June 2010, a report on the "Three Enters and Three Togethers" movement was included in the Party's classified internal reference materials. After reviewing it, China's then Vice President Xi Jinping issued a written directive (*pi shi*) stating that Chongqing's experience "should be studied and emulated."[114] Subsequently, during a visit to Chongqing, Li Yuanchao, then head of the Central Organization Department, which oversees the Party's personnel and nomenklatura system, also affirmed the value of Bo's party-building initiatives, adding that Chongqing's local experience "has set a good example for the entire country to follow."[115]

Bo Xilai's populist turn in Chongqing reflected the broader political climate in China at the time. Toward the end of Hu Jintao's second term (2010–2012), reviving the spirit of the Mass Line became increasingly prominent on the Party center's political agenda. Just as the two-year party rectification campaign centered on Hu Jintao's Scientific Development concluded in early 2010, a follow-up campaign was launched in May of the same year. This new initiative, known as Chuang Xian Zheng You (CXZY), was a shorthand for the campaign to "establish advanced grassroots party organizations and strive to be outstanding party members." The central logic of the campaign held that "party members should be rooted in the masses, serving as the primary agents sustaining the Party's blood-and-flesh ties with the people." Unlike the preceding Scientific Development campaign, which mobilized the Party as a whole, the CXZY campaign specifically targeted grassroots cadres working directly with the masses. In 2012, this mandate was further highlighted when the year was officially designated as the "Year of Grassroots Organization Building" (*jiceng zuzhi jianshe nian*).[116]

Accordingly, Bo Xilai moved swiftly to introduce another Mass Line campaign. As a direct policy response to the new rectification initiative launched by the Party's central leadership in 2010, Chongqing claimed to have "innovated" a new approach to grassroots party building. In practice, however, the measures were largely conventional, consisting of self-reporting, evaluation, ranking, and the public disclosure of assessment results (*yi jiang er ping san gong shi*).[117]

What most clearly testified to the heightened politicization of the Mass Line campaigns in Chongqing, as Bo embraced a more populist turn, was the Mao-style mobilization of college students. This initiative evoked the Mao-era "rustication" movement, commonly known as the "Down to the Countryside" campaign (*shang shan xia xiang*). Launched in late 2010, the campaign urged local college students "to once again learn from workers, peasants, and soldiers" (*zai xue gong nong bing*).[118] Specifically, the official plan required each university student in Chongqing to complete six tasks prior to graduation: planting 100 trees; undertaking a one-month paid internship; living and working with peasants in rural villages for one month; working in an enterprise or service position for one month; participating in a one-month military drill; and completing a social research report. According to Bo, "it is commendable that students of the new generation carry forward the fine traditions of the 1950s and 1960s, and remain connected with the masses, including workers and peasants, even while still in school."[119] Elsewhere, Bo claimed that for students who had the opportunity to work in what Mao called the "vast and open world" (*guangkuo tiandi*), that is, the countryside, the experience was "no less valuable than pursuing a master's degree." He further urged students to "be willing to learn as humble pupils" and to "learn from the masses with humility,"[120] once again invoking Maoist language for symbolic effect.

4.3.2 *Rhetorical Rebranding*

With the Mass Line emerging as the defining core of the Chongqing Model, Bo's other major policy initiatives underwent a further process of radicalization. A populist layer was superimposed on top of earlier socialist framings.

First, Bo's Common Prosperity agenda possessed an inherent affinity for populist politicization. It was no longer merely a socialist economic program aimed at improving the conditions of the poor and disadvantaged; more importantly, it was cast as a testament to the Party's legitimacy as the true representative of the people's interests. Bo was explicit on this point, noting that the "core and essence" of Socialism with Chinese Characteristics lay in common prosperity, which he presented as a concrete embodiment of the Party's fundamental principle of "serving the people."[121] In the words of a leading conservative theoretician, common prosperity was tied to the Party's "legitimacy and re-legitimation." It was argued that while Western democracies sustain their legitimacy through elections, China's political system "remains legitimated" by "improving people's livelihoods."[122]

Second, the Sing Red movement, as a rhetorical chameleon, acquired an additional populist coloration alongside its earlier dimensions—motivational, developmental, moral, educational, cultural, and ideological. This populist element had already been discernible during Bo's earlier leftist turn, but it became more pronounced as he assumed the mantle of a conservative vanguard, asserting that the essence of the Socialist Core Value System was ultimately "the people."[123] In this vein, he argued that "singing red songs is serving the people," which, in turn, "is precisely what the Party is meant to do."[124] As Bo further stated, "we Communists must have the confidence and courage to hold high the red banner, sing red songs, uphold our ideals and convictions, and serve the people with honesty and openness."[125]

Semi-official voices further elaborated Chongqing's official populist framing. As Su Wei pointed out, when both society at large and party cadres sang red songs, they were in effect praising the Party's altruistic spirit of serving the public good—embodied in the tradition of "not taking so much as a needle or a thread from the masses." At the same time, these songs served to remind cadres of their obligations and to warn against misconduct.[126] According to Zhu Jiamu, a leading conservative theoretician who helped articulate Xi Jinping's "Two Thirty Years" thesis (*liang ge san shi nian*), which seeks to whitewash and legitimize the Maoist past, "protecting and safeguarding the interests of the masses" constituted the "foundation" of the Sing Red movement. "Red songs are not something that the masses will sing wherever and whenever they are told to do so," Zhu further elaborated. "If the issues that the masses strongly complain about are not resolved, and if no concrete benefits are delivered to ordinary people, the songs will not be sung; even if they are, they will lack spirit."[127] Not unlike the Common Prosperity project, the Sing Red movement was also portrayed as crucial to the Party's political legitimacy. It was claimed that the movement "has once again made the Party's glorious 'Serve the People' brand shine," thereby "fundamentally consolidating the legitimacy of the Party's rule." Conversely, "abandoning the red banner of 'Serve the People' would fundamentally undermine the foundation of the Party's governance."[128]

To be sure, the populist turn of the Sing Red movement did not displace its other framings. Rather, by intensifying the overall politicized atmosphere, it further accentuated the role of the red culture campaign in the Party's politico-ideological struggle against the influence of Western capitalism. Both the tone and the language grew increasingly bellicose, evoking the class struggles of earlier decades. In particular, the Sing Red movement was portrayed as emblematic of what China required to counter "peaceful evolution" and "color revolutions" allegedly orchestrated by hostile Western forces.[129] Given that "the global configuration, where the two major social systems [i.e., socialism and capitalism] develop through comparison and struggle, will not change in the short term," the Party was said to need a strengthened ideological bulwark against "infiltration through culture and values" from the West. This was framed as essential to ensuring that China's reform would not devolve into a kind of "reform and opening-up that abandons principles and the socialist system in pursuit of bourgeois liberalization."[130] In practice, Bo Xilai reshaped programming on Chongqing Satellite TV in March 2011. From that point on, the channel "eliminated all commercials during broadcasts" and "focused exclusively on disseminating advanced socialist culture."[131] This highly symbolic move was praised by leftist commentators as "a concrete effort to compete for the masses, especially the youth, in the ideological sphere against erroneous trends of thought."[132]

Third, the framing of the Strike Black campaign also underwent a populist upgrading. It was no longer a mere cliché of righteous law enforcement defeating criminal elements; rather, it was recast as a manifestation of the Party's capacity to remain accountable to the people. In this reframing, the anti-organized-crime campaign was elevated into an anti-corruption initiative. Citing Hu Jintao's remarks as an authoritative endorsement, Bo Xilai argued that Chongqing's Strike Black campaign owed its success not only to its crackdown on organized crime but also to its targeting of their "protective umbrellas"—the political cover provided by corrupt Party officials—thereby integrating it with broader anti-corruption efforts.[133] Through this linkage, the Strike Black campaign was transformed into a project of party building. Given that corruption, within the Party's political discourse, is conceptually associated with a weakening of the Mass Line spirit—that is, a loss of connection with the masses—what began as a law-and-order initiative evolved into a movement of political rectification and moral cleansing.[134]

Su Wei particularly emphasized that "anti–organized-crime campaigns had been carried out in the past, but they failed to uproot the 'protective umbrellas.'" In his view, it was precisely this extension of the crackdown into officialdom, both in practice and in conceptual framing, that endowed the Strike Black campaign with distinctive political significance. As he put it, "Chongqing's Strike Black is not an anti–organized-crime campaign in the ordinary sense, because such campaigns are in themselves neither 'socialist' nor 'communist.'"[135] From a class-struggle perspective, Su Wei further argued that anti-corruption was fundamentally about resisting capitalist encroachment. Corruption, in this view, originated from morally degenerate entrepreneurs who "launched large-scale attacks on party and state power holders with 'sugar-coated bullets'" (*tang yi paodan*). More importantly, by "taking the anti–organized-crime campaign to a deeper level," the movement touched upon a broader issue: the Party's effort to preserve its "purity"—that is, its legitimacy as the representative of the Chinese people it claims to serve.[136] Accordingly, Su Wei argued that the Strike Black campaign ultimately contributed to "consolidating the foundation of the Party's rule," insofar as successful anti-corruption "demonstrates that the Party is fully capable of purifying itself through its own efforts."[137] Echoing this view, another leftist theoretician contended that "the Strike Black is not merely a form of protectionism, but a manifestation of the nature of the political regime." At stake, in this rhetoric, was whether "political power remains in the hands of the people."[138] By invoking the idea of a "people's regime," the underlying message was that anti-corruption efforts constituted a form of Party-led realization of popular sovereignty, carried out in the name of and for the benefit of the people.

Fourth, accompanying Bo Xilai's populist move, which rebranded virtually every major component of his political agenda, was a proliferation of politically charged symbolism that glorified the Party's revolutionary traditions, particularly those of the Mao era. A central message was that what made the Maoist past a "golden era" (albeit in a largely mythologized sense) could also secure China's future, insofar as the Party had been, remained, and would continue to be committed to serving the people wholeheartedly. A series of commemorative events celebrated iconic Mao-era figures and narratives, including the "War to Resist U.S. Aggression and Aid Korea" (*kang mei yuan chao*), i.e., China's participation in the Korean War,[139] as well as Dr. Norman Bethune (Bai Qiu En) and Lei Feng.[140] On these occasions, Bo repeatedly stressed that "spiritual forces can be transformed into material ones," echoing Mao's formulation in his 1963 text "Where Do Correct Ideas Come From?"[141] Emphasizing the Maoist ethos of self-sacrifice for the communist cause, Bo also urged cadres to learn from model workers of the Mao era, such as the "Iron Man" Wang Jinxi of Daqing.[142]

Accordingly, Bo sought to portray himself as the living embodiment of the Party's revolutionary legacy, emphasizing in particular the political credentials derived from his revolutionary lineage. In *Yu Lun*, Bo was praised for his frequent and effective use of Mao's quotations in speeches—an ability attributed to his identity as a "Red Descendant" and the life and work experiences associated with it. Maoist thought was said to have shaped Bo's worldview and to have provided him with continuous spiritual guidance, thereby constituting the sole correct ideological framework for governing Chongqing.[143] Within this logic, Bo's project of building a "Red Chongqing" was framed not merely as an effort to carry forward the Party's revolutionary spirit, but also as an attempt to transmit the governing philosophy of the communist forefathers to a new era.[144]

In general, Bo Xilai sought to transform Chongqing into a contemporary symbol of the Party's political legitimacy. During his Maoist phase of governance, Chongqing hosted a series of central-level conferences attended by leading party theoreticians, serving as a form of political endorsement. The city was selected to host a seminar on party historiography on the grounds that "Chongqing is a city of revolution and heroes."[145] According to the director of the Central Party History Research Office (*zhongyang dangshi yanjiu shi*), from the perspective of Party history, what was unfolding in Chongqing under Bo Xilai "amounts to nothing less than a continuation of the magnificent history written by the masses under the leadership of the Chinese Communist Party."[146] On the occasion of the Party's 90th anniversary, the Central Party School and the National Society for Party Building Studies (*quanguo dangjian yanjiu hui*) also selected Chongqing to host a symposium on Party building. This choice was said to reflect "high-level attention to and full recognition of Chongqing's practices in party building."[147] The success of Chongqing's overall development was attributed to Bo Xilai's emphasis on party building, which "provided political and organizational support for economic development."[148]

Seizing this opportunity to reinforce the populist framing of his anti-organized-crime and anti-corruption campaigns, Bo invoked the Party's revolutionary heroism, imbued with a mythologized symbolism of popular support. "During the revolutionary wars, thanks to the heartfelt support of the masses, our Party was like a fish in water, invincible wherever it went."[149] Around the same time, another conference was convened to promote the efforts to "carry forward revolutionary spirit."[150] There, "Hongyan Spirit," rooted in Chongqing's local revolutionary history, was elevated to a status on par with centrally canonized revolutionary traditions. Alongside "Jinggangshan Spirit," "Yan'an Spirit," and the "Long March Spirit," it was now celebrated as one of the "radiant and exemplary" traditions cultivated by the Party within its "grand garden of revolutionary spirit."[151] In this way, Chongqing's local revolutionary ethos was incorporated into the Party's ideological pantheon.

Bo Xilai's defense of his Chongqing program also appealed to a populist justification. In response to reformist criticism, he argued that the satisfaction of the majority of the people constituted the sole criterion for evaluating a leader's performance. "Let others say whatever they will, but what truly matters is that the people are satisfied," Bo asserted, "A governing official should never expect to receive 100 percent support. As long as the majority of the people express approval and satisfaction, one should press ahead with determination."[152]

4.4 Mass Spontaneity

According to the Mass Line doctrine, the Party claims, on the one hand, to represent and serve the people, while, on the other hand, the masses are expected to welcome and cooperate with the Party as it descends to lead them. The first element of the Mass Line is evident in Bo Xilai's effort to reorient his political programs around the rhetoric of "Serve the People." The second element can be found in the same body of propaganda, much of which was devoted to highlighting "mass spontaneity" within these state-led campaigns.

By foregrounding the notion of "mass spontaneity," Bo once again positioned Chongqing's local practice of the Mass Line ahead of the Party center's agenda, much as the Common Prosperity initiative in Chongqing outpaced the Hu–Wen leadership's People's Livelihoods program, and as the so-called Chongqing Model extended beyond the conventional framework of local experimentation.

Bo's vanguardism manifested itself in two key respects. First, although Chongqing's Mass Line policies initially emerged from Bo Xilai's proactive alignment with the central agenda, particularly the two major waves of rectification campaigns, his distinctly populist approach and framing were eventually taken up by the Party center. In this sense, the direction of political guidance was effectively reversed: a local initiative set the tone, and the center followed suit. More importantly, this was not a matter of policy-level experimentation and innovation, but a declaration of political ambition and an arrogation of agenda-setting authority. Second, with the Sing Red and Strike Black campaigns becoming fully politicized, and with the added emphasis on "mass spontaneity," Chongqing effectively became a pioneer in reviving the Mao-era practice of "mass movements" (*qunzhong yundong*). Historically, large-scale, top-down mobilizations in post-Mao China had taken the form of rectification campaigns aimed primarily at party cadres rather than at mobilizing the general populace. By contrast, this renewed form of mobilization in the early 2010s reintroduced elements of mass participation, even if it stopped short of explicitly endorsing overtly antagonistic rhetoric—that is, it did not invoke the kind of "life-and-death struggle" discourse characteristic of the Mao era. Nevertheless, the strong conservative critique of China's market-oriented reforms, particularly pronounced during Hu Jintao's second term, provided an unsettling backdrop, making this resurgence of mass mobilization appear to echo, at least implicitly, the more confrontational movements of the 1960s.

"Mass spontaneity" is less a substantive phenomenon than a political construct, largely derived from a politicized framing of the routine mode of governance under party rule—namely, the top-down mobilization of a hierarchically organized bureaucracy and society into ad hoc campaign-style action in pursuit of specific policy goals. Following a directive issued by party leaders at the apex of power, political pressure is transmitted down the bureaucratic hierarchy, ultimately reaching street-level officials and the general populace, who are compelled to carry out the assigned tasks.

As is often the case, state propaganda presents the leader's decisions as enjoying broad popular support, frequently reinforced through orchestrated public displays of approval. This familiar trope was clearly evident in Chongqing during Bo Xilai's early tenure, particularly in official reporting on the Mind Emancipation campaign. Party mouthpieces claimed that public participation unfolded in several stages—beginning with initial observation, followed by attentive engagement, and ultimately culminating in active involvement—which "reflected Chongqing citizens' strong desire to break through ideological constraints and pursue further [economic] development."[153]

In the case of the Sing Red movement, early claims that top-down mobilization responded to popular demand largely resembled a conventional form of justification. The rhetoric did little to move beyond the familiar cliché of the state asserting mass support, whether or not such support genuinely existed. Chongqing's Sing Red campaign was said not to have been initiated by "hotheaded" party leaders, nor to have been imposed as "an administrative fiat" from above. Rather, it was portrayed as resting on "a broad and solid popular foundation," characterized by the voluntary participation of ordinary people.[154] In this sense, the movement was framed as a perfect alignment of supply and demand: "when official intentions closely converged with popular aspirations."[155]

The rhetorical transformation was fully on display when official discourse highlighted a self-reinforcing *loop* between top-down cultivation and bottom-up internalization. This narrative closely followed the logic of the Mass Line: the Party that claims to know what is best for the people (i.e., red songs) descends to raise mass consciousness (through the Sing Red movement), after which the masses embrace the policy and, in turn, call for its further expansion. "Red songs have transformed mainstream values and culture into the people's voluntary pursuit, producing an effect like rain that nourishes things silently."[156] When socialist values "are no longer confined to the understanding of a few, but are grasped and consciously put into practice by the broad masses," a powerful current of public opinion would emerge as "a real ethical force that permeates social life, shaping and regulating it by fostering a moral atmosphere and exerting invisible constraints and norms." Ultimately, "those who have gained ideological benefit from [the Sing Red movement] will, in turn, propel the activity to deeper levels."[157] According to an official summary issued by the Chongqing Propaganda Department in late 2011, the success of the Sing Red movement depended on "a mechanism capable of generating lasting effects." The process began with state-led organization, shifted to popular response and participation, and then returned to state coordination for the initiation of a new cycle, forming what was described as "an endogenous chain that reproduces itself through continual repetition while spiraling upward."[158] At its core, this mechanism "consistently foregrounds the principal position of the masses and relies on their conscious willingness and voluntary participation."[159] In late 2010, a group of party theoreticians from the Chinese Academy of Social Sciences visited Chongqing to lend ideological endorsement, characterizing the Sing Red movement as "a mass-based innovation in party theory and socialist practice."[160]

Bo Xilai's use of the state apparatus and top-down mobilization was indispensable in producing a self-reinforcing reality on the ground, which in turn fed into the populist framing of mass enthusiasm. From the outset, the local state machinery was fully engaged. For example, choruses were established in virtually every state unit, and red songs were formally incorporated into school curricula.[161] As Bo moved further along a leftist path, the Chongqing state assumed an increasingly prominent role in sustaining the Sing Red movement. The annual workload of the Chongqing Propaganda Department was outlined as follows: at least 10 major events at the national level, over 100 large-scale events organized by municipal-level departments, and more than 1000 events of significant scale across Chongqing's 40 districts and counties. In addition, the Department was tasked with guiding and mobilizing over 10,000 activities in communities, schools, military units, and enterprises, as well as co-hosting at least one national-level large-scale event each year in collaboration with relevant central ministries.[162] Over time, the red culture campaign became more deeply institutionalized within the bureaucratic structure. Additional state agencies were brought into the effort, expenditures were formally incorporated into the state budget, and Sing Red–related performance was integrated into the cadre evaluation system.[163]

In addition, the populist promotion of red culture incorporated Chongqing's anti-organized-crime campaign into a broader framework of populist politics. Bo Xilai characterized the Strike Black campaign as one that "relied on the masses while handling cases strictly in accordance with the law throughout the entire process."[164] Moreover, it was officially framed as a genuine "people's war" (*renming zhanzheng*).[165] In response to reformist criticism that Chongqing's crackdown on organized crime resembled a Cultural Revolution–style political struggle, Su Wei of the Chongqing Party School offered a distinctive interpretation of the relationship between the Sing Red and Strike Black campaigns. According to Su,[166] the shortcomings of China's legal system stemmed largely from the fact that many people "have lost their faith, morality, and even a basic sense of courage" and therefore "are unwilling to come forward as witnesses." Consequently, any attempt to "raise China's law-based governance to a level comparable to that of the West" required not only institutional development but also moral transformation, namely that "citizens must be reshaped and a sense of faith must be instilled," a task far more difficult than merely "creating legal statutes." In practice, this entailed "filling the vacuum of belief with spiritual resources drawn from China's own [cultural traditions]." Su Wei claimed that "this is precisely the significance of promoting Sing Red in Chongqing." With regard to safeguarding social justice and public security, the underlying logic was that only after the ideological vacuum among the populace had been filled by the Party's red culture would individuals become sufficiently emboldened to report crimes. "How can the masses be mobilized to serve as witnesses? It is precisely through Sing Red that the faith and courage already present among the people can be discovered and further strengthened." Su Wei further argued that by "first mobilizing mass participation through traditional ideological resources, and then proceeding in accordance with the law," Chongqing's Strike Black campaign represented, in a broader sense, a distinctly Chinese approach that "combines faith with institutions."

Su Wei also highlighted the role of charismatic leadership in the populist framing of the Strike Black campaign. The underlying argument was that, in the absence of a fully institutionalized democratic system in China, the most effective means of combating corruption—embodied, in Chongqing's case, by the expanded scope of the Strike Black campaign—was to rely on a so-called "upright and incorruptible official" (*qing tian*), a quasi-heroic figure who is benevolent, wise, and committed to crushing evil forces in order to restore justice.[167]

Toward the end of Hu Jintao's tenure, the Party center appeared to be following Chongqing's lead, as the notion of "mass spontaneity" began to surface in both central-level political rhetoric and policy initiatives. Mass mobilization was identified as one of several effective practices in successful party-building efforts. In a speech delivered at a meeting marking the official conclusion of the Chuang Xian Zheng You campaign in late 2012, Li Yuanchao, then head of the Party's Central Organization Department, highlighted seven practices worthy of emulation and further development.[168]

- Integrating party-building efforts closely with central tasks of local party units
- Delivering more tangible benefits to the masses
- Striving for excellence in one's own position and responsibilities
- Strengthening party building at the grassroots level
- Promoting a dynamic pattern in which party organizations lead non-party actors and party members lead the masses (*dang nei dai dang wai, dangyuan dai qunzhong*), thereby fostering a broad-based joint effort between the Party and the people to strive for excellence
- Leveraging exemplary models to provide guidance and demonstration effects
- Closely integrating party-building work with professional and operational responsibilities

The fifth point appeared to introduce a new emphasis, subtly embedded among the other six largely formulaic talking points on party rectification. The examples provided included Chongqing, where "more than 200,000 Party members took the lead in mobilizing 560,000 ordinary citizens" to participate in the "Hongyan Volunteer Action." There was also the case of Jilin, where party cadres implemented a "Red Cell Project" in collaboration with local residents, and that of Liaoning, where more than 7300 volunteer groups were organized under the leadership of 190,000 Party members. According to Li Yuanchao, such Mass Line–style, party-led mobilization of the populace was both exemplary and desirable, because party members "should not only maintain their own advanced character, but also influence the whole of society and lead others to strive for advancement." To be sure, the lexical roots of this emphasis on cadre-led mass mobilization can be traced back to the party document that launched the CXZY campaign in May 2010, just as Bo Xilai was about to push Chongqing into its more vanguardist phase.[169] That document stated that "party members should serve as role models, using exemplary conduct to influence the masses and lead them in accomplishing all assigned tasks."

It was unprecedented in reform-era China for such an explicit and positive endorsement of mass mobilization to appear in central-level political documents. A close reading of party documents on earlier rectification campaigns suggests that, although mass participation was at times rhetorically encouraged as a mechanism for bottom-up feedback and supervision—namely, the so-called open-door rectification (*kaimeng zheng feng*)—the masses were never granted meaningful agency. In other words, post-Mao rectification campaigns were primarily designed to discipline cadres and compel them to better serve the people, who were positioned largely as passive recipients rather than active participants. The rationale behind this arrangement was straightforward. The trauma of Mao's Cultural Revolution left a lasting imprint on party leaders, leading them to conclude that the masses should not be allowed a substantial role in party rectification, for fear that such participation might spiral out of control and turn against the party leadership in the name of popular sovereignty. Against this backdrop, Li Yuanchao's concluding remarks in 2012, embracing a more populist form of mass mobilization, represented a conspicuous departure from reform-era practice.

Particularly worth noting here is that Li's speech was delivered after Bo Xilai's fall from power. It corroborates the view that the rising conservative wave during the Hu Jintao era was independent of Bo, who appeared to be fighting for his own power and future by aligning himself with the ascending leftism and chose to be a conservative spokesman. The leftist vendetta against reformism went on relentlessly even after Bo was shot down.

The populist spirit on display in Chongqing found another policy vehicle at the central level in March 2012, just two weeks before Bo Xilai's fall from power. The "Learn from Lei Feng" campaign can arguably be understood as a central-level counterpart to Bo's Sing Red movement.

According to official elaborations, the campaign was intended to "promote the development of the Socialist Core Value System" and to "raise citizens' moral standards and the level of social civility."[170] Notwithstanding these ideological and moral objectives, a *political* agenda underlay the initiative: by urging society as a whole to emulate Lei Feng—the exemplary communist figure—the campaign effectively functioned as a form of populist mobilization aligned with the Mass Line spirit. With Lei Feng cast as a moral exemplar embodying the "going to the masses" dimension of the narrative, ordinary citizens were called upon to assume the role of enlightened participants, expected to "love the Party, the motherland, and socialism," just as Lei Feng did.

Methodologically, as with the Sing Red movement, the Lei Feng campaign emphasized a combination of top-down organization and bottom-up initiative. It called on local governments to "fully mobilize the masses by activating their enthusiasm and initiative" and to "integrate centrally organized activities with those arising spontaneously from the masses." It was further stipulated that the campaign be embedded in the everyday work and lives of both cadres and the broader public, with "social volunteer service as a vehicle." By "combining concentrated campaigns with routine daily work," the initiative was intended to permeate society as a whole.

From a historical perspective, the political significance of the 2012 Lei Feng campaign should not be underestimated. Campaigns centered on Lei Feng and initiated by the Party center have been rare throughout the Party's history (see Table 4.2), and their timing has not been arbitrary. On each occasion when Lei Feng was invoked, unusual dynamics were unfolding within the party leadership. The underlying logic is straightforward: although Lei Feng has often been portrayed as a model of moral virtue, he has fundamentally functioned as a symbol of *political loyalty*.

Table 4.2 "Learn from Lei Feng" campaigns

When a Lei Feng campaign started	*Corresponding events*
1964 (Lei Feng was made a role model for the first time)	Mao started the Great Proletarian Cultural Revolution in 1966
1973	Lin Biao, who was once the heir apparent to Mao, died in a plane crash in 1971 and was later charged with a coup attempt
1977	The Gang of Four was arrested in 1976
1983	The "Democracy Wall" movement took place from 1978 to 1979. The Twelfth Party Congress, held in 1982, removed Mao's Cultural Revolution theory from the Party's Constitution
1990	Chinese students staged protests at Tiananmen Square in 1989
2012	Bo Xilai launched Mao-style mass campaigns in Chongqing

Notes

1. Part of Sect. 4.1 is adapted from Lin Le, *China's Conservative Turn: The Origins of Xi Jinping's New Era* (Lynne Rienner Publishers, 2025), 120–124.
2. External Propaganda Office of the Chongqing Party Committee (EPOCPC) and Chongqing Center for Internet News Research (CCINR), *Yu lun 2008* [Public Opinion in Chongqing 2008] (self-published, 2009); Chongqing Leading Small Group for Internet Regulation (CLSGIR), EPOCPC, and CCINR, *Yu lun 2009* [Public Opinion in Chongqing 2009] (self-published, 2010); CLSGIR, EPOCPC and CCINR, *Yu lun 2010* [Public Opinion in Chongqing 2010] (self-published, 2011).
3. EPOCPC and CCINR, *Yu lun 2008*, preface.
4. EPOCPC and CCINR, *Yu lun 2008*, preface.
5. EPOCPC and CCINR, *Yu lun 2008*, preface.
6. CLSGIR, EPOCPC, and CCINR, *Yu lun 2009*, preface.
7. CLSGIR, EPOCPC and CCINR, *Yu lun 2010*, preface.
8. CLSGIR, EPOCPC and CCINR, *Yu lun 2010*, preface.
9. Xiao Zhu, "Ba zan Chongqing jian de geng meihao, rang baixing de shenghuo geng xingfu" [Making Chongqing Better and the People's Lives Happier], *Chongqing ribao*, November 18, 2010.
10. Yu Yan, "Cong genben shang zhuanbian jingji fazhan fangshi" [Changing the Mode of Economic Development in a Fundamental Way], *Chongqing ribao*, January 12, 2011.

11. Xiao Zhu, "Jianding bu yi zou gongtong fuyu daolu" [Firmly Following the Path of Common Prosperity], *Chongqing ribao*, July 25, 2011.
12. Xiao Zhu, "Ba zan Chongqing jian de geng meihao."
13. "Bai jia meiti, jujiao Chongqing" [Hundreds of Media Groups Focusing on Chongqing], *Chongqing ribao*, March 12, 2011.
14. Xiao Zhu, "Ba zan Chongqing jian de geng meihao."
15. "Wang Yang: bei wudu de 'dangao lun'" [Wang Yang: The Misinterpreted "Cake Theory"], *Liaowang Dongfang Zhoukan*, July 25, 2011, https://news.sohu.com/20110725/n314471558.shtml.
16. Propaganda Department of Chongqing Party Committee (PDCPC), *Goujian hexie Chongqing* [Building a Harmonious Chongqing] (Chongqing chubanshe, 2006).
17. PDCPC, *Goujian hexie Chongqing*, 17.
18. PDCPC, *Goujian hexie Chongqing*, 18.
19. PDCPC, *Goujian hexie Chongqing*, 31.
20. PDCPC, *Goujian hexie Chongqing*, 43.
21. PDCPC, *Goujian hexie Chongqing*, 44.
22. PDCPC, *Goujian hexie Chongqing*, 44–45.
23. Chongqing Daily Commentator, "Fen hao dangao cai neng zuo da dangao" [Only by Dividing the Cake Fairly Can We Make the Cake Bigger], *Chongqing ribao*, December 1, 2010.
24. "Shi di kan yi kan, jiu geng xihuan Chongqing" [Come and Visit in Person, and You'll Love Chongqing Even More], *Jinri Chongqing*, no. 9 (2011): 15–16.
25. Xiao Zhu, "Suo cha gong fu, wei renmin fuwu" [Narrowing the Gaps, Realizing Common Prosperity, and Serving the People], *Chongqing ribao*, September 29, 2011.
26. "Wen Jiabao: fen hao shehui caifu zhe ge 'dangao' shi zhengfu de liangzhi" [Wen Jiabao: The Conscience of the Government Requires that the "Cake" of Social Wealth Be Divided Fairly], *Zhongguo zhengfu wang*, February 27, 2010, http://www.gov.cn/zlft2010/content_1543394.htm.
27. Wang Weiguang and Zhao Jianying, "Kexue fazhan guan wei shenme, shi shenme, zenme ban" [The Scientific Outlook on Development: Why, What, and How], in *Zhongguo makesi zhuyi yanjiu qianyan 2008* [Frontier of Marxism Research in China, 2008], ed. Zhao Jianying, Wu Bo, and Zheng Xiangfu (Zhongguo shehui kexue chubanshe, 2009), 25–36. To be sure, books on redistribution and poverty reduction that have the term "common prosperity" in their titles have existed long before the term became politicized during Hu Jintao's second term.
28. "Gongtong fuyu yu Zhongguo tese shehui zhuyi lilun yantaohui zhuanjia fangtan" [Interviews with Experts at the Seminar on Theories of Common

Prosperity and Socialism with Chinese Characteristics], *Chongqing ribao*, June 27, 2011; Liu Guoguang, "Zhongguo caifu zouxiang" [The Prospect of China's Wealth], *Renmin luntan*, no. 22 (2011).

29. Zhang Xuefeng and Wang Xiaolei, "Zou nong hu, jie qiong qin, wei jiceng qunzhong ban shishi" [Visiting Rural Households, Building Ties with the Poor, and Accomplishing Practical Work for Grassroots Communities], *Chongqing ribao*, January 4, 2010.
30. Xiao Zhu, "Zhuahao 10 jian da shi, qieshi gaishan minsheng" [Focusing on Ten Major Tasks and Effectively Improving People's Livelihoods], *Chongqing ribao*, June 28, 2010.
31. Liu Changfa and Zhang Xuefeng, "Chongqing qidong si jian da shi" [Chongqing Started Working on Four Major Tasks], *Jinri Chongqing*, no. 4 (2010): 10–11.
32. "Bai jia meiti, jujiao Chongqing."
33. Xiao Zhu, "Jianding bu yi zou gongtong fuyu daolu."
34. I.e., the gaps between rural and urban areas, between developed and underdeveloped regions, and between the rich and the poor.
35. Xiao Zhu, "Yi gaishan minsheng wei dongli, tuidong Chongqing kexue fazhan" [Promoting the Scientific Development of Chongqing, with Improving People's Livelihoods as the Driving Force], *Chongqing ribao*, December 22, 2010.
36. Xiao Zhu, "Jianding bu yi zou gongtong fuyu daolu."
37. Xiao Zhu, "Jianding bu yi zou gongtong fuyu daolu."
38. Xiao Zhu, "Yi gaishan minsheng wei dongli."
39. Ke Ti Zu, "Queli minsheng youxian fazhan fangzhen tiaozheng guomin shouru fenpei geju—cong 'zhongdeng shouru xianjing' tanqi" [Establishing the Developmental Guideline of Prioritizing People's Livelihoods and Adjusting the Structure of National Income Distribution—A Discussion Starting with the "Middle-Income Trap"], *Hongqi wengao*, no. 18 (2011).
40. Deng Xiaoping, *Deng Xiaoping wen xuan* [Selected Works of Deng Xiaoping], vol. 3 (Renmin chubanshe, 1993), 373.
41. Literature Research Office of the Central Committee of the Chinese Communist Party (LROCCP), *Deng Xiaoping nianpu 1975–1997* [The Chronicle of Deng Xiaoping, 1975–1997], vol. 2 (Zhongyang wenxian chubanshe, 2004), 1356–1357.
42. LROCCP, *Deng Xiaoping nianpu*, vol. 2, 1317.
43. Li Shenming, ed., *Gongtong fuyu yu Zhongguo tese shehui zhuyi* [Common Prosperity and Socialism with Chinese Characteristics] (Zhongguo shehui kexue chubanshe, 2011).
44. What seemed particularly bizarre about the seminar was that several reform-minded Chinese economists, such as Li Yining, had also been

invited. Ostensibly, their presence may have served to shield the event from accusations of being purely political or ideologically partisan. In reality, however, their incongruous voices were completely drowned out by the leftist chorus. Their marginalized presence instead functioned as an almost theatrical foil, reinforcing the impression of an unstoppable leftist tide. Whether this outcome was deliberately orchestrated remains unclear.

45. Xiao Zhu, "Ba zan Chongqing jian de geng meihao."
46. Xiao Zhu, "Minsheng, minzhu, chang hong, da hei" [People's Livelihoods, Democracy, Singing Red, Striking Black], *Chongqing ribao*, May 2, 2011.
47. Xiao Zhu, "Suo xiao 'san ge chaju', shixian gongtong fuyu" [Narrowing the "Three Gaps" and Realizing Common Prosperity], *Chongqing ribao*, June 27, 2011.
48. Xiao Zhu, "Gao Zhongguo tese shehui zhuyi, zou gongtong fuyu zhi lu" [Practicing Socialism with Chinese Characteristics and Following the Path of Common Prosperity], *Chongqing ribao*, September 22, 2011.
49. "Rang baixing dedao gengduo de shihui" [Let the People Receive More Tangible Benefits], *Chongqing ribao*, July 28, 2011.
50. Xiao Zhu, "Gao zhongguo tese shehui zhuyi."
51. Xiao Zhu, "Jianding bu yi zou gongtong fuyu daolu."
52. Xiao Zhu, "Gao zhongguo tese shehui zhuyi."
53. Guoguang Wu, *China's Common Prosperity Program: Causes, Challenges, and Implications* (Asia Society Policy Institute, 2022); Xin Sun, *Decoding China's "Common Prosperity" Drive* (LSE IDEAS, 2022); Minxin Pei, "The Origins and Implications of Xi Jinping's 'Common Prosperity' Agenda," *China Leadership Monitor* 70 (Winer 2021).
54. Mary E. Gallagher, "China's Struggle for Common Prosperity," *China Leadership Monitor* 75 (Spring 2023).
55. Barry Naughton, "'Common Prosperity' as Revealed in the Documents," *Interpret: China*, Center for Strategic and International Studies, 2021, https://interpret.csis.org/common-prosperity.
56. Xi Jinping, "Zhashi tuijin gongtong fuyu" [Solidly Promoting Common Prosperity], *Qiushi*, no. 20 (2021), http://www.qstheory.cn/dukan/qs/2021-10/15/c_1127959365.htm.
57. Le, *China's Conservative Turn.*
58. For a detailed review of various leftist discourses on the Chongqing Model, see Edmund Downie, "One City, Many Models: The Chinese Left's Debates over Chongqing," *Academia.edu*, April 14, 2014, https://www.academia.edu/8919324/One_City_Many_Models_The_Chinese_Left_s_Debates_over_Chongqing.

59. Ji Shuoming, "Chongqing moshi chuang Zhongguo jingji fangong xin lujing" [The Chongqing Model Created a New Path for China's Economic Comeback], *Yazhou Zhoukan*, no. 6 (2009).
60. "Zhong wai meiti jujiao Chongqing" [Chinese and Foreign Media Focusing on Chongqing], *Chongqing ribao*, March 11, 2009.
61. "Zhong wai meiti jujiao Chongqing."
62. Liao Xuemei, "Chongqing moshi quan guo zhumu" [The Chongqing Model Attracting Nationwide Attention], *Chongqing ribao*, March 19, 2007.
63. Zhou Qin and Guan Yuanyuan, "'Chongqing moshi': gouzhu tengfeng de paodao" ["The Chongqing Model": Building a Runway for Takeoff], *Chongqing ribao*, November 30, 2007.
64. "Zuo qiang zuo da guoqi guanjian zai dang" [The Key to Making State-Owned Enterprises Stronger and Bigger Lies with the Party], *Chongqing ribao*, June 11, 2007.
65. Luo Chengyou and Deng Chunxi, "Yi gongye linian yinling xiandai nongye" [Leading the Development of Modern Agriculture through Industrial Concepts], *Chongqing ribao*, January 23, 2007; Li Weifan, "Yubei nongye keji yuan tuxian 'Chongqing moshi'" [Yubei Agricultural Science and Technology Park Highlights the "Chongqing Model"], *Chongqing ribao*, June 13, 2007.
66. "Yongxin bianzhi Chongqing xian ji gonglu wang" [Devotedly Weaving Chongqing's Inter-County Road Network], *Chongqing ribao*, May 22, 2007.
67. Peng Yu and Zhao Tong, "Huajie Zhong xian chanye fazhan 'pinxue' zhi tong" [Alleviating the "Anemia" of Industrial Development in Zhong County], *Chongqing ribao*, December 21, 2007.
68. Li Yuman, "Fuwu hexie nongcun shangye baoxian da you ke wei" [Serving a Harmonious Rural Society, Commercial Insurance Has Great Potential], *Chongqing ribao*, August 15, 2007; Qin Shiyou, "Tan bei zhengdi nongmin yanglao baoxian tansuo de yiyi" [Discussing the Significance of Exploring Pension Insurance for Land-Expropriated Farmers], *Chongqing ribao*, February 6, 2007.
69. Meng Dongfang, "You biyao chuangli Chongqing xue" [It Is Necessary to Establish a Chongqingology], *Chongqing ribao*, August 20, 2007.
70. Propaganda Department of Chongqing Party Committee (PDCPC), *Tanlu chengxiang tongchou* [Exploring the Way toward Urban–Rural Integration] (Chongqing chubanshe, 2008), 11.
71. Li Zhihui, Zhang Qin, and Liu Yuanxu, "'Xin te qu' wei Zhongguo gaige xia yi ge 30 nian xunqiu tupo" [The "New Special Zones" Seeking Breakthroughs for China's Next Thirty Years of Reform], *Chongqing ribao*, January 3, 2009.

72. PDCPC, *Tanlu chengxiang tongchou*, 12.
73. PDCPC, *Tanlu chengxiang tongchou*, 13.
74. Li, Zhang and Liu, "'Xin te qu' wei zhongguo."
75. PDCPC, *Tanlu chengxiang tongchou*, 10–11.
76. For a full list of Chongqing Model policies, see Su Wei, Yang Fan, and Liu Shiwen, *Chongqing moshi* [The Chongqing Model] (Zhongguo jingji chubanshe, 2011) and Yi Xiaoguang, *Pojie Zhongguo fazhan zhi kunju: Chongqing shijian lun* [Cracking the Problem of Development in China: A Thesis on Chongqing's Practices] (Zhongguo jingji chubanshe, 2012). For a thorough review of Bo Xilai's Chongqing policies, see Philip C. C. Huang, "Chongqing: Equitable Development Driven by a 'Third Hand'?" *Modern China* 37, no. 6 (2011): 569–622, https://doi.org/10.1177/0097700411419966.
77. CLSGIR, EPOCPC, and CCINR, *Yu lun 2009*, preface.
78. "'Chongqing moshi' te zai 'shi'" ["The Chongqing Model" Is Special Because It Is "Practical"], *Chongqing ribao*, September 20, 2010.
79. "'Chongqing moshi' te zai 'shi'."
80. Yang Fan and Zhang Xiangdong, "Chongqing ban de kexue fazhan guan" [The Chongqing Version of the Scientific Outlook on Development], *Chongqing ribao*, September 20, 2010.
81. Ji Shuoming, "Chongqing tanxun Zhongguo gongtong fuyu moshi xin lujing" [Chongqing Is Exploring a New Path for China's Model of Common Prosperity], *Yazhou Zhoukan*, no. 12 (2010).
82. Yang and Zhang, "Chongqing ban de kexue fazhan guan."
83. Ji Shuoming, "Chongqing guanzhu minsheng you redu geng you sudu—yi ge Xianggang jizhe de guancha" [Chongqing's Attention to People's Livelihoods Is Strong in Both Intensity and Speed—An Observation by a Hong Kong Journalist], *Chongqing ribao*, October 8, 2010.
84. Yang and Zhang, "Chongqing ban de kexue fazhan guan."
85. Hu Angang, ed., *Kexue fazhan guan de fangfa lun: yi Chongqing wei li* [The Methodology of the Scientific Outlook on Development: A Case Study of Chongqing] (Dangjian duwu chubanshe, 2010), 202.
86. Su, Yang and Liu, *Chongqing moshi*, 2–4.
87. "Gongtong fuyu yu zhongguo tese shehui zhuyi lilun yantaohui."
88. Zhou Jigang and Long Zaiyu, "Shehui zhuyi shijian de Chongqing tansuo" [Chongqing's Exploration of the Practice of Socialism], *Chongqing ribao*, January 7, 2011.
89. Zhou Jigang and Long Zaiyu, "Chongqing shijian quanshi 'jihua he shichang dou shi jingji shouduan'" [The Chongqing Practice Illustrates that "Both Planning and the Market Are Economic Tools"], *Chongqing ribao*, January 5, 2011.

90. Zhao Qizheng, "Guanyu Chongqing chuangxin yiyi de ganhuai" [Reflections on the Significance of Chongqing's Innovation], in *Gongtong fuyu yu Zhongguo tese shehui zhuyi* [Common Prosperity and Socialism with Chinese Characteristics], ed. Li Shenming (Zhongguo shehui kexue chubanshe, 2011), 14–18.
91. Zhao Qizheng, "Chongqing moshi de chuangxin dian" [Innovative Aspects of the Chongqing Model], *Renmin luntan*, no. 22 (2011): 39.
92. "Yang Lujun: ri zhao Chongqing—Bo Xilai yu 'Chongqing moshi'" [Yang Lujun: The Sun Shines on Chongqing—Bo Xilai and "The Chongqing Model"], December 8, 2010, https://m.aisixiang.com/data/37711.html.
93. Zhou Jigang and Long Zaiyu, "Dui 'xin ziyou zhuyi' de Chongqing fansi" [Chongqing-Inspired Reflections on "Neoliberalism"], *Chongqing ribao*, January 13, 2011.
94. Renmin University Project Team on Chongqing (RUPTC), *Chongqing xin shi* [New Things in Chongqing] (Zhongguo renmin daxue chubanshe, 2011), 43–44.
95. Hu, *Kexue fazhan guan*, 196.
96. Dai Juan, "Chongqing wei gongtong fuyu tanlu" [Chongqing Is Exploring the Way to Common Prosperity], *Chongqing ribao*, July 21, 2011.
97. Zhang Sha, "Chongqing tanlu suo xiao san ge chaju zhi de jiejian" [Chongqing's Exploration of Narrowing the Three Gaps Is Worth Learning From], *Chongqing ribao*, July 26, 2011.
98. Hu, *Kexue fazhan guan*, 188; Li Xiguang, "Kexue fazhan guan shiye de Chongqing shijian" [The Chongqing Practice from the Perspective of the Scientific Outlook on Development], *Gaige*, no. 7 (2010): 6–15.
99. Hu Angang, Yan Longyi, and Wei Xing, *2030 Zhongguo maixiang gongtong fuyu* [China Marching toward Common Prosperity in 2030] (Zhongguo renmin daxue chubanshe, 2011), 186–187.
100. Hou Huiqin and Xin Xiangyang, eds., *Wenhua minsheng de shidai jiedu—Chongqing "chang du jiang chuan" huodong kao* [A Contemporary Interpretation of Culture and People's Livelihoods: An Investigation of Chongqing's "Sing, Read, Say, Spread" Activities] (Renmin chubanshe, 2011), 6.
101. Luo Jingwen, Dai Juan, and Chen Bo, "Di shi yi jie guo shi xueshu nianhui zhuanjia fangtan" [Interviews with Experts at the 11th Annual Academic Conference on National History], *Chongqing Ribao*, September 29, 2011; Li Jie, "Daodi zenme kan Chongqing moshi" [How, After All, Should the Chongqing Model Be Viewed?], *Renmin luntan*, no. 11 (2011): 30–31.

102. Cheng Enfu, "Makesi zhuyi quyu hua de dianxing" [A Typical Case of the Regionalization of Marxism], *Renmin luntan*, no. 22 (2011): 33.
103. Wen Jing, "Chongqing zhuazhu le dang quan xin quan yi wei renmin fuwu zhe ge 'dao'" [Chongqing Closely Follows the Party's "Way" of Serving the People Wholeheartedly], *Chongqing ribao*, October 6, 2011.
104. Xiao Zhu, "'Zi qiang bu xi,' 'liang shou dou yao ying'" ["Be Relentless in Striving for Self-Improvement," "Be Tough with Both Hands"], *Chongqing ribao*, October 5, 2011.
105. Hu, *Kexue fazhan guan*, 48–52.
106. "Chongqing guo zi: di san caizheng shijian" [State-Owned Assets in Chongqing: The Practice of the Third Source of Fiscal Revenue], *Liaowang*, no. 67 (2010). Also see Zhiyue Bo and Gang Chen, "Bo Xilai and the Chongqing Model," *East Asian Policy* 1 (2009): 42–49.
107. Ivan Szelenyi, "Third Ways," *Modern China* 37, no. 6 (2011): 672–683, https://doi.org/10.1177/0097700411420799.
108. Su, Yang and Liu, *Chongqing moshi*, 232.
109. In early 2012, Su Wei made a lengthy refutation against this view. See Su Wei, "'Chongqing moshi' shi zenyang bei wudu de" [How the "Chongqing Model" Has Been Misinterpreted], *Guancha zhe wang*, February 2, 2012, https://www.guancha.cn/politics/2012_02_02_64993.shtml.
110. Su Wei, "Lun xin de lishi qidian shang de Chongqing xinzheng yu Chongqing moshi" [On the New Policies of Chongqing and the Chongqing Model at a New Historical Starting Point], *Tansuo*, no. 4 (2010): 21–28.
111. Yang and Zhang, "Chongqing ban de kexue fazhan guan."
112. Ji, "Chongqing tanxun zhongguo."
113. Su, "Lun xin de lishi qidian."
114. Meng Dongfang, "Chongqing shi kaizhan 'san jin san tong' huodong de sikao" [Reflections on Chongqing's "Three Enters and Three Togethers" Activities], in *Chongqing lan pi shu: Zhongguo Chongqing fazhan baogao* [The Blue Book on Chongqing: A Report on Development in Chongqing, China], by Chongqing Academy of Social Science and Center for Development Research of the Chongqing Government (Chongqing chubanshe, 2011), 46–58.
115. Xiao Zhu, "Chongqing mingtian hui geng hao, renmin shenghuo geng xingfu" [Chongqing's Tomorrow Will Be Better, and the People's Lives Will Be Happier], *Chongqing ribao*, April 19, 2011.
116. Qiu Shi, "Chuang xian zheng you huodong de shenhou shijian jichu he jianshi lilun zhicheng" [The Deep Practical Foundation and Firm Theoretical Support for the "Chuang Xian Zheng You" Activities], *Qiushi*, no. 9 (2012): 41–44.

117. Propaganda Department of Chongqing Party Committee (PDCPC), *Chongqing zhuiqiu* [Chongqing's Pursuit] (Chongqing chubanshe, 2012), 199–200.
118. Guo Hong, "Chongqing guanfang cu 75 wan daxuesheng zai xue 'gong, nong, bing'" [The Chongqing Government Urging 750,000 University Students to Learn from Workers, Peasants, and Soldiers Once Again], *Zhongguo xinwen wang*, November 9, 2010, http://www.chinanews.com.cn/edu/2010/11-09/2644946.shtml.
119. "Bai jia meiti, jujiao Chongqing."
120. "Bo Xilai: daxuesheng dao nongcun shijian bu ya yu du yanjiu sheng" [Bo Xilai: University Students' Rural Practice Is No Less Beneficial than Pursuing a Master's Degree], *Chongqing ribao*, May 6, 2010.
121. Xiao Zhu, "Ji gefang zhihui, tansuo gongtong fuyu" [Gathering Wisdom from All Sides and Exploring the Path to Common Prosperity], *Chongqing ribao*, December 5, 2011; Xiao Zhu, "Xiang xiongdi shengshi xuexi, nuli shixian kexue fazhan" [Learning from Other Provinces and Cities, Striving to Achieve Scientific Development], *Chongqing ribao*, October 28, 2011; Xiao Zhu, "Chongqing hai hui you geng da de fazhan" [Chongqing Will See Even Greater Development], *Chongqing ribao*, October 13, 2011.
122. Hu, *Kexue fazhan guan*, 197.
123. Xiao Zhu, "Jianchi shehui zhuyi hexin jiazhi, tuidong wenhua da fazhan da fanrong" [Upholding Socialist Core Values and Promoting the Great Development and Prosperity of Culture], *Chongqing ribao*, October 23, 2011.
124. Liu Kang, Zhang Guilin, and Tang Yaoguo, "Zhuanxing Zhongguo de Chongqing tupo" [The Chongqing Breakthrough in a Transforming China], *Liaowang*, April 19, 2010.
125. Xiao Zhu, "Ba zan Chongqing jian de geng meihao."
126. Su, "Yu san pi faguo jizhe."
127. Zhang Sha, "Chongqing shijian de hexin shi quan xin quan yi wei renmin fuwu" [The Core of the Chongqing Practice Is Serving the People Wholeheartedly], *Chongqing ribao*, October 6, 2011.
128. Hu, *Kexue fazhan guan*, 198.
129. Zhang, "Chongqing shijian de hexin"; Hou and Xin, *Wenhua minsheng*, 246.
130. Hou and Xin, *Wenhua minsheng*, 37–45.
131. "Shi shi" [Current Affairs], *Jinri Chongqing*, no. 4 (2011): 2.
132. Zhang, "Chongqing shijian de hexin."
133. Xiao Zhu, "Yao zhen de zhu huairen bang de liao baixing guan de zhu ziji" [One Must Be Able to Restrain Wrongdoers, Help the People, and Govern Oneself], *Chongqing ribao*, January 8, 2011; Xiao Zhu, "Yingzao

feng qing qi zheng de zhengzhi huanjing" [Creating a Clean and Upright Political Environment], *Chongqing ribao*, January 28, 2011.

134. Xiao Zhu, "Chongqing hai hui you geng da de fazhan"; "Yu renmin qunzhong da cheng yi pian, feng yu tong zhou" [Staying Close to the People and Sharing Both Hardships and Triumphs], *Jinri Chongqing*, no. 6 (2011): 14–15.
135. Su, "Lun xin de lishi qidian."
136. Su, Yang and Liu, *Chongqing moshi*, 26.
137. Su, Yang and Liu, *Chongqing moshi*, 37–44.
138. "Di shi yi jie guo shi nianhui" [The 11th Annual Conference on National History], *Renmin luntan*, no. 33 (2011): 61.
139. Xiao Zhu, "Mianhuai na xie zui keai de ren" [Remembering Those Who Are the Most Lovable], *Chongqing ribao*, October 27, 2010.
140. Xiao Zhu, "Xingcheng jiankang gaoshang de shehui fengqi" [Fostering a Healthy and Noble Social Atmosphere], *Chongqing ribao*, March 2, 2011.
141. Mao Zedong, "Ren de zhengque sixiang shi cong nali lai de?" [Where Do Correct Ideas Come From?], May 1963, https://marxistphilosophy.org/maozedong/mx8/061.htm.
142. Xiao Zhu, "Xuexi tieren jingshen, jianshe meihao Chongqing" [Learning from the Iron Man Spirit and Building a Wonderful Chongqing], *Chongqing ribao*, May 9, 2011.
143. CLSGIR, EPOCPC and CCINR, *Yu lun 2009*, 187–188.
144. CLSGIR, EPOCPC and CCINR, *Yu lun 2010*, 105.
145. He Fang, "Quan guo dang shi bumen dang shi yu ren gongzuo yantao hui zai Chongqing zhaokai" [A Seminar on Party History Education Was Held in Chongqing, Attended by Party History Departments across the Country], *Chongqing ribao*, November 23, 2010.
146. Xiao Zhu, "Bo Xilai huijian Zhongyang dang shi yanjiu shi zhuren Ouyang Song" [Bo Xilai Met Ouyang Song, Director of the Central Office for Party History Research], *Chongqing ribao*, November 23, 2010.
147. Chongqing Daily Commentator, "Shijian yong wu zhi jing, lilun zhi shu chang qing" [Practice Knows No Bounds, and the Tree of Theory Remains Evergreen], *Chongqing ribao*, June 8, 2011.
148. Yu Yunyao, "Chongqing shi de 'san xiang zhidu' yu xin xingshi xia de qunzhong gongzuo" [Chongqing's "Three Institutions" and Mass-Related Work under New Circumstances], in *Jinian Zhongguo gongchandang chengli 90 zhounian dang jian lilun yu shijian Chongqing yantaohui lunwen ji* [Papers of the Chongqing Symposium on Party Building Theories and Practices in Commemoration of the Chinese Communist Party's 90th Anniversary], vol. 1 (Dangjian duwu chubanshe, 2011), 22–23.

149. Xiao Zhu, "Yu renmin qunzhong da cheng yi pian, feng yu tong zhou" [Staying Close to the People and Sharing Both Hardships and Triumphs], *Chongqing ribao*, June 9, 2011.
150. Dai Juan and Zhang Sha, "Hongyang geming jingshen, tuidong kexue fazhan, jianshe hexie shehui" [Carrying Forward the Revolutionary Spirit, Promoting Scientific Development, and Building a Harmonious Society], *Chongqing ribao*, June 18, 2011.
151. Zhang Sha and Dai Juan, "Li Zhongjie and Zhou Yong jieshou Xinhua wang Chongqing pindao caifang" [Li Zhongjie and Zhou Yong Interviewed by the Chongqing Channel of XinhuaNet], *Chongqing ribao*, June 18, 2011.
152. Xiao Zhu, "Chongqing hai hui you geng da de fazhan."
153. "Jiefang sixiang tuidong Chongqing da kaifang" [Mind Emancipation Driving Chongqing toward Greater Opening-Up], *Jinri Chongqing*, no. 9 (2008): 14–15.
154. "Zhong wai meiti jujiao Chongqing."
155. Deng Quanlun, "Chongqing, rang wenhua wei chengshi su hun" [Chongqing: Let Culture Shape the Soul of the City], *Chongqing ribao*, April 14, 2009.
156. Zhang Qin, "Chang xiang zhu xuanlü, ningju jing qi shen" [Singing the Main Melody Aloud and Rallying Collective Spirit], *Chongqing ribao*, October 30, 2010.
157. Zhang Xuefeng, "Zhuliu wenhua wei fazhan jiayou" [Mainstream Culture Contributing to Development], *Chongqing ribao*, June 18, 2009.
158. Yu Xuanwen, "Chongqing 'chang du jiang chuan' yinfa de hongse shishang" [The "Sing, Read, Say, Spread" Movement in Chongqing Sparked a Red Cultural Trend], *Chongqing ribao*, November 22, 2011.
159. "'Chang hong' shi jiankang youyi de qunzhong xing wenhua huodong" ["Sing Red" Is a Healthy and Beneficial Mass Cultural Activity], *Chongqing ribao*, July 11, 2011.
160. Hou and Xin, *Wenhua minsheng*, preface.
161. Guan Yuanyuan and Wen Jia, "Rang hongse gequ chang xiang Ba Yu dadi" [Let Red Songs Resonate across the Land of Bayu], *Chongqing ribao*, July 25, 2008.
162. Lan Shiqiu, "Gao biaozhun kechixu tuijin 'chang du jiang chuan' huodong" [Promoting the "Sing, Read, Say, Spread" Activities Sustainably with High Standards], *Chongqing ribao*, January 15, 2011.
163. Hou and Xin, *Wenhua minsheng*, 105–112.
164. Xiao Zhu, "Jiaqiang minzhu fazhi jianshe, tuidong Chongqing kexue fazhan" [Advancing the Construction of Democracy and the Rule of Law and Promoting Chongqing's Scientific Development], *Chongqing ribao*, December 21, 2011.

165. PDCPC, *Chongqing zhuiqiu*, 168.
166. Su, Yang and Liu, *Chongqing moshi*, 258–260.
167. Su, Yang and Liu, *Chongqing moshi*, 57; Su, "Lun xin de lishi qidian."
168. "Quan guo chuang xian zheng you huodong zongjie jiaoliu hui guanche Hu Jintao zhongyao pishi" [The Summary and Exchange Conference on the National "Chuang Xian Zheng You" Campaign Emphasized the Implementation of Hu Jintao's Important Directives], October 15, 2012, https://www.gov.cn/jrzg/2012-10/15/content_2244332.htm. The original full text of Li Yuanchao's speech was once available online but it is no longer accessible now. The author has an electronic copy of Li's full speech.
169. "Zhongyang zuzhi bu, Zhongyang xuanchuan bu guanyu zai dang de jiceng zuzhi he dangyuan zhong shenru kaizhan chuang xian zheng you huodong de yijian" [Opinions of the Central Organization Department and the Central Propaganda Department on Carrying Out "Chuang Xian Zheng You" Activities within the Party's Grassroots Organizations and among Party Members], April 5, 2010, in *Shi qi da yi lai zhongyao wenxian xuan bian* [Selected Important Documents since the Seventeenth Party Congress, i.e., *SID17PC*], vol. 2 (Zhongyang wenxian chubanshe, 2011), 622–628.
170. "Zhonggong zhongyang bangong ting yinfa" [The General Office of the Chinese Communist Party Central Committee Issued "Opinions on Comprehensively Carrying Out the Learn from Lei Feng Campaign"], March 2, 2012, http://www.moe.gov.cn/jyb_xxgk/moe_1777/moe_1778/201203/t20120314_132124.html.

CHAPTER 5

Opportunistic Ambivalence

Between late 2011 and early 2012—just months before the disgraceful end of his political career—Bo Xilai publicly claimed that he had never proposed anything resembling the Chongqing Model. This created the impression that he was backpedaling and perhaps attempting to distance himself from the conservative line.

5.1 Denying, Distancing, and Decoupling

First, Bo hastened to emphasize that Chongqing was merely a typical case of local experimentation, stating that "we are simply trying to conduct more experiments."[1] If Chongqing could "successfully make this path work," it would constitute "a concrete and practical exploration toward realizing socialist ideals" and could potentially offer useful "lessons" for other western provinces. In short, rather than presenting an established model for emulation, Chongqing was engaged in an ongoing process of exploration. "There is nothing of a conclusive nature, and it is even less the time to 'draw a full stop.'"

Second, Bo stressed that nothing in Chongqing had gone beyond the policy parameters set by the Party center.[2] "If there is anything distinctive about Chongqing's development," Bo claimed, "it is simply that [we] have faithfully followed the central authorities' requirements and worked to pursue a people's-livelihoods-oriented path."

L. Le, *Revival of Maoism in Reform-Era China*,
https://doi.org/10.1007/978-981-92-4606-9_5

There is strong evidence that Bo Xilai did somewhat temper the Maoist momentum of his political campaigns in his final days, although he maintained his broader alignment with the Chinese Left.

However, Bo's *denial* of any intention to construct a "Chongqing Model" does not, in itself, provide a sufficiently clear indicator of this subtle shift in course. Rather, his handling of the discourse surrounding the Chongqing Model can be seen as an act of strategic *distancing*, allowing him to avoid formal commitments while retaining sufficient flexibility for tactical maneuvering whenever necessary. This logic of distancing was also evident in the way Bo defended Chongqing's Maoist agenda against reformist criticism, by leveraging the multi-layered framing of key political concepts.

On the one hand, Bo Xilai was not being untruthful if his denial referred specifically to a formal, explicit articulation of a "Chongqing Model." He never made such a claim. On the contrary, at the outset he explicitly rejected the notion: "It does not yet rise to the level of what could be called a 'Chongqing Model.'"[3] Even at the height of Chongqing's propagandistic promotion of common prosperity, Bo's close associate, Chongqing mayor Huang Qifan, reiterated that "we have simply addressed problems as they arise and have never intended to create any so-called Chongqing Model." Huang further stressed that everything "was and is being carried out in accordance with the central government's requirements."[4] According to *Yu Lun*, Chongqing's official propaganda handbook, the city's beyond-expectation developmental achievements were ultimately attributed to strict adherence to the policy guidelines set by the Party center.[5] Just as reform in Chongqing was said to have always been implemented "within the existing political framework," local propaganda was quick to point out that the goal of achieving common prosperity had "already been clearly articulated" in the Party's Twelfth Five-Year Plan.[6]

On the other hand, Bo was not being entirely truthful, as he rejected the label of the "Chongqing Model" while simultaneously affirming the substance that defined it. In other words, Bo Xilai was effectively pursuing the model without formally naming it. This is evident in his stated ambitions.

First, Bo intended his Chongqing program to be pathbreaking. "If Chongqing can truly narrow the urban–rural divide and the gap between rich and poor, then we would be making history and putting into practice the Party's fundamental purpose."[7] Second, Chongqing was meant to serve as a pioneer. "While there are many models for expanding the size of the economy, there is still no ready-made experience to draw upon when it comes to reducing inequality and achieving common prosperity."[8] Third, Chongqing's efforts were framed not only in national terms but also in relation to the future of humanity. If China succeeded in realizing common prosperity, "this would not only mark the success of the Party and the Chinese nation, but also constitute a major contribution to humanity."[9] Echoing Bo, Huang Qifan likewise emphasized Chongqing's historic contributions to China's reform, even as he denied the existence of a "Chongqing Model." According to Huang, Chongqing had become a "pathbreaker" in reform and opening up.[10] "What Chongqing has been undertaking is, in terms of its innovative contributions to reform and opening up, no less significant than the development of Shenzhen in the 1980s and Shanghai's Pudong in the 1990s."[11]

As noted earlier, the rhetorical promotion of the "Chongqing Model" was carried out through semi-official channels and intellectual endorsement. By explicitly titling his book *The Chongqing Model*, Su Wei of the Chongqing Party School was tasked with articulating what Bo refrained from stating publicly.

The strategy was to create a buffer—namely, to put in place a delegate who could represent the patron without formal authorization, while retaining the ability to assert independence whenever the implicit relationship of representation became a liability. One internal report by the Chongqing government advised that local leaders should "exercise caution in handling the current controversy over the 'Chongqing Model'" and "refrain from intervening in the debate or making statements in an official capacity."[12] Failure to do so, the report warned, would expose Chongqing to the risk of "misinterpretation and harm resulting from mislabeling." The report further observed that "as comparative analyses of the 'Chongqing Model' and related discussions spread from the public sphere to academia, and from the domestic arena to the international stage, some actors with ulterior motives are seizing the opportunity to fan the flames, revealing a clear intention to force the Chongqing authorities to take an official stance." Although it remains unclear whether Bo derived this approach from the report or had independently adhered to such a no-commitment strategy, the report nonetheless illustrates the political logic that likely motivated him to avoid formalizing the "Chongqing Model" as an official objective.

Moreover, in justifying the terminology, Su Wei introduced an additional layer of insulation by claiming that the choice of the label

"Chongqing Model" was made simply because no available alternative was more appropriate. First, he noted that the term "model" itself carries an undertone of dogmatism and is therefore not particularly "scientific."[13] Second, labels such as "experience" or "exploration" were deemed insufficiently broad, as narrowly defined "practices" or "experiences" in specific domains could also be described as a "Chongqing Model."[14] Therefore, given that Bo Xilai's Chongqing "New Deal" was intended to be innovative in a comprehensive sense, there appeared to be no option but to "borrow" the label "Chongqing Model," which, to some extent, conveyed that Chongqing's efforts were "systematic," "comprehensive," and "methodical."

With this buffer in place, Bo could readily distance himself from the issue whenever necessary. He reportedly told a fellow party princeling in early 2012 that "we truly do not want to call it the 'Chongqing Model,' but the term has already gained wide currency." In effect: I did not initiate this; others did. As Bo further claimed, "we have indeed accomplished a great deal, but what we lack most is theoretical articulation."[15] In other words: what I intended was something else; any confusion may have arisen from miscommunication or misrepresentation.

The same logic of distancing and decoupling underpinned Bo's denial of pursuing a "leftist" agenda. Despite extensive rhetoric and policy initiatives promoting leftism and Maoist themes in practice, there was no formal declaration or explicit commitment. However, this logic operated somewhat differently in this context. Decoupling was not framed as a simple yes-or-no question; rather, it hinged on distinguishing between different variants of leftism—orthodox versus heterodox. Accordingly, the "delegate" to be sacrificed and decoupled from when necessary consisted of those elements deemed to deviate from the correct line, rather than something wholly opposed to the Left, or leftism itself.

Taking advantage of Mao's enduring political status, Bo often demonized his critics as challengers to the Party itself, while sidestepping the question of whether he was in fact pursuing a Maoist path. He charged that some people harbored hostility toward the Party's "communist ideology."[16] He dismissed the view as "utter nonsense and bizarre talk," namely the claim that "only learning from the West counts as 'moving forward,' whereas inheriting and carrying forward the Party's fine traditions is nothing but 'leftist' and a 'return to the past.'"[17] Elsewhere, he posed a rhetorical question: "If the [Chinese] Communist Party does not sing red [songs], is it supposed to lead the people in singing grey, yellow, or even black [songs]?"[18]

Meanwhile, Bo Xilai had to manage an additional complication: how to prevent his Maoist positioning from being hijacked by China's neo-Maoist radicals. He made it clear that a revival of socialist fundamentalism had nothing to do with embracing another Cultural Revolution. Whereas the former concerned safeguarding the Party's rule through the consolidation of political orthodoxy, the latter represented a perverse version of Maoism. Under Mao's influence, some radicals came to believe that "it is right to rebel" against the entire officialdom. Fully aware of this potential threat from the left, Bo was quick to emphasize the distinction between two forms of Maoism. He told the media, "speaking of the Cultural Revolution, both my family and I were deeply victimized and carry a pain that cuts to the bone."[19] Echoing Bo, the head of the Chongqing Propaganda Department likewise stressed that "the 'Sing Red' campaign does not preclude people from singing other songs they enjoy; therefore, there is no question of left versus right, much less a return to the Cultural Revolution."[20] In light of this logic of decoupling, the fact that radical neo-Maoists were at one point warmly received by Chongqing's public security authorities when they visited the city to express support may be better understood as an effort by Bo to monitor, and, if necessary, contain, these radicals during their stay, rather than as evidence of any substantial alignment between Bo and grassroots neo-Maoist groups.[21]

On the other hand, there was another fine line to walk: decoupling Chongqing from the radical wing without signaling any wavering commitment to orthodox Mao Zedong Thought. Through a degree of rhetorical legerdemain, Su Wei of the Chongqing Party School managed to shield Bo Xilai from the political liabilities associated with radical Maoism while avoiding alienation of Maoist supporters more broadly.[22] To this end, Su Wei began by asserting that Chongqing's Sing Red movement "has consistently drawn a clear boundary between itself and the 'mistakes' of the Cultural Revolution." He then emphasized the need to distinguish between the Cultural Revolution "mistakes" (*wen ge cuowu*) and the Cultural Revolution "period" (*wen ge qijian*). While the former must be "completely repudiated," the latter should not be treated in the same way. In effect, by ostensibly opposing the radical variant of Maoism, Su Wei simultaneously reaffirmed Chongqing's commitment to the Party's Maoist orthodoxy. As he noted, "the Chinese Communist Party has upheld the banner of Mao Zedong Thought ever since the beginning of reform and opening up." Chongqing's Sing Red movement, he argued, "carries the Party's banner, of which Mao Zedong Thought is an integral part." Su Wei further warned that "the voices praising Mao Zedong in Chongqing may still not be strong enough to counterbalance the global discourse that demonizes Mao Zedong."

With these demarcation lines in place, radical leftists, as an "othered" group, provided an additional layer of insulation for Bo Xilai's Chongqing agenda. According to Su Wei,[23] among those who viewed Chongqing as moving in a Maoist direction, some "do not know the full picture and remain traumatized by the Cultural Revolution," others harbored ulterior motives and were eager to see China take a "rightist turn," and still others were genuinely "leftist," believing that "reform and opening up has 'gone too far' and deviated from the socialist path." Su Wei attributed the problem primarily to the last group, namely the radical neo-Maoists, accusing them of having "misrepresented" Chongqing's practices as "leftist" and of "sowing misunderstanding among those who are critical of leftism." In contrast to these distracting foils, Chongqing was portrayed as proceeding neither to the left nor to the right, but rather along the "correct" direction endorsed by the Party center.

Thus, the tension between what Bo Xilai was actually attempting to accomplish and what he verbally disclaimed created an illusory gap. Bo's sympathizers sought to bridge this gap by rationalizing the contradiction through variations of the argument that "Bo was not aligned with these groups" and/or "Bo did not mean what he appeared to say."

At a symposium held in late 2011, a group of Chinese intellectuals convened to assess the Chongqing Model through "non-ideological" approaches.[24] One argument held that Chongqing had adopted a flawed strategy of political communication. With regard to the Sing Red movement, many leftists "over-interpreted Chongqing and even regarded it as the embodiment of their own beliefs." Although Chongqing's policies did not appear substantively leftist in practice, its propaganda style created the impression that the city was the "headquarters" of radical Maoism, thereby alienating both ideological moderates and those who harbored strong aversion to the Cultural Revolution. Another view attributed Bo's unintended association with the Chinese Left to structural constraints within China's marketplace of ideas. Leftist ideologies were said to dominate the field. When "confronted with something new like the Chongqing Model," Bo Xilai had no choice but to "articulate new ideas through an outdated ideological language." This perspective further suggested that "by appropriating the Chongqing Model, the radical left was steering China onto an erroneous path." Given that "leftist discourse has dominated research on Chongqing," Chongqing's leadership was seen as partly responsible for this situation and was therefore urged to guard against being hijacked. A third view went even further, speculating that Bo deliberately adopted a Janus-faced strategy to mislead conservatives while preparing to advance reformist initiatives once resistance from the left subsided. From this "packaging strategy" perspective, Bo was portrayed as "a shrewd strategist."

What made this hedging-by-distancing strategy possible was the multi-layered framing of Bo's key political concepts. As more politicized layers of interpretation were added, earlier layers were not simply overridden. Instead, they remained active and were invoked from time to time, either positively, as part of the concept's broader semantic range, or negatively, as a defensive clarification in response to criticism. This helps explain why, even during Bo Xilai's Maoist phase, he and other Chongqing officials occasionally defended the Sing Red movement as nonpolitical. In such instances, the educational function of the red culture campaign was often emphasized.[25] With these multiple layers of framing in place, Bo could readily retreat from the most politicized interpretation to less politicized ones when necessary. This maneuver allowed him to avoid rolling back or repudiating his program in its entirety. Instead, he could selectively shed a particular layer of political framing. In this way, the political cost was minimized. In particular, the Chongqing Model can be understood as consisting of three layers: local implementation, local experimentation, and a vanguardist or status-quo-transcending model. The appeal to leftism was likewise multi-layered, encompassing Hu Jintao's pro-poor policy orientation, Deng Xiaoping's conservative considerations, Marxist and socialist principles, the Party's revolutionary traditions, and Maoism. The Sing Red movement appeared to possess the greatest number of layers: it functioned as a branding tool for urban development, a source of developmental motivation, a moral corrective, an educational supplement, a cultural transmitter, an ideological purifier, a mobilizational call, and a political symbol. One of Bo's sympathizers once cautioned against "indiscriminate promotion of 'singing red [songs]'" (*longtong chang hong*). Recognizing that "redness" was a shared element across radical leftism, communist revolutionary heritage, and even certain strands of Chinese traditional culture, the scholar suggested that Chongqing should either disentangle these different layers of "redness" or replace the red culture altogether with an alternative, such as "new civilization," to serve as the city's cultural "main melody."[26]

To sum up, Bo Xilai's public denial of pursuing a "Chongqing Model" or engaging in a leftist or Maoist project, in itself, does not provide sufficient inferential leverage to substantiate claims of a political realignment in the final phase of his career. This is because such denials were an integral part of the hedging-by-distancing strategy he adopted to minimize potential risks. Bo's repeated denials in late 2011 may signal change, but they may also not. After all, similar denials had appeared throughout, and his posture of strategic non-commitment remained consistent. At most, these denials suggest that, by late 2011, the conditions were not yet ripe for a more decisive move forward. In this regard, there is substantial evidence that Bo Xilai remained committed to his leftist agenda until the end of his political career.

However, more compelling evidence lies elsewhere—Bo Xilai did adjust his policy orientation in response to shifting political winds, although these changes do not necessarily indicate a fundamental reversal.

5.2 Repositioning

Any substantial shift in course would necessarily be reflected in the policy agenda and in the ways it was (re)framed. Here, two indicators are particularly instructive. First, we examine the central theme of Chongqing's Tenth Party Plenum, convened in December 2011, and how existing programs were repositioned in relation to the new agenda. This meeting was the last local plenum before Bo Xilai's downfall. Second, we consider the most recent official articulation of Bo's Chongqing political project, published by the Chongqing Propaganda Department in early March 2012—just two weeks before his removal. The book, titled *Chongqing's Pursuit* (*Chongqing zhuiqiu*) and edited by Su Wei of the Chongqing Party School, was intended to "faithfully document this extraordinarily important period in Chongqing's development...with a focus on theoretical reflection and practical exploration, in order to comprehensively review, summarize, and distill the major initiatives, their substantial achievements, and the valuable experience they generated."[27] Presumably designed to promote Bo's Chongqing "New Deal" while he was attending a national conference in Beijing, the book provides a useful reference point for identifying which policies were ultimately *retained*, *revised*, or *marginalized*.

The key finding is that Bo moderated his leftist vanguardism on multiple fronts while continuing to assert his unparalleled contributions to Chinese socialism. These mixed signals are best understood as reflecting both shifting political dynamics at the top and the persistent ambiguities, opacity, and uncertainties that characterize China's authoritarian elite politics.

5.2.1 Socialist Democracy

To begin with, Chongqing's Tenth Party Plenum was devoted to promoting "socialist democracy and the rule of law" (*shehui zhuyi minzhu fazhi*). This official theme appeared to be an ad hoc addition to an otherwise routine conference agenda. As Table 4.1 shows, the plenum had originally been expected to reiterate the guidelines and policies set forth at the Party's Sixth Plenum of the Seventeenth Central Committee. Instead, cultural development not only ceded its place to another topic but was replaced by one that bore little relation to culture. This shift was highly unusual. In post-Mao Chinese politics, discourse on democracy and the rule of law has largely been the domain of reformist actors. Conservatives, by contrast, have generally refrained from placing political development explicitly on the official agenda. Rather, they have focused primarily on safeguarding the Party's absolute authority, maintaining ideological purity, and ensuring political loyalty.

Beyond the agenda-setting itself, the need for Chongqing's leadership to graft their earlier leftist and populist policies onto a reformist framework, and to parrot the talk of "institutionalization," appears to support the observation that reformism was on the rise during the final years of Hu Jintao's tenure, a shift that Bo Xilai could not afford to ignore. That said, it did not seem to be a viable option for Bo to dismantle wholesale the leftist political persona he had been cultivating since he chose to lean in that direction.

Bo had to tread a fine line as he navigated mixed signals from the Party center. Despite the rise of leftist tendencies during the 2009–2011 period, the political winds suddenly shifted in favor of the reformist camp.[28] Beginning with the Party's Sixth Plenum of the Seventeenth Central Committee, reformists appeared to have regained significant control over the political agenda. Leftist ideological discourse was increasingly depoliticized.[29] At the same time, alongside continued references to the Mass Line, Hu Jintao's "July 1st Speech," delivered in 2011 to commemorate the Party's 90th anniversary, introduced a reformist approach to party building centered on the notion of "scientification" (*kexue hua*)—that is, the supervision and regulation of party affairs through institutionalization, standardization, and proceduralization.

With the benefit of hindsight, we can clearly observe that the reformist pushback—already underway while Bo was still in power—became increasingly conspicuous around the Eighteenth Party Congress held in late 2012. Reformist elements were further reflected in the agendas of the Third and Fourth Plenums of the Eighteenth Central Committee, convened in 2013 and 2014, respectively—by which time Bo had long been politically deceased. Together, the party congress and the two plenums elevated market-oriented economic reform and political reform to top priorities, creating the impression that the reformist blueprint outlined at the Sixteenth Party Congress in 2002 was being revived after a decade-long hiatus. In particular, the proposed political reforms sought to advance the "rule of law" by giving meaningful effect to China's Constitution. Echoing the unofficial advocacy of "constitutionalism" championed by Chinese liberals, the official agenda placed renewed emphasis on "institutionalization." From this historical vantage point, it becomes clear that Bo Xilai's repositioning at Chongqing's Tenth Party Plenum was neither coincidental nor whimsical. Rather, it represented an effort to keep pace with shifting political dynamics within the Party center.

Bo's leftist supporters were likely bewildered when Chongqing leaders claimed in late 2011 that "democracy and the rule of law have been an important driving force behind, and a key guarantee of, the achievements Chongqing has made in recent years."[30] After all, democracy and the rule of law are typically associated with reformist discourse and sit uneasily with a leftist logic of authoritarianism that foregrounds the Party's unconstrained power. Yet this was precisely what unfolded in practice: with democracy and the rule of law enshrined as the central theme of the plenum, a process of extensive conceptual grafting was set in motion. "People's Livelihoods" was now described as the "foundation and prerequisite" of democracy, while the Strike Black campaign was incorporated into the project of developing democracy and the rule of law. More awkwardly, the high-profile Mass Line campaigns that dispatched cadres to rural areas were reframed as efforts to "improve mechanisms for ensuring that public opinion can be expressed smoothly and addressed in a timely manner," on the grounds that "the expression of public opinion is the starting point of democracy."[31] As for the Common Prosperity initiative,

Bo Xilai invoked Deng Xiaoping's definition of the "nature" of socialism, juxtaposing Marxist egalitarianism with "democracy and the rule of law" as the twofold essence of socialism.[32] However, Deng's original formulation, cited by Bo to reconcile these elements, made no reference to democracy or the rule of law.[33] Elsewhere, Chongqing Mayor Huang Qifan invoked "[socialist] core values" rather than the "nature" of socialism and offered a different rhetorical formulation of their relationship: socialism, he argued, is built upon the economic foundation of common prosperity, upon which democracy and the rule of law constitute the superstructure.[34]

Alongside such clumsy grafting, Chongqing's leadership was compelled to embrace the new agenda of "institutionalization." Ironically, this rhetoric resembled a veiled critique of Bo Xilai's entire political program. According to Huang Qifan, "the crux of democracy and the rule of law lies in getting institutional arrangements right." This did not mean that "leading cadres or managers should simply perform good deeds," nor did it refer to "a rule-of-man system in which power rests in the hands of morally upright individuals." Rather, the emphasis was on establishing "a law-based government" and "governance according to law."[35]

Despite this apparent thematic shift away from the left, Bo Xilai appeared determined to hold his leftist ground. He sought to qualify his discussion of political reform with socialist language. This awkward straddling can be explained in two ways. First, the balance of power between leftist and reformist factions within the top party leadership remained opaque and uncertain. There were signs of change. Bo, as a member of the top ruling circle, was likely quick to perceive them. But the prevailing uncertainty did not warrant a decisive realignment. Hedging by appealing to both sides thus appeared to be a prudent strategy. Second, even if Bo had recognized a strong reformist resurgence poised to gain the upper hand, he had already invested too heavily in the leftist camp to break with it at that stage. Constrained by this position, he could only resort to selective conceptual grafting to mitigate potential losses. Ultimately, however, Bo had little choice but to remain aligned with the left until the end. By late 2011, it was simply too late for him to engineer a fundamental political realignment.

In particular, even as he upheld the banner of democracy and the rule of law, Bo made clear that he was referring specifically to *socialist* democracy. China's socialist polity, he argued, must be safeguarded against "Western capitalist democracy," and democracy in China must embody

Chinese characteristics, since "there is no such thing as abstract, universal democracy in the world."[36] Bluntly rejecting the reformist view that China's political reform was lagging and therefore required urgent action, Huang Qifan argued that liberal advocacy was grounded in idealism and dogmatism. "Most of these [liberal ideas] come from bookish intellectuals who toy with concepts drawn from texts without understanding what is actually happening in society," Huang contended. "Detached from social reality, they take theories they read 20 or 50 years ago and present them as issues for discussion." Instead, Huang pointed to "opening up" as China's top priority, thereby sidestepping the issue of political reform while maintaining a pro-reform posture. "For China at present, I believe the foremost issue is how the Chinese economy should further open up and integrate globally within a new world order," Huang argued, "Failing to seize these opportunities would constitute the greatest historical mistake."[37]

Furthermore, embedded within the defense of socialist democracy was a concurrent promotion of the principle of common prosperity. As Bo stated, "we have consistently emphasized common prosperity, because it is an issue that Western politicians are reluctant to address, and one they would be unable to realize even if they did raise it." This, Bo argued, was why socialist democracy was "fundamentally different" from its Western counterpart.[38] Echoing Bo's rhetoric, Huang Qifan elaborated on class struggle as a precondition for democracy. "Capitalism and privatization inevitably lead to social polarization, and under such conditions there can be no genuine democracy." According to Huang, electoral democracy in the West "appears democratic, but in reality it is driven by wealth, as well as by compromises and alliances among economic and political elites."[39] Therefore, Huang argued, genuine democracy necessarily depends on common prosperity; without it, one person, one vote cannot deliver justice.[40]

5.2.2 *Chongqing's Pursuit*

Another indicator of Bo Xilai's difficult political repositioning was the book *Chongqing's Pursuit*, published in March 2012. It arguably represented the final version of the political manifesto through which Bo sought to promote his agenda in the run-up to the Party's cross-generational leadership transition at the Eighteenth Party Congress. As a useful point of reference, *Chongqing's Pursuit* enables us to compare how specific formulations and policies were retained, revised, or discarded just two weeks before Bo's fall from power.

First, there was a noticeable rhetorical shift toward emphasizing the guiding role of central-level policies in Chongqing's local achievements. To be sure, claims that Chongqing's policies were aligned with central directives and expectations had long been a standard feature of the city's official propaganda. For instance, even during Bo Xilai's Maoist heyday, Chongqing was still portrayed as exploring the frontier of Hu Jintao's Scientific Development concept.

However, the wording employed by Chongqing's leadership in March 2012 appeared qualitatively different, recalling Bo's rhetoric from his earlier reformist phase. Once again, full credit was attributed to Hu Jintao's "3–14 Overall Arrangement" and "Document No. 3" issued by the State Council under Wen Jiabao.[41] In Bo's words, these two policy packages were "magic weapons" that made Chongqing's recent "healthy development" possible.[42] As if such indirect signaling through policy alignment were insufficient, Chongqing's leaders also explicitly affirmed their compliance. As Bo put it, his Chongqing policies "constituted concrete practices fully in line with the party line established by the central leadership."[43]

Similarly, Huang Qifan told the media that "Chongqing is striving to advance reform, exploration, and development in accordance with the requirements of the central leadership," reiterating that "the party committee and municipal government of Chongqing have never approached issues in terms of a so-called 'Chongqing Model.'"[44] In particular, Huang highlighted Chongqing's designated role as a local experimental zone for the "coordinated development of urban and rural areas." As he explained, "the most salient feature of Chongqing's work in recent years is that, in accordance with the Party center's requirements under the 'Scientific Outlook on Development,' we have undertaken significant exploratory efforts in the comprehensive reform of urban–rural integration." Huang thus concluded that "there have been two primary focal points in Chongqing's development and exploration in recent years": one was exploring more effective forms of urban–rural integration, and the other was transforming Chongqing into an "inland high ground for opening up"—that is, an inland, labor-intensive manufacturing hub envisioned in the "domestic flying geese" framework. Moreover, Huang sought to depoliticize Bo's "New Deal." When confronted with a media question suggesting that Chongqing's prominence stemmed more from the red culture movement and the anti-organized-crime campaign than from its economic achievements, Huang attributed this perception to the media's tendency to favor sensational reporting, which, he argued, had skewed public attention toward the Sing Red and Strike Black campaigns. By contrast, Huang insisted that "our work is comprehensive in scope and addresses a full range of issues."

Second, the mass-centered framing of the Sing Red movement was noticeably toned down. In *Chongqing's Pursuit*, the final version of this framing outlined the movement's mobilization method as comprising five interconnected steps.[45]

1. Providing content
2. Cultivating the main actor, with the masses as the principal participants
3. Exercising active leadership over major state-organized events
4. Providing propaganda and guidance
5. Mobilizing, expanding, and forming a "chain of activities" by embedding the red culture campaign into everyday life and work.

Both the state-nurtured mass initiative and the daily embeddedness of the campaign were retained, along with other layers of framing associated with the Sing Red movement, including revolutionary legacies, Chinese cultural traditions, developmental motivation, and socialist ideology.[46]

What was conspicuously *missing* was the rhetoric of mass enthusiasm that was supposed to feed back into and reinforce state efforts, which were said to raise mass consciousness in the first place. In this sense, Bo took a step back and effectively demobilized his Mass Line policies by downplaying the element of "mass spontaneity." This bottom-up "awakening," conceived as a response to the top-down "enlightenment" provided by political leaders, had until recently been prominently emphasized, lending these nonviolent, post-Mao campaigns a distinctly Maoist tint, reminiscent of the mob-like justice meted out against class enemies during the Mao era.

Nevertheless, the Sing Red movement continued to occupy a central place in Bo Xilai's overall political program, even though it proved difficult to reconcile the red culture campaign with a reformist agenda centered on democracy and the rule of law. While these two themes were enshrined as the focus of Chongqing's Tenth Party Plenum, the leadership simultaneously adopted a separate resolution to accelerate efforts to "build a culturally strong city" (*wenhua qiang shi*).[47] This echoed the Party's Sixth Plenum of the Seventeenth Central Committee, which had called for "making culture develop and prosper"—the same theme that had guided Chongqing's Fifth Party Plenum in mid-2009. Having once stolen the Party center's thunder, Bo could conceivably have done so again in 2011 by further politicizing socialist culture, had he not needed to hedge against shifting political dynamics by tempering earlier approaches with a new emphasis on "democracy and the rule of law." In this context, the red culture movement was reframed as a means of "facilitating the integration of rule by virtue and rule of law."[48]

Third, a stand-alone anti-corruption program that had been under development for some time was ultimately dropped. This was the "Clean Chongqing" (*lianjie Chongqing*) initiative. Bo Xilai formally placed it on the agenda in early 2010, just as the Strike Black campaign was undergoing a discursive elevation—namely, the reframing of anti-organized-crime efforts as anti-corruption in particular and party building more broadly.[49]

This line of thinking was endorsed by a party theoretician in mid-2011, when a high-level symposium on party building was convened in Chongqing to mark the Party's 90th anniversary.[50] In November 2011, a research team from Tsinghua University, led by the prominent left-leaning scholar Hu Angang, published a book on Bo's "Clean Chongqing" agenda.[51] The book sought to further legitimize the Chongqing Model by introducing a new policy initiative to complement existing programs. Chongqing's anti-corruption efforts were portrayed as central to the "Chongqing Experience," serving as a "political guarantee" for refining and strengthening the local model.[52] To be sure, as the book itself suggests, the Chongqing approach to anti-corruption did not appear particularly novel or innovative in technical terms. Its contribution was instead framed at the conceptual level: Chongqing's anti-corruption efforts extended beyond targets punishable through the Party's internal disciplinary mechanisms, such as the Central Discipline and Inspection Commission, to encompass forms of corruption embedded in China's political system and social culture.[53] With this discursive groundwork in place, Bo Xilai formally announced the program in early 2012 through a newly adopted resolution.

Notably, "Clean Chongqing" disappeared from *Chongqing's Pursuit*. The book downplayed anti-corruption as a stand-alone local policy program. The Clean Chongqing initiative was not mentioned at all,[54] even though, at the time of its official launch, it had been presented as one of the key themes defining Bo's broader political campaign. In its initial conception, anti-corruption was accorded a status equal to other major policy priorities, including people's livelihoods, common prosperity, and democracy and the rule of law.[55] At that time, the Sing Red movement also acquired an additional layer of framing, becoming a tool for anti-corruption.[56] Taken together, these developments underscore the central importance that the Clean Chongqing initiative was originally intended to hold.

Why, then, was it removed? One possible explanation is that Bo scaled it back for the same reason he toned down the mass-centered framing of the Sing Red movement. In short, this was an act of hedging through the selective removal of the most politicized elements. Like proclaiming ideological innovation, launching a systematic anti-corruption campaign is a prerogative reserved for the Party's general secretary. Local governments are expected to faithfully implement initiatives put forward by the central leadership. Another possible factor was less deliberate and more contingent: the Wang Lijun incident that erupted in February 2012.

5.2.3 *Staying the Course*

These concessions notwithstanding, Bo Xilai continued to hold fast to his core program and ambitions. The Common Prosperity initiative remained firmly in place. The overarching framework of Chongqing's policies was summarized in *Chongqing's Pursuit* as follows: "pioneering a path of Scientific Development oriented toward people's livelihoods, reducing inequality, and promoting common prosperity."[57] Although, by this point, common prosperity had been relegated to a secondary position and subsumed under the primary emphasis on people's livelihoods, its political significance remained evident. This Marxist egalitarian ideal continued to serve as a defining element of Bo's political program. At the same time, the conservative dimension of Deng Xiaoping's thought was still invoked as a source of legitimacy: the "nature" of socialism was said to require the realization of common prosperity.[58]

More indicative of Bo Xilai's determination to remain on the left was the way he framed Chongqing's contributions. Paradoxically, he claimed that he had consistently followed the lead of the Party center, even as he emphasized the vanguardist character of Chongqing's policy experimentation. In particular, Bo arrogated to himself the authority to declare a historic turning point in China's development: the transition from "partial prosperity" to "common prosperity" was framed as the "new task of our time." Chongqing, in turn, was portrayed as the pioneer taking the lead in initiating this "strategic transformation."[59]

Furthermore, Bo asserted that he had achieved "theoretical innovation"—a prerogative typically reserved for the Party's top leadership. He made it clear that, as a local official, he deserved credit for the foresight and resolve demonstrated in Chongqing's policy initiatives. In his view, since "common prosperity is a vast and highly challenging undertaking, with little existing experience to draw upon," the reason Chongqing "took the initiative to tackle this thorny issue" was that "its decision-makers possessed a clear and sober understanding [of what was at stake]."[60]

In *Yu Lun*, Chongqing's "reform" under Bo was described as having made a significant contribution to China's local political reform.[61] In particular, Chongqing's "political and economic practice" was no longer framed as a narrow case of local experimentation; rather, it had become a focal point drawing public attention to a set of "fundamental questions," including how China might successfully upgrade its development strategy, how local governments should preserve the "nature" of socialism, and how they could contribute to Socialism with Chinese Characteristics.[62] The Common Prosperity initiative in Chongqing was said to embody the Party's proletarian identity, signify China's historic transition from "letting some get rich first" to "achieving prosperity for all," and provide a model for broader emulation, thereby reflecting Bo's strong sense of political responsibility and historical mission.[63] The so-called "Chongqing Pathway" was further presented as a blueprint for "the Chinese Way." Ideologically, Chongqing's practice was claimed to be highly successful because it "absorbs the strengths of both planned and market economies while discarding the shortcomings of each."[64] In this rhetoric, socialism was defended and vindicated despite its failures under Mao, while capitalism was criticized despite its successes under Dengist reform.

In *Chongqing's Pursuit*, Bo reiterated his "new" theories, originally advanced at the height of his flirtation with Maoism, asserting that they "provide a vivid elaboration of the Party's fundamental purpose and basic theories."[65] Much like the Common Prosperity initiative itself, these theories posed a direct challenge to the Party's reform-era doctrines. For instance, pro-poor redistribution was promoted as a major "driver" of economic growth, in contrast to the Dengist emphasis on market reform. Communist ideals were translated into concrete policy prescriptions: "now is indeed the time to seriously consider [the realization of] common prosperity." The most provocative example was an explicit repudiation of Deng Xiaoping's well-known reformist dictum. Whereas Deng asserted that "development is the absolute principle," Bo challenged this claim head-on, arguing that without the realization of common prosperity, "development would not be an 'absolute principle' (*ying daoli*), but rather 'nonsense' (*mei daoli*)." Alluding to the populist underpinnings of this egalitarian stance, Bo further emphasized that "the issue of people's livelihoods, especially the question of distribution, is essentially a matter of the relationship between the Party and the people," and that communists must "side with the masses on questions of distribution."[66]

Following the pattern of other top leaders in reform-era China, whose achievements became associated with specific localities, Bo Xilai sought to elevate Chongqing to a status comparable to Shenzhen, Pudong, and Binhai. These three locations are widely regarded as milestones of China's reform under Deng Xiaoping, Jiang Zemin, and Hu Jintao, respectively. Bo's ambition was unmistakable. As he put it, "one should certainly not miss [the opportunities in] Chongqing if one has already missed [those in] Pudong and Binhai."[67] Chongqing was cast as a "front-runner" rather than a follower.[68] As *Yu Lun* observed, the "Shenzhen Dream" ushered China into its industrial age, while the "Chongqing Dream" was leading the country into "an age of people's livelihoods," with the two "dreams" jointly contributing to the realization of the Chinese Dream.[69]

Finally, Bo did not neglect to issue a pointed warning to Chongqing's local cadres who were considering, or had already decided, to distance themselves from his conservative agenda, as they may have perceived subtle shifts in the political winds. At a local conference on propaganda work held in February 2012, Bo stressed the importance of the Sing Red movement as an ideological bulwark against hostile forces, employing unusually belligerent language.[70] "The hostile forces have been devoting considerable effort to [shaping] public opinion and [controlling] the information sphere," Bo noted. "Whenever something happens on our side, they spare no effort to mislead the public and spread rumors, with the aim of sowing confusion." As Bo put it, "this 'battlefield' is invisible, but the struggle is fierce." Bo then rebuked those who were not following his directives, urging them to stand firm and faithfully implement existing policies. "There are indeed a few among us who, whether due to ideological confusion or overconfidence in their own judgment, adopt a straddling stance, engage in opportunistic grandstanding, and lack the courage to uphold the truth and adhere to the Party center's policies."

Indeed, there is evidence that some Chongqing officials were playing it safe and not closely aligning themselves with Bo. In particular, not all propaganda materials produced locally in Chongqing framed Bo's governance in the same way as those by Su Wei of the Chongqing Party School. Two books published in November 2011 and March 2012 are especially instructive in this regard. Both offered their own formulations of the Chongqing Model and were collectively authored by scholars within Chongqing's local establishment.

The first was compiled by the editorial team of *Chongqing Governance* (*Chongqing xingzheng*), a journal published by the Chongqing Academy of Governance (*Chongqing xingzheng xueyuan*).[71] The second was produced by the "Research Team on Chongqing's Local Conditions" (*Chongqing shi qing yanjiu keti zu*) at the Chongqing Research Center for Comprehensive Economics (*Chongqing shi zonghe jingji yanjiu yuan*).[72] Overall, both adopted a relatively depoliticized approach, praising Bo's achievements without amplifying his broader ambitions. In some instances, their arguments even appeared to serve as an implicit corrective to Su Wei's claims about the Chongqing Model. For example, while echoing Bo's strategic denial, one volume diverged from Su Wei's semi-official promotion by arguing that it would take time to determine whether Chongqing's local experimentation could evolve into a mature and fully developed "model."[73] At most, the so-called Chongqing Model was described as a "model of local development"—a "product" that required years to take shape. The authors further emphasized that this process had in fact begun when Chongqing was designated a provincial-level municipality in 1997, although the contours of the model "only became recognizable in recent years."[74] The underlying message was clear: Bo did not merit the exceptional credit often attributed to Chongqing's development.

The second book went further by conveying a degree of veiled criticism.[75] It began by asserting that "the Chinese Way is the prerequisite, foundation, and condition for the Chongqing Practice," and that the latter represents "an extension, deepening, and innovation" of the former. Having established this relationship, the book emphasized that the Chinese Way was none other than "the path of Socialism with Chinese Characteristics [that has been followed] since the Third Plenum of the Eleventh Central Committee." In effect, this amounted to a reformist statement that pushed back against leftist claims that foregrounded China's uniqueness and the legacy of the Mao era. The most explicit expression of dissent was arguably the claim that Chongqing had experienced four waves of "Mind Emancipation" since attaining its status as a municipality. The most recent of these was said to have occurred in the second half of 2006. In other words, the book did not credit Bo with contributing to Chongqing's reform and development, despite his highly publicized "Mind Emancipation" campaign during his early tenure in the city.

5.3 "Rob the Rich to Help the Poor"

Toward the end of his political career, Bo Xilai adjusted the framing of his political campaign as part of a hedging strategy in response to subtle shifts in the political dynamics at the top. Yet, on the whole, he preserved the leftist core of his program and sustained his broader ambitions. Bo signaled his determination to remain aligned with the Left not only through *rhetoric* but also through concrete *actions*. In particular, he sought to implement the Common Prosperity blueprint by extracting resources from private entrepreneurs and redistributing them to lower-income groups, ostensibly in the name of promoting the development of the private sector.

The prototype of this "exploiting the rich" approach may be traced to a nationwide initiative launched by the Party's Central Department of United Front (*zhongyang tong zhan bu*) in mid-2010.[76] This campaign was later formalized as the "Initiative of Promoting Well-being and Prosperity for the People, and Assisting Society." Under this program, private entrepreneurs were paired with socially disadvantaged and economically impoverished households and tasked with providing financial assistance. According to official propaganda, the origins of this initiative can be further traced back to March 2008, when Shanxi Province pioneered the so-called "Initiative of Ten Thousand Shanxi Entrepreneurs Connecting with Ten Thousand Households in Gratitude." The local government "organized" 30 individuals from the "non-state sector" to assist three groups facing financial hardship: elderly veterans, senior party members, and retired model workers. Such rich–poor partnerships were portrayed as serving a dual purpose: on the one hand, they provided a platform for private entrepreneurs to "develop in a healthy manner," presumably with the help of this peculiar political education; on the other hand, they fostered a sense of respect and gratitude toward these revolutionary constituencies in society while promoting the Party's fine traditions. In July 2010, Du Qinglin, head of the United Front Department, elevated this local practice to the level of a "national strategy." Subsequently, a campaign titled the "Gratitude and Social Contribution Initiative of Non-State-Sector Entrepreneurs" was rolled out nationwide. In Hebei Province, for example, 870 private enterprises were paired with approximately 9000 low-income households.

In Chongqing, the campaign was titled the "Initiative of Ten Thousand Chongqing Entrepreneurs Expressing Gratitude to Hongyan." It had three specific targets: ten thousand entrepreneurs from the non-state sector were to participate, ten thousand individuals in need were to receive assistance, and each beneficiary was to receive no less than 10,000 yuan per year. Among the 50,000 veteran party members selected for assistance, approximately one-fifth were living at or below the poverty line. In terms of implementation, private entrepreneurs were encouraged to deliver their support through five channels: direct monetary donations, job opportunities, the provision of basic necessities, vocational training, and investment in poverty alleviation projects.[77]

The early version of the campaign called on private entrepreneurs to "express gratitude by reflecting on the sources of their wealth" (*si yuan gan'en*).[78] Chongqing's state media highlighted two representative cases to illustrate how this poverty alleviation program operated.[79] First, companies were required to provide financing and training to help low-income individuals establish local farms or small businesses. They were also expected to purchase goods produced by these ventures; when market conditions were unfavorable, purchases were to be made at prices that ensured a minimum profit margin for local producers. The rationale was that "those who become prosperous first have an obligation to help others achieve prosperity as well." In particular, so-called "dragon-head enterprises" (*longtou qiye*)—that is, leading firms within an industry—were said to bear responsibility for enabling the poor to "generate their own income" (*zao xue*), rather than merely providing a temporary "lifeline" (*shu xue*). Second, beyond direct monetary transfers to low-income households, companies were tasked with providing housing for employees, safeguarding their welfare and social security, and ensuring access to education and training. In effect, responsibilities typically associated with the state were shifted onto the private sector. It was claimed that Chongqing's private sector would collectively invest 20 billion yuan to raise incomes in rural, impoverished areas. In total, 171 companies "voluntarily" registered to participate in the campaign.[80]

The emergence of the rich–poor partnership program coincided with Bo Xilai's reorientation toward leftist policies. In terms of its format, the campaign closely resembled Chongqing's Mass Line initiatives launched in mid-2009, which dispatched party officials to rural areas and paired leading cadres with poor households for poverty alleviation—the so-called "forming ties with poor relatives" program (*jie qiong qin*). The key difference, however, was that this time it was not party members but private entrepreneurs who were "sent down." The "exploiting the rich" program was also thematically linked to the People's Livelihoods agenda that Bo advanced at Chongqing's Seventh Party Plenum in mid-2010.

Foreshadowing the subsequent Common Prosperity initiative, the so-called "Ten People's Livelihoods Policies" introduced after Chongqing's Seventh Party Plenum not only encompassed the provision of public goods and social welfare but also included targeted measures to address economic inequality. One component, the "10,000 Yuan Income Increase" program (*wan yuan zeng shou*), largely overlapped with the United Front initiative launched in mid-2010, which effectively forced private entrepreneurs to contribute to poverty alleviation. Another component was a plan to develop tens of thousands of "micro-enterprises" (*weixing qiye*). Initially framed within the people's livelihoods agenda due to its focus on employment, this policy was later conveniently incorporated into the Common Prosperity framework. Micro-enterprises were defined as private businesses "with registered capital below 100,000 yuan and fewer than 20 employees."[81] Chongqing's state media explicitly asserted that "[the development of] micro-enterprises is an effective means of reducing inequality between rich and poor."[82]

For all the idealistic rhetoric, the greatest challenge facing Chongqing's leadership was securing sufficient funding to realize their ambitious promises. Bo Xilai, however, appeared largely unconcerned about the fiscal constraints. When asked how the government could possibly sustain such a high level of investment, he responded to this technical question with a political argument: "since the people are the 'parents' who provide for us, how can anyone question whether money should be spent on them?"[83] In November 2010, shortly after Chongqing's Eighth Party Plenum, at which common prosperity was elevated to a position of priority task, Bo reassured the public that funding would not be an issue so long as the government was determined to act.[84] "Our country is now a large and prosperous household, and Chongqing's fiscal situation has improved significantly," he stated. "If the goal is to deliver more tangible benefits to the people, what is truly lacking is not money, but capable and diligent officials." In Bo's opinion, the primary obstacle was not financial but administrative. "Some of our cadres suffer from two problems: first, bureaucratism and inaction; second, a lack of expertise and professional competence." In short, Bo suggested that the time was ripe to address inequality, even though Chongqing was not among China's most developed regions. "Some say Chongqing is poor, but in fact it is quite resource-rich if one knows where to look," Bo asserted, "What we must do is improve management and extract these resources to better the lives of low- and middle-income groups."

There appeared to be a division of labor: Chongqing Mayor Huang Qifan focused on devising technical solutions, while Bo Xilai provided overall political direction. Huang's initial approach combined state revenue with private investment. He explicitly noted that "the government cannot shoulder the entire burden and must therefore adopt market-based mechanisms to share the costs of reform."[85] More specifically, "with government investment serving as a catalyst and market-based operations as the channel, both profit-making and non-profit entities, as well as individuals, are encouraged to invest [in the social welfare sector] to help solve the people's livelihoods problems."[86] A second measure involved extracting resources from state-owned enterprises (SOEs)—unsurprisingly, a characteristic Leninist approach to economic management. Chongqing's SOEs collectively issued a "Letter of Initiative," declaring it their responsibility to support people's livelihoods.[87] Among the proposals outlined in the document, one emphasized job creation and vocational training, while others focused on supporting micro-enterprises. The SOEs agreed to "allocate 100 million yuan annually from their capital returns for five consecutive years and remit it to the public treasury for unified allocation," integrate micro-enterprises into their industrial supply chains, and provide financial services to them.

However, these measures ultimately proved insufficient to achieve the stated goals. In March 2011—four months before Chongqing's Ninth Party Plenum, at which common prosperity was elevated to the official theme—Huang Qifan told the media that the leadership was still struggling to identify a feasible approach to reducing economic inequality.[88] As Huang noted, "what concerns me now is how to sustain economic growth while gradually narrowing the 'Three Gaps.'" He framed the challenge in terms of two questions: (1) "what measures can address the root causes of the problem?" and (2) "to what extent must such measures be implemented to achieve meaningful reductions [in inequality]?" Huang admitted that he had yet to find clear answers. "At present, I still do not have a clear picture; I feel unsettled and under considerable pressure." He added that this issue was precisely what Bo Xilai was "most concerned about and thinking about."

With the benefit of hindsight, it becomes clear that Huang Qifan's first question was largely rhetorical. The answer, in his view, was evident: developing the private sector. This was a point Huang had already raised earlier and would elaborate on further. Discussing the Common Prosperity agenda unveiled at Chongqing's Ninth Party Plenum,[89] Huang emphasized that "without full employment, the goal of narrowing the Three Gaps would remain a mere castle in the air," and that "entrepreneurship is the path to prosperity." The principal reason, he argued, was that "the rich–poor divide stems not only from disparities in wages, but more importantly from differences in capital gains." Accordingly, Huang maintained that effectively addressing inequality requires "vigorously promoting entrepreneurship across society—using it to generate employment and facilitate wealth creation—so that more people can acquire assets and derive capital gains." To support this argument, Huang presented a brief comparison using descriptive statistics. Chongqing, with a population of 32 million, was said to have only 200,000 enterprises and 700,000 small, family-run businesses. By contrast, the figures for Shanghai were 20 million, 600,000, and 1.2 million, respectively; for Zhejiang Province, they were 40 million, 800,000, and 2.2 million. Huang thus pointed directly to the underlying monetary constraint: for small and micro-enterprises, the principal barriers to development were access to finance and the availability of start-up capital.

If Huang's first question was rhetorical, his second was misleading. The real issue was not "what" measures to take or "how much" to implement, but how *quickly* results could be delivered. In other words, the question appeared genuine only because pursuing a "proper" path in accordance with economic principles would take too long. By that point, Bo had less than a year remaining in Chongqing before the leadership reshuffle scheduled for late 2012. Hence, to realize common prosperity within such a limited timeframe, he was compelled to pursue a more "perverse" approach.

The idea of enlisting private entrepreneurs to incubate "micro-enterprises" can be understood as arising from the combination of the United Front's rich–poor partnership initiative and Bo Xilai's People's Livelihoods agenda. In the former, the objective shifted from poverty alleviation to the development of business entities. In the latter, an additional source of funding was introduced alongside the state sector.

Evidence suggests that Bo made up his mind to pursue this course in the summer of 2011. At an annual conference on Chongqing's private sector development, both Bo Xilai and Huang Qifan emphasized a market-oriented approach to "enriching the people" and the importance of supporting private entrepreneurs.[90] However, behind the scenes, Bo was working on a markedly different agenda. Shortly after the pro-market conference, Bo convened a "heart-to-heart" meeting with Chongqing's private entrepreneurs. Many of them were members of China's so-called "democratic parties" that participate in China's People's Political Consultative Conference—a consultative body often presented as evidence of China's democratic credentials. At this informal gathering, Bo signaled what was to come.[91] "Is it contradictory for private entrepreneurs to talk about common prosperity?" he asked rhetorically. He then answered that "only those entrepreneurs who truly understand common prosperity can be regarded as possessing wisdom and a long-term vision." To render this position more economically persuasive, Bo offered further reasoning: "if enterprises pursue excessively high profit margins while workers' incomes remain low, social consumption will be insufficient, and accumulated tensions may lead to significant problems at both the micro and macro levels." Bo thus urged these entrepreneurs to interpret his economic strategy through the lens of common prosperity.

To be sure, during his early reformist phase, Bo also called upon private entrepreneurs to contribute to the development of Chongqing's poorer regions. However, the economic logic he emphasized at that time was clearly reformist. At an annual conference with the private sector in 2008, Bo encouraged the redirection of private capital toward underdeveloped areas of Chongqing, not only because doing so would "make contributions to society," but also because it would allow firms to "secure a share of future markets and create opportunities for long-term development."[92] Even when Bo praised these entrepreneurs for their "patriotism," he appealed to their entrepreneurial incentives. In his words, "investing in the western regions is both highly challenging and deeply meaningful."[93]

In contrast, by late 2011, Chongqing's private sector had been assigned a *paternal* role, as entrepreneurs were expected to redistribute their own resources to lower-income groups. Following Bo's "heart-to-heart" meeting in August, Chongqing's United Front Department convened a "promotion conference" in November 2011. There, private entrepreneurs were called upon to actively contribute to the socialist project of Common Prosperity; they were urged to "deepen their ideological understanding and voluntarily participate."[94] In particular, the Chongqing government issued a document titled "Ten Actions for the Non-State Sector to Promote Inequality Reduction and the Realization of Common Prosperity," which outlined the responsibilities expected of private business owners.[95] The key points are summarized as follows.

1. Large enterprises should continue to expand.
2. Enterprises must conduct their business with "responsibility" and "integrity," including paying all taxes due to local authorities.
3. Enterprises should cultivate "harmonious" employer–employee relations, including establishing reasonable mechanisms for workers to negotiate their remuneration.
4. Enterprises should support the development of "micro-enterprises" by providing financial resources, technology, supply chain support, and a broadly defined favorable business environment. The goal was to create 1.5 million jobs by 2015.
5. Enterprises should provide "stable employment" as well as relevant training for migrant workers.
6. Enterprises should continue to contribute to poverty reduction in Chongqing's rural regions by investing 15 billion yuan by 2015 and ensuring that each of the one million targeted households achieved an annual income increase of 10,000 yuan.
7. Enterprises should contribute to economic development across all counties in Chongqing, primarily through investment.
8. Enterprises should assist rural villages in improving infrastructure.
9. Enterprises should provide direct financial assistance to those in need.
10. Enterprises should cultivate a business culture grounded in a "culture of gratitude" (*gan'en wenhua*), defined as "a normative ethos in which employers express gratitude to employees, employees express gratitude to employers, and both express gratitude to the Party, the state, and the people."

It is unclear how the first objective could be achieved in light of the eight subsequent *extractive* tasks. This apparent contradiction may help explain the inclusion of the unusual tenth requirement. The underlying message seemed to be: "do what you are told to do and do not complain."

Corresponding to these Ten Tasks, a "Letter of Initiative" was issued in the name of private entrepreneurs as a bottom-up response.[96] The document asserted that supporting the development of "micro-enterprises" was an "objective requirement" that the private sector had to fulfill in order to contribute to the Common Prosperity project; it was presented as the proper way for private entrepreneurs to "give back to society." The letter outlined six specific proposals detailing their expected actions, largely reiterating the extractive measures imposed by the local state. A week later, Chongqing Mayor Huang Qifan issued a similar call,[97] effectively providing *government* endorsement for an initiative first introduced through the *United Front* system—a sequence that reflected a subtle and strategic political maneuver, whereby a sensitive and possibly controversial policy was initially advanced through a lower-profile channel before receiving formal backing from a higher-level authority.

The "exploiting the rich" policy took on a more dramatic form in December 2011, when Chongqing's state media published what appeared to be a "forced" confession by a local private entrepreneur.[98] Yin Mingshan, chairman of Chongqing's leading motorcycle manufacturer, Lifan, described how his company had contributed to Bo's Common Prosperity initiative. The effort included a 50 million yuan financial transfer to a state-owned enterprise in Wanzhou, which was said to have enabled the firm to complete its restructuring and achieve full employment for more than 1000 workers. Moreover, Yin told the media that he felt "guilty" for three reasons: first, "I became wealthy by benefiting from the tailwinds of reform, but have not done enough to help others become prosperous"; second, "[our company] still falls short compared with state-owned enterprises and other private firms that have done more in this regard"; and third, "two-thirds of Lifan's employees cannot afford to purchase housing." Yin thus announced additional measures to make amends, including the construction of dormitories capable of housing up to 10,000 workers, the provision of subsidized meals in company canteens, free shuttle bus services, and, most importantly, wage increases. Echoing official rhetoric, he further stated that "private entrepreneurs who became wealthy first should reflect on the sources of their prosperity and consider how to continue progressing."

One month later, the Chongqing government staged an awards ceremony to honor "model" entrepreneurs who had "generously contributed funds while also creating employment and paying taxes."[99] Official propaganda further emphasized that "although capital is inherently driven to maximize profit, entrepreneurs with a strong sense of responsibility do not regard wealth accumulation as the primary goal of life." It was also stressed that "participating in the great endeavor of reducing inequality and achieving common prosperity constitutes a historical mission assigned to private entrepreneurs in this new era."[100] Similarly, another "Letter of Initiative" was issued in the name of these model entrepreneurs, presented as a bottom-up endorsement of a top-down state initiative.[101] According to the letter, "it is not prosperity when only one entrepreneur makes money, nor when only one company turns a profit; enterprise development must strike a balance between profit-seeking and moral responsibility, with the latter taking priority; true prosperity can only be achieved when the vast majority of society enjoys a good standard of living."

This "rob the rich to help the poor" initiative, however, was not mentioned in *Chongqing's Pursuit*, the promotional volume Bo Xilai intended to use to showcase his achievements to the Party's top leadership. Strictly speaking, it fell within the domain of the *United Front* and therefore did not necessarily need to be presented alongside formal *government* policies or *party* affairs. In practical terms, it was politically prudent to avoid prominently highlighting such a radical practice in March 2012, given the uncertainty of elite politics and the ongoing public controversy surrounding the Wang Lijun incident.

Bo Xilai's decision to pursue this "perverse" path of poverty reduction was arguably one of the key factors behind his political downfall—perhaps even the principal cause. Translating common prosperity into concrete policy inevitably entailed far greater risks than merely endorsing it rhetorically. The former likely crossed the bottom line of the reformist camp, which continued to wield substantial political influence at the time.

Zhang Dejiang, the Politburo member dispatched to assume temporary control of Chongqing following Bo's removal, moved swiftly to halt Bo's extractive measures and to reassure local private entrepreneurs of the Party's continued commitment to supporting the private sector. At a 2012 conference on private sector development, Zhang emphasized that "countless examples have demonstrated that wherever the private sector is vibrant, the economy prospers."[102] More importantly, in an effort to reassure entrepreneurs who had been adversely affected under Bo, Zhang effectively dismantled the justification for the Common Prosperity agenda. As he stated, "Chongqing remains at a stage of underdevelopment (*qian fada jieduan*) and is still a region of underdevelopment (*qian fada diqu*)."[103] This position was further elaborated by the Chongqing

Propaganda Department in a booklet published in late 2012.[104] The earlier eight-character summary of Bo's political program—"oriented toward people's livelihoods, reducing inequality, and realizing common prosperity" (*min sheng dao xiang, suo cha gong fu*)—was subsequently replaced by a reformist formulation: "scientific development, enriching the people, and revitalizing Chongqing" (*ke xue fa zhan, fu min xing yu*).[105]

The booklet openly criticized Bo's transgressions in unusually direct language. "The existence of problems is not in itself alarming, but what is alarming is failing to approach them with a 'seeking truth from facts' attitude and pursuing quick results by exceeding the limits of the current stage of development." In this context, Zhang Dejiang's "Two Underdevelopments" assessment was presented as a "sobering reminder."[106] Leaders, it stressed, "must never become hotheaded, must never issue directives based on assumptions, and must never indulge in grandstanding or superficial displays."[107]

Notes

1. Xiao Zhu, "Ji gefang zhihui, tansuo gongtong fuyu" [Gathering Wisdom from All Sides and Exploring the Path to Common Prosperity], *Chongqing ribao*, December 5, 2011.
2. Xiao Zhu, "Tantao gaige kaifang, reyi gongtong fuyu" [Discussing Reform and Opening Up and Vigorously Debating Common Prosperity], *Chongqing ribao*, January 12, 2012.
3. "Zhong wai meiti jujiao Chongqing" [Chinese and Foreign Media Focusing on Chongqing], *Chongqing ribao*, March 11, 2009.
4. "Bai jia meiti, jujiao Chongqing" [Hundreds of Media Groups Focusing on Chongqing], *Chongqing ribao*, March 12, 2011.
5. Chongqing Leading Small Group for Internet Regulation (CLSGIR), External Propaganda Office of the Chongqing Party Committee (EPOCPC), and Chongqing Center for Internet News Research (CCINR), *Yu lun 2010* [Public Opinion in Chongqing 2010] (self-published, 2011), 238.
6. CLSGIR, EPOCPC, and CCINR, *Yu lun 2010*, 210.
7. Xiao Zhu, "Yi gaishan minsheng wei dongli, tuidong Chongqing kexue fazhan" [Promoting the Scientific Development of Chongqing, with Improving People's Livelihoods as the Driving Force], *Chongqing ribao*, December 22, 2010.
8. Xiao Zhu, "Jianding bu yi zou gongtong fuyu daolu" [Firmly Following the Path of Common Prosperity], *Chongqing ribao*, July 25, 2011.

9. "Rang baixing dedao gengduo de shihui" [Let the People Receive More Tangible Benefits], *Chongqing Ribao*, July 28, 2011; Xiao Zhu, "Gao Zhongguo tese shehui zhuyi, zou gongtong fuyu zhi lu" [Practicing Socialism with Chinese Characteristics and Following the Path of Common Prosperity], *Chongqing ribao*, September 22, 2011.
10. Shang Yu, "Kaifang gaige tiaokong shi Chongqing fazhan de hexin dongli" [Reform, Opening-Up, and Regulation Are the Core Driving Forces behind Chongqing's Development], *Chongqing ribao*, December 9, 2011.
11. Ren Rui, Shang Yu, and He Qingping, "Xianggang zhuliu meiti guanzhu Chongqing gaige yu fazhan" [Mainstream Hong Kong Media Focusing on Chongqing's Reform and Development], *Chongqing ribao*, October 12, 2011.
12. Propaganda Department of Chongqing Party Committee (PDCPC) and Chongqing Office of Internet and Information (COII), *Chongqing yuqing huibian*, vol. 8 [Collection of Chongqing's Public Opinion, vol. 8] (self-published, 2012), 19.
13. Deng Bin, Peng Weimin, and Huang Xiaohua, "'Chongqing moshi yu Zhongguo tese shehui zhuyi' xueshu yantao hui shuyao" [A Summary of the Academic Seminar on the "Chongqing Model and Socialism with Chinese Characteristics"], *Tansuo*, no. 1 (2012): 179–181.
14. Su Wei, "'Chongqing moshi' shi zenyang bei wudu de" [How the "Chongqing Model" Has Been Misinterpreted], *Guancha zhe wang*, February 2, 2012, https://www.guancha.cn/politics/2012_02_02_64993.shtml.
15. Yang, Fan. "Yong fei yishixingtai fangfa yanjiu Zhongguo moshi yu Chongqing moshi" [Studying the China Model and the Chongqing Model Using Non-Ideological Methods]. January 5, 2012. https://m.aisixiang.com/data/48866.html.
16. Xiao Zhu, "Fayang geming chuantong, laoji dang de zongzhi" [Carrying Forward Revolutionary Traditions and Keeping Firmly in Mind the Party's Principles], *Chongqing ribao*, July 3, 2011.
17. Xiao Zhu, "Ji gefang zhihui."
18. Xiao Zhu, "Gao zhongguo tese shehui zhuyi."
19. Xiao Zhu, "Chongqing hai hui you geng da de fazhan" [Chongqing Will See Even Greater Development], *Chongqing ribao*, October 13, 2011.
20. "'Chang hong' shi jiankang youyi de qunzhong xing wenhua huodong" ["Sing Red" Is a Healthy and Beneficial Mass Cultural Activity], *Chongqing ribao*, July 11, 2011.
21. Yang, "Yong fei yishixingtai."
22. Su, "'Chongqing moshi' shi zenyang bei wudu de."

23. Su Wei. "Yu san pi faguo jizhe tan Chongqing 'chang hong', 'da hei'" [A Talk with Three Groups of French Journalists about Chongqing's "Sing Red" and "Strike Black"], *Wu You Zhi Xiang*, June 21, 2011, https://www.wyzxwk.com/Article/shidai/2011/06/234683.html.
24. Yang, "Yong fei yishixingtai."
25. Shang Yu and He Qingping, "Zhong wai meiti jujiao Chongqing gaige fazhan" [Chinese and Foreign Media Focusing on Chongqing's Reform and Development], *Chongqing ribao*, March 5, 2011; Xiao Zhu, "Jixu tuijin Chongqing kexue fazhan" [Continuing to Advance Chongqing's Scientific Development], *Chongqing ribao*, March 6, 2011; Xiao Zhu, "Minsheng, minzhu, chang hong, da hei" [People's Livelihoods, Democracy, Singing Red, Striking Black], *Chongqing ribao*, May 2, 2011; Xiao Zhu, "Gao zhongguo tese shehui zhuyi."
26. Yang, "Yong fei yishixingtai."
27. Propaganda Department of Chongqing Party Committee (PDCPC), *Chongqing zhuiqiu* [Chongqing's Pursuit] (Chongqing chubanshe, 2012), 209.
28. Lin Le, *China's Conservative Turn: The Origins of Xi Jinping's New Era* (Lynne Rienner Publishers, 2025).
29. Le, *China's Conservative Turn.*
30. Xiao Zhu, "Jiaqiang minzhu fazhi jianshe, tuidong Chongqing kexue fazhan" [Advancing the Construction of Democracy and the Rule of Law, Promoting Chongqing's Scientific Development], *Chongqing ribao*, December 21, 2011.
31. Xiao Zhu, "Jiaqiang minzhu fazhi jianshe"; "Guanyu jiaqiang shehui zhuyi minzhu fazhi youguan wenti de jueding" [Decision on Questions Related to Strengthening Socialist Democracy and the Rule of Law], *Chongqing ribao*, December 26, 2011.
32. Xiao Zhu and Shang Yu, "Jiaqiang minzhu fazhi, gao hao wenhua jianshe, fuwu Chongqing renmin" [Strengthening Democracy and the Rule of Law, Promoting Cultural Development, and Serving the People of Chongqing], *Chongqing ribao*, December 22, 2011.
33. The original text of Deng's quote is that "the nature of socialism is to liberate and develop the productive forces, eliminate exploitation and extreme economic polarization, and finally achieve common prosperity."
34. "Chongqing zhengzai anzhao Zhongyang yaoqiu nuli gaige tansuo fazhan" [Chongqing Is Striving to Reform, Explore, and Develop in Accordance with Central Requirements], *Chongqing ribao*, March 6, 2012.
35. Xiao Zhu and Shang, "Jiaqiang minzhu fazhi."
36. Xiao Zhu, "Jiaqiang minzhu fazhi jianshe."
37. "Chongqing zhengzai anzhao zhongyang yaoqiu."

38. Xiao Zhu and Shang, "Jiaqiang minzhu fazhi."
39. Xiao Zhu and Shang, "Jiaqiang minzhu fazhi."
40. "Chongqing zhengzai anzhao zhongyang yaoqiu."
41. PDCPC, *Chongqing zhuiqiu*, 4.
42. Zhang Xuefeng, Li Peng, and Shang Yu, "Jujiao Chongqing redian gong hua kexue fazhan" [Focusing on Hot Topics in Chongqing and Jointly Discussing Scientific Development], *Chongqing ribao*, March 11, 2012.
43. Xiao Zhu, "Minsheng daoxiang, suo cha gong fu de Chongqing shijian" [The Chongqing Practice Oriented toward People's Livelihoods, Reducing Inequality, and Realizing Common Prosperity], *Chongqing ribao*, March 1, 2012.
44. "Chongqing zhengzai anzhao zhongyang yaoqiu."
45. PDCPC, *Chongqing zhuiqiu*, 141–146.
46. PDCPC, *Chongqing zhuiqiu*, 18.
47. "Guanyu guanche luoshi dang de shi qi jie liu zhong quanhui jingshen jia kuai jianshe wenhua Qing shi de jueding" [Decision on Implementing the Spirit of the Party's Sixth Plenum of the Seventeenth Central Committee and Accelerating the Construction of a Culturally Strong City], *Chongqing ribao*, December 23, 2011.
48. Xiao Zhu and Shang, "Jiaqiang minzhu fazhi."
49. *Lianjie Chongqing—Shi qi da yi lai Chongqing shi tuijin fanfu changlian jianshe de tansuo yu shijian* [Clean Chongqing: Exploration and Practice of Anti-Corruption and Clean Governance in Chongqing since the Seventeenth Party Congress, i.e. *CCEPACCG*] (Hongqi chubanshe, 2011), 7.
50. Shi Zhongquan, "Jixu jianjue geili yufang he chengzhi fubai" [Continuing to Firmly Strengthen the Prevention and Punishment of Corruption], in *Jinian Zhongguo gongchandang chengli 90 zhounian dang jian lilun yu shijian Chongqing yantao hui lunwen ji* [Papers of the Chongqing Symposium on Party Building Theories and Practices in Commemoration of the Chinese Communist Party's 90th Anniversary], vol. 1 (Dangjian duwu chubanshe, 2011), 71–80.
51. I.e., *CCEPACCG.*
52. *CCEPACCG*, 8.
53. *CCEPACCG*, 2–3.
54. PDCPC, *Chongqing zhuiqiu*, 202–205.
55. Xiao Zhu, "Baochi dang de chunjie xing, nuli jianshe 'lianjie Chongqing'" [Maintaining the Party's Purity and Striving to Build "Clean Chongqing"], *Chongqing ribao*, January 18, 2012.
56. "Guanyu tuijin 'lianjie Chongqing' jianshe de jueding" [Decision on Promoting the Construction of "Clean Chongqing"], *Chongqing ribao*, January 18, 2012; Lan Shiqiu and Wang Tian, "'Chang du jiang chuan'

hong bian Chongqing" ["Sing, Read, Say, Spread" Becomes Popular across Chongqing], *Chongqing ribao*, January 23, 2012.

57. PDCPC, *Chongqing zhuiqiu*, Chapter 1 title.
58. PDCPC, *Chongqing zhuiqiu*, 4.
59. PDCPC, *Chongqing zhuiqiu*, 5.
60. Xiao Zhu, "Minsheng daoxiang, suo cha gong fu."
61. CLSGIR, EPOCPC, and CCINR, *Yu lun 2010*, 211, 232.
62. CLSGIR, EPOCPC, and CCINR, *Yu lun 2010*, 233.
63. CLSGIR, EPOCPC, and CCINR, *Yu lun 2010*, 233.
64. CLSGIR, EPOCPC, and CCINR, *Yu lun 2010*, 223.
65. PDCPC, *Chongqing zhuiqiu*, 50.
66. PDCPC, *Chongqing zhuiqiu*, 24.
67. PDCPC, *Chongqing zhuiqiu*, 108.
68. PDCPC, *Chongqing zhuiqiu*, 6.
69. CLSGIR, EPOCPC, and CCINR, *Yu lun 2010*, 206.
70. Xiao Zhu, "Qizhi xianming de jianchi zhenli, tisheng shimin de zhengti suzhi" [Unequivocally Upholding the Truth and Enhancing the Overall Quality of Citizens], *Chongqing ribao*, February 4, 2012.
71. Zhang Xinhua and Song Yingjun, eds., *"Zhongguo daolu" yu "Chongqing shijian"* [The "Chinese Path" and the "Chongqing Practice"] (Chongqing daxue chubanshe, 2011).
72. Yi Xiaoguang, *Pojie Zhongguo fazhan zhi kunju: Chongqing shijian lun* [Cracking the Problem of Development in China: A Thesis on Chongqing's Practices] (Zhongguo jingji chubanshe, 2012).
73. Yi, *Pojie zhongguo fazhan*, 252.
74. Yi, *Pojie zhongguo fazhan*, 1–4.
75. The cited content below comes from the journal-article version of the book. Full text is available from the *Chongqing Xingzheng* Journal (no. 1–3 of 2011).
76. Wu Baotong, Hu Zhaolin, and Jin Xianfeng, "'Shi da xingdong' feng sheng shui qi tongyi zhanxian fenli qianxing—2010 nian Zhongyang tong zhan bu shishi 'shi da xingdong' zongshu" [The "Ten Major Initiatives" Gaining Momentum and the United Front Moving Forward—A Summary of the Implementation of the "Ten Major Initiatives" by the Central United Front Department in 2010], *Zhongguo tongyi zhanxian*, no. 12 (2010): 14–21.
77. Li Xing, "Zhashi tuijin wan ming Yu shang Hongyan gan'en xingdong" [Steadily Advancing the Initiative of Ten Thousand Chongqing Entrepreneurs Expressing Gratitude to Hongyan], *Chongqing ribao*, August 30, 2010.
78. In fact, Chongqing implemented this exploit-the-rich strategy four months before the national campaign began. Together with Hebei,

Chongqing likely took its cue from Shanxi. The Central United Front Department later stated that the national campaign was launched after drawing on the local experiences of these three localities.

79. Dai Juan and Wen Feng, "Xian fu zhe you yiwu daidong dajia gongtong zhifu" [Those Who Become Prosperous First Have a Duty to Help Others Achieve Common Prosperity], *Chongqing ribao*, March 12, 2010.
80. Xiao Zhu, "Min ying qiye 200 yi yuan zhutui 'liang yi' nonghu zeng shou" [Private Enterprises Investing 20 Billion Yuan to Boost Income Growth for Farmers in the "Two Wings" Region], *Chongqing ribao*, April 23, 2010.
81. Yang Bing, "Chongqing zai quan guo shuaixian chutai zhengce fuchi weixing qiye" [Chongqing Took the Lead Nationwide in Introducing Policies to Support Micro-Enterprises], *Chongqing ribao*, June 8, 2010.
82. Chongqing Daily Commentator, "Peiyu weixing qiye, cujin baixing chuangye" [Fostering Micro-Enterprises and Promoting Entrepreneurship among the People], *Chongqing ribao*, June 8, 2010.
83. Yang Bing, "Minsheng shi tiao: rang qunzhong gongxiang gaige fazhan chengguo" [The Ten Policies for People's Livelihoods: Allowing the Public to Share in the Benefits of Reform and Development], *Chongqing ribao*, August 28, 2010.
84. Xiao Zhu, "Ba zan Chongqing jian de geng meihao, rang baixing de shenghuo geng xingfu" [Making Chongqing Better and the People's Lives Happier], *Chongqing ribao*, November 18, 2010.
85. Yang, "Minsheng shi tiao."
86. Theoretical Research Team of the Propaganda Department of Chongqing Party Committee, "Yong gaige chuangxin de siwei ban hao minsheng shi shi" [Addressing People's Livelihoods Issues with a Mindset of Reform and Innovation], *Chongqing ribao*, August 19, 2010.
87. Commission of State-Owned Assets of Chongqing Party Committee, "Changyi shu" [Letter of Advocacy], *Chongqing ribao*, August 8, 2010.
88. Shang and He, "Zhong wai meiti jujiao Chongqing."
89. Shang Yu and He Qingping, "Cujin gongfu de Chongqing lujing" [The Chongqing Path to Promoting Common Prosperity], *Chongqing ribao*, July 25, 2011.
90. Liao Xuemei and Zhang Jie, "Minjian touzi jiang chengwei Zhongguo weilai jingji fazhan de neisheng dongli he yuanquan" [Private Investment Will Become the Endogenous Driving Force and Source for China's Future Economic Development], *Chongqing ribao*, July 6, 2011; He Qingping, "Shi Chongqing chengwei xibu qiye fazhan zui ju huoli de difang" [Making Chongqing the Most Dynamic Place for Business Development in the Western Region], *Chongqing ribao*, July 6, 2011; Xiao Zhu, "Shi lingdao huijian 2011 Zhongguo (Chongqing) min ying

jingji fazhan luntan can hui jiabin" [Municipal Leaders Met with Participants of the 2011 China (Chongqing) Private Economy Development Forum], *Chongqing ribao*, July 7, 2011.

91. Xiao Zhu, "Juji gefang liliang, qixin tuidong 'gong fu'" [Gathering Forces from All Sides and Working Together to Promote "Common Prosperity"], *Chongqing ribao*, August 19, 2011.
92. Tao Weihong and Zhang Xuefeng, "Min ying qiye yao zai kaifang zhong jiakuai fazhan" [Private Enterprises Must Accelerate Development through Opening Up], *Chongqing ribao*, April 11, 2008.
93. Liu Changfa and Zhang Xuefeng, "Min ying qiye zai da xi nan da you ke wei" [Private Enterprises Have Great Potential in the Southwestern Region of China], *Chongqing ribao*, July 14, 2008.
94. Wu Gang, "Chongqing fei gong jingji yao zai gaishan minsheng, 'suo cha gong fu' zhong you geng da zuowei" [Chongqing's Non-State Economy Should Play a Greater Role in Improving People's Livelihoods and in "Narrowing the Gaps and Realizing Common Prosperity"], *Chongqing ribao*, November 17, 2011.
95. "'Shi da xingdong' liang xiang, quanli zhutui 'suo cha gong fu'" [The "Ten Major Initiatives" Launched, Fully Driving the Effort to "Narrow the Gaps and Realize Common Prosperity"], *Chongqing ribao*, November 17, 2011.
96. "Quan shi fei gongyou zhi jingji lingyu zhutui weixing qiye fazhan changyi shu" [Letter of Advocacy from the Non-State Sector of the City for Promoting the Development of Micro-Enterprises], *Chongqing ribao*, November 17, 2011.
97. Shang Yu, "Dali fuchi wei qi fazhan, cujin suo cha gong fu gaishan minsheng" [Vigorously Supporting the Development of Micro-Enterprises and Promoting Efforts to Narrow the Gaps, Realize Common Prosperity, and Improve People's Livelihoods], *Chongqing ribao*, November 25, 2011.
98. Li Xing and Wang Lijuan, "Fei gong renshi yao chengwei 'suo cha gong fu' zhong liu di zhu" [People from the Non-State Sector Must Become the Backbone of the Effort to "Narrow the Gaps and Realize Common Prosperity"], *Chongqing ribao*, December 7, 2011.
99. "Chongqing xuyao geng duo min ying qiyejia touru dao 'suo cha gong fu' de weida shijian zhong" [Chongqing Needs More Private Entrepreneurs to Invest in the Great Practice of "Narrowing the Gaps and Realizing Common Prosperity"], *Chongqing ribao*, January 16, 2012.
100. Wu Gang, "Suo cha gong fu shi min ying qiyejia de xin shiming" [Narrowing the Gaps and Realizing Common Prosperity Is the New Mission for Private Entrepreneurs], *Chongqing ribao*, January 16, 2012.

101. "Min ying qiye suo cha gong fu tong xin tong xing changyi shu" [Letter of Advocacy from Private Entrepreneurs for Working Together to Narrow the Gaps and Realize Common Prosperity], *Chongqing ribao*, January 16, 2012.
102. "Quan li cujin Chongqing min ying jingji xin fazhan" [Making Every Effort to Advance the New Development of Chongqing's Private Economy], *Jinri Chongqing*, no. 6 (2012): 14–15.
103. Zhang Dejiang, "Shenru guanche luoshi kexue fazhan guan wei zai xibu shuaixian shixian quanmian jianshe xiaokang shehui mubiao er fendou" [Thoroughly Implementing the Scientific Outlook on Development and Striving to Achieve the Goal of Building a Moderately Prosperous Society in All Respects in the Western Region], *Chongqing ribao*, June 25, 2012.
104. Propaganda Department of Chongqing Party Committee (PDCPC), *Qian fada jieduan, qian fada diqu: kaiqi "kexue fazhan, fu min xing Yu" xin zheng cheng* [A Phase and an Area of Underdevelopment: Starting a New Journey toward "Scientific Development, Enriching the People and Prospering Chongqing"] (Chongqing chubanshe, 2012).
105. PDCPC, *Qian fada jieduan*, 61.
106. PDCPC, *Qian fada jieduan*, 1.
107. PDCPC, *Qian fada jieduan*, 2.

CHAPTER 6

Rectification and the Masses

The unusual political significance of Bo Xilai's populist mobilization and revival of "mass spontaneity" becomes evident when his political maneuvering is placed within the broader context of the Party's rectification campaign.

Rectification, by definition, targets Party cadres rather than the broader population. Yet the role that the masses should play has long been a closely related and politically sensitive question. Since rectification is designed to deal with "public servants" who have failed the "masters" they are meant to serve, the issues of popular sovereignty and mass participation in politics are inherently embedded in the process. This underlying logic enabled Bo to politicize the concept of mass spontaneity by symbolically and rhetorically linking it to key elements of rectification, such as anti-corruption, popular supervision, and cadre accountability. The Party center subsequently followed Bo's lead and adopted aspects of his local initiative, incorporating the ideal of mass spontaneity into rectification campaigns launched at the central level.

Within the Party's discourse and practice of rectification, the role of the masses has long been a thorny issue, as it raises the question of how to reconcile bottom-up supervision of officials with the need to ensure that the Party's absolute power would not be diluted or challenged. Viewed against this backdrop, Bo's emphasis on the masses' voluntary, bottom-up, pro-regime input into state-led *mobilization* marked an explicit break with the post-Mao pattern of political *demobilization*. Mao-style mass

L. Le, *Revival of Maoism in Reform-Era China*,
https://doi.org/10.1007/978-981-92-4606-9_6

movements had largely disappeared in reform-era China until Bo revived them in Chongqing in the 2010s.

Bo's mass mobilization in Chongqing appeared to take place at a critical turning point in the CCP's high-level power struggle: Bo's political campaign started at the height of elite contention, and by the time it ended, the balance of power had already begun to shift toward the dominance of one faction. In other words, Bo's Chongqing episode was an integral part of a major confrontation and showdown within the central leadership during Hu Jintao's final years. This extraordinary timing is illustrated by mapping a negative correlation between the ups and downs of elite-level power struggles and the *intensity* of Party rectification campaigns in the post-Mao era, as measured by their changing formats and varying scopes. More specifically, a high intensity of rectification usually indicates the presence of a dominant political force within the Party, whereas rectification intensity tends to remain relatively low during periods when elite power struggles are deadlocked. In short, political strength lies behind rectification. Thus, contextualizing the political significance of Bo's Chongqing policies leads to a renewed understanding of reform-era rectification itself. Rectification is not only a political tool for regulating Party cadres; it can also serve as a barometer of elite-level power struggles among Chinese autocrats behind the scenes.

6.1 Rectification in Post-Mao China

When the Party launched rectification campaigns in the reform era, what *political* rationale lay behind such personnel reshuffles and organizational cleansing, beyond the ostensibly *technical* objective of disciplining cadres? What explains the varying formats and scopes in which rectification campaigns have been conducted? Existing studies on reform-era rectification in China remain scarce and underdeveloped.

First, a major obstacle is that researchers sometimes mistakenly conflate rectification with anti-corruption campaigns, on which much scholarly attention has been concentrated. In fact, anti-corruption, although historically a punitive arm of rectification, has been institutionally separated and turned into an independent operation during the reform era. The two should therefore be analytically distinguished rather than treated as interchangeable. Although the Party's anti-corruption efforts undeniably take the form of campaigns,[1] they are not rectification campaigns. Nor is a rectification campaign simply a component of an anti-corruption campaign, or vice versa, in the strict sense in the context of reform-era China. In short, rectification campaigns are not reducible to anti-corruption drives.

A brief historical background helps clarify the relationship between the two. In Mao's time, the intensity of rectification campaigns varied along a coercive–persuasive continuum.[2] In the reform era, however, the coercive and punitive functions of rectification were largely transferred to the Central Discipline and Inspection Commission.[3] This institutional shift aligned with the broader trend toward legalization and bureaucratic rationalization during China's reform process. As documented in several single-case studies,[4] the 1983–87 Rectification appears to represent a transitional case, in which some punitive measures were still carried out within the campaign.[5]

In this light, with its coercive arm separated, the rectification observed in reform-era China shows only the persuasive dimension of the original Maoist model. It is therefore unsurprising that contemporary rectification campaigns are officially described by the Party as "educational activities" (*jiaoyu huodong*). By the same logic, just as anti-corruption campaigns target violations that have reached a "criminal" level, focusing exclusively on them risks overlooking the other part of the story—rectification campaigns, which are intended to correct those still "curable" cadres who have committed relatively "minor" mistakes.[6]

Second, another important reason why post-Mao rectification campaigns have received so little attention is that, from a macro perspective, China studies has long been under the influence of a mythical assumption: state-led campaigns, typically involving top-down political mobilization, are relics of the Maoist past, extinct and forever gone. By contrast, post-Mao China under Party rule is widely portrayed as being characterized by technocracy and rationalization, manifested in the growing bureaucratization of governance and institutionalization of political authority.

This view has been effectively debunked by recent studies showing that the Maoist legacy of mobilization and campaign-style governance,[7] as an enduring feature of Chinese politics, continues to exert significant influence.[8] The reason for this continuity is that campaigns, as a specific governing technique, have a strong affinity with China's hierarchical political system.[9] By leveraging the pressure-transmitting design of a hierarchy-based bureaucratic structure, campaigns enable one-time bursts of resource mobilization and intensified enforcement of directives from above. In this way, campaigns empower the state by allowing it to transcend its routine organizational limits, often in pursuit of short-term and ad hoc policy goals.[10] Yet the effects of such campaigns frequently fall short of their intended outcomes. Not only are any positive achievements difficult to sustain once campaigns end, but policy implementation also remains difficult to monitor because the party-state possesses only limited supervisory vision at the grassroots level of governance. Ironically, this latter limitation is itself one of the key reasons why the Chinese authoritarian regime relies on campaign-style governance in the first place. In a system where power is concentrated at the top and officials are incentivized to follow central mandates rather than remain accountable to ordinary citizens, the patron–client problem created by information asymmetry becomes a structural constant.[11] This also explains why the Chinese party-state deploys campaigns not only for policy implementation but also as a corrective mechanism for addressing cadre misconduct and bureaucratic noncompliance.[12]

However, campaigns differ in their goals, target groups, punitive intensity, and organizational styles.[13] Recent scholarship emphasizing the continuing relevance of campaigns in China has mainly focused on *policy*-oriented cases—for example, the One-Child Policy,[14] and the New Socialist Countryside initiative[15]—rather than on *disciplinary* campaigns primarily aimed at ensuring the compliance of Party cadres.

Third, the analytical depth and validity of the few works that examine reform-era rectification comparatively are seriously limited by their case selection. The main problem is either that anti-corruption campaigns are mistakenly juxtaposed with rectification campaigns for comparison,[16] or that a comprehensive study encompassing all post-Mao rectification cases is curiously absent,[17] even though the universe of cases is actually quite small. In this regard, Chinese-language studies on the same topic by Party theoreticians in China have done a much better job of identifying and including all relevant cases,[18] although their analyses are often produced for propaganda purposes or constrained in both scope and depth by self-censorship.

6.2 Rectification in Comparison

My analysis examines all 11 major rectification campaigns launched by the Party's central leadership in post-Mao China through 2022 (Table 6.1).

The *Intensity* of a reform-era rectification campaign is measured along two dimensions. The first concerns the focus of rectification: whether it is *political* or *practical*. A political focus means that rectification is intended

Table 6.1 Rectification campaigns in post-Mao China

Case	*Time*	*Focus*	*Scope*	*Intensity*
The Rectification 整党	1983–1987	Political	All	1
"Three Talks" 三讲	1998–2000	Political –	Leaders	5
Studying the Three Represents in Rural Areas 农村学习三个代表	2000–2002	Practical +	Grassroots	9
Maintaining the Party's Advanced Nature & Studying the Three Represents 三个代表&保持先进性	(2004–2005) 2005–2006	(Political) Practical +	All	(1) 7
Scientific Outlook on Development 科学发展观	2008–2010	Practical	All	10
Chuang Xian Zheng You (Establishing Advanced Party Organizations & Competing to become Good Party Members) 创先争优	2010–2012	Practical +	Grassroots	9
The Mass Line 群众路线	2013–2014	Political –	All	4
Three Stricts and Three Honests 三严三实	2015	Political	Leaders	2
Two Studies and One Action 两学一做	2016–2017	Political	All	1
Staying True to the Original Aspiration and the Founding Mission 不忘初心, 牢记使命	2019–2020	Political	All	1
Studying the Party History 党史	2021–2022	Political	All	1

to address problems related to party members' ideological commitment and political loyalty. In other words, a political rectification campaign represents an effort at "soul making." By contrast, practical rectification aims at correcting the misbehavior of party cadres.

To be sure, the agenda of any political rectification campaign always includes a practical component, since rectification is officially framed as addressing concrete problems in cadre behavior. The focus of rectification is therefore best conceptualized as varying along a political–practical spectrum. This dimension measures the extent to which a given rectification campaign is politically oriented. Even at the "political" extreme of the spectrum, a case of political rectification does not imply that the practical element has entirely disappeared. Rather, it indicates that the political element constitutes the dominant theme, to which practical tasks are oriented and subordinated.

In this study, the focus of rectification is qualitatively determined by analyzing the Party's official documents that outline the planning of each campaign. The measurement employs a four-level ordinal scale (Table 6.2). "Political–" and "Practical+" refer to intermediate cases along the political–practical spectrum.

Second, what is the *scope* of rectification? In other words, which group of party members does a rectification campaign target? As party documents indicate, a rectification campaign may be launched at three levels: the whole party (*quan dang*), party leaders at or above the county level (*xian chu ji yi shang lingdao ganbu*), and the Party's grassroots organizations and members (*jiceng*). The analytical assumption here is that broader coverage indicates stronger rectification intensity, since large-scale political mobilization requires commensurate political strength. In Table 6.2, the three scopes are denoted as "All," "Leaders," and "Grassroots," respectively.

Based on the information regarding the focus and scope of a rectification campaign, its intensity level can be determined. The coding rule is that each first-order measurement of rectification focus is paired with a second-order measurement of rectification scope. In total, this procedure generates 12 levels of rectification intensity (Table 6.2). Figure 6.1 presents the resulting distribution.

The figure reveals a clear trajectory: during Jiang Zemin's final years and throughout Hu Jintao's decade in power, rectification intensity

Table 6.2 Intensity of rectification campaigns

Intensity level	*Focus*	*Scope*
1	Political	All
2	Political	Leaders
3	Political	Grassroots
4	Political –	All
5	Political –	Leaders
6	Political –	Grassroots
7	Practical +	All
8	Practical +	Leaders
9	Practical +	Grassroots
10	Practical	All
11	Practical	Leaders
12	Practical	Grassroots

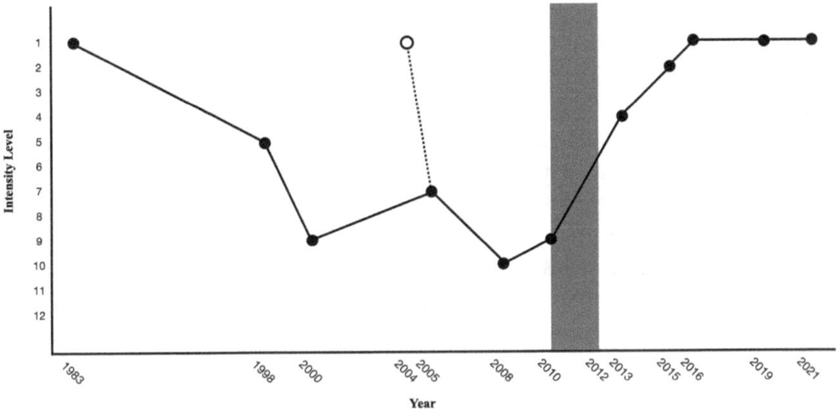

Fig. 6.1 Rectification intensity in post-Mao China, 1983–2022. Note: Each black dot denotes a major rectification campaign. The hollow dot represents the stillborn version of the "Maintaining the Party's Advanced Nature" campaign, initially scheduled for 2004–2005. The dotted line indicates the relegation of this campaign's significance in terms of its intensity level. The gray area highlights the 2010–2012 period when Bo Xilai revived the Maoist mass movement in Chongqing

remained relatively low, except for a near-miss case of high intensity that ultimately reverted to another low-intensity data point. By contrast, both the Deng era and the Xi era show high rectification intensity.

A broad pattern emerges when the rise and fall of rectification intensity are linked to the level of political tension in China's elite politics. Specifically, there appears to be a negative correlation between the two. High rectification intensity corresponds to low political tension, suggesting the presence of a dominant political force within the Party's central leadership capable of imposing order and maintaining a relatively high degree of elite unity. Conversely, low rectification intensity corresponds to high political tension, indicating unresolved struggles among competing political elites. This pattern generally aligns with the conventional view that Hu Jintao was a relatively weak leader throughout his tenure, as well as with the observation that intense left–right contestation characterized Hu's decade in power and Xi's early years, which eventually ended with conservative forces achieving a decisive victory over the reformers.[19]

This pattern suggests that launching a rectification campaign in authoritarian China is never merely a matter of personnel management, but rather a politically motivated and politically empowered undertaking. In other words, a leader and their coalition can launch high-intensity rectification campaigns—those covering broader scopes and incorporating more political agendas—only after they have established political dominance over their rivals. When power is balanced or factions of roughly equal strength are locked in a tug-of-war, rectification efforts tend instead to target lower-level cadres and focus on less political objectives. Because rectification involves disciplining political subordinates, the capacity to "mold" party members inherently signals a higher degree of political control by the ruler, compared with merely compelling them to fulfill policy tasks. Likewise, demonstrating the ability to make rectification compulsory for all party members, rather than limiting it to lower-ranking cadres, appears to be a clear display of political authority.

6.3 Rectification in Historical Context

The 1983–1987 Rectification serves as a typical case of the highest level of rectification intensity, characterized by highly politicized objectives and comprehensive coverage of party cadres. By that time, Deng Xiaoping and his fellow party elders had firmly consolidated their power. They subsequently launched a Mao-style rectification campaign to cleanse the Party of the lingering influence of the Cultural Revolution and to curb the growing advocacy of political liberalism during the early reform period—an ideological current that had caught the Party leadership off guard,[20] particularly during the 1978–79 Democracy Wall movement.

The next major rectification campaign did not emerge until 1998, when China's state-owned enterprise reform was in full swing and corruption within the officialdom had become rampant. The political rhetoric of the "Three Talks" campaign (*san jiang*) carried a distinctly conservative tone. At the time, it raised considerable concern among China's reformers that Jiang Zemin was appealing to conservative forces and positioning himself to reverse the momentum of further reform. In addition to commonly observed misbehavior, cadres were accused of "wavering in their commitment to the ideals of socialism and communism, lacking political sensitivity and political discernment, failing to distinguish right from wrong on major issues of principle, and even following erroneous tendencies."[21] Amid the ongoing left–right contestation over the "direction" of

China's reform—whether it should remain socialist or move toward capitalism (*xing she xing zi*)—Jiang appeared to side with the conservatives. In retrospect, however, the Three Talks campaign can be understood as a strategic hedge implemented by Jiang before introducing his Three Represents theory, which was widely denounced by leftists as a profound assault on the Party's communist orthodoxy.

The 2000 campaign, which combined the study of Jiang's new theory with rectification in rural areas, appeared to be part of Jiang's early effort to promote the Three Represents in a relatively low-profile manner. Probably anticipating strong resistance from the Left, Jiang embedded an ideological agenda within a campaign framed in practical terms: "effectively address the prominent problems facing rural areas."[22] Moreover, advancing the politically controversial proposal of inviting capitalists to join the Party, i.e., "to absorb the advanced elements of the new social strata who meet the qualifications for communist party membership into the Party,"[23] was likely to encounter less opposition among grassroots cadres. In the end, Jiang managed to overcome conservative opposition, at least temporarily. The Three Represents theory was formally enshrined at the Sixteenth Party Congress, when Hu Jintao formally assumed the top position while Jiang and his allies still retained overwhelming political influence.

A rectification campaign dedicated to promoting the Three Represents under the banner of maintaining the Party's "Advanced Nature" was initially scheduled to begin in early 2004. However, the campaign, tasked with proselytizing what was arguably the most progressive reform blueprint since the 1989 Tiananmen protests, failed to materialize and effectively became stillborn, as indicated by the hollow dot in Fig. 6.1. It was postponed for one year, most likely as a result of conservative resistance. When the Advanced Nature campaign finally began in early 2005, Jiang's Three Represents was no longer the central theme, although it was still formally retained in the campaign's official title. Most importantly, the campaign that had originally sought to transform the Party from a Leninist political organization into a post-communist, modernized political party was ultimately downgraded into a cadre education program focused primarily on policy implementation: "remain committed to linking theory with practice and striving for practical results."[24]

Hu Jintao's second five-year term witnessed a rise in leftist influence, although the reformist camp still retained considerable political weight as a counterbalance.[25] The fact that Hu's signature party ideology—Scientific Outlook on Development—was presented primarily in policy rather than political terms was telling, reflecting the conservatives' inability at the time to push their broader ideological agenda. Given the depoliticized nature of Hu Jintao's Scientific Outlook on Development, the rectification campaign launched under its banner in 2008 could have had little more than a practical focus: "[we must] update our developmental outlook, transform our approach to development, resolve major challenges of development, and improve institutions and mechanisms."[26]

However, conservative forces had been steadily gaining strength during Hu's final years. The rectification campaign known as Chuang Xian Zheng You, launched in 2010, succeeded in politicizing the disciplinary operation somewhat by linking grassroots cadres' conduct to the task of "strengthening commitment to socialism with Chinese characteristics."[27] A more explicit revival of the spirit of the Mass Line, however, had to wait until 2013, when Xi Jinping assumed the top office and, more importantly, aligned himself with the conservative camp. Although the 2013 Mass Line rectification campaign ostensibly focused on motivating cadres to serve the people—"Serve the People, Be Practical, and Be Clean" (*wei min, wushi, qinglian*)—its real emphasis lay in political discipline, namely maintaining the Party's "advanced nature" and "purity."[28] In Xi's own words, the campaign enabled cadres to "replenish" themselves with "spiritual calcium" (*jingshen shang bu le gai*).[29]

Around 2015–2016, Xi appeared to have won a decisive battle against the reformist camp.[30] Ambitious political and economic reforms proposed at the Third and Fourth Plenums of the Eighteenth Party Central Committee in 2013 and 2014 were cast into limbo, while *Yan Huang Chun Qiu*, the flagship journal of Chinese liberals, was forcibly shut down in 2016. Since the launch of the "Three Stricts and Three Honests" campaign (*san yan san shi*) in 2015, rectification under Xi has remained highly politicized, testifying to his consolidated power and political dominance within the Party. After more than three decades of reform, the Party's rectification campaigns appeared to be returning to their classic Maoist form. These campaigns were said to address problems such as "wavering ideals and convictions, confusion of faith, and spiritual disorientation," as well as "disregard for the Party's political discipline and political rules, and disloyalty to the Party."[31]

6.4 The Masses

The timing of Bo's political mobilization in Chongqing is politically suggestive, as shown in Fig. 6.1 (the 2010–2012 period marked by the gray area). More significant, however, is the political symbolism of Bo's effort to revive the idea of *mass spontaneity*. To fully grasp this significance, this section briefly reviews how the role of the masses has evolved in the Party's discourse on rectification, drawing on relevant primary sources including party documents, speeches by party leaders, and official Party histories written by party theoreticians.

The role of the masses in rectification highlights a perennial dilemma for party leaders, who must ensure that subordinates remain compliant with directives while also staying clean and competent in local governance. Party leaders understand that without some degree of bottom-up input or popular participation, the principal–agent problem cannot be satisfactorily resolved. Yet allowing the people to play a substantive role in rectification carries its own risks—most notably the possibility that the Party may lose control over the masses and its monopoly of power may be challenged and eroded.

Party leaders had already experienced such backfire during the 1947–1949 rectification campaign. Probably owing to inexperience, the leadership decided to "open the door" (*kaimen*) to the masses—inviting local people to participate in the rectification process targeting grassroots party cadres. According to official Party historiography, in some places local residents effectively took over party organizations and assumed complete control of local affairs. This mistake was later characterized as "removing the stones" (*ban shitou*), referring to "treating party organizations and party members as 'stones' that obstruct the way, and moving them aside,"[32] and as "tail-ism" (*weiba zhuyi*), meaning "doing whatever the masses demand."[33] What truly alarmed the Party was that party organizations were stripped of their authority over the masses. The resulting problems were described as "placing the Poor Peasant Associations above the proletarian vanguard, blurring the principled boundary between the proletarian vanguard and the peasantry, and diminishing—or even abolishing—the Party's leading role."[34] Terrified by these developments, the party leadership quickly moved to close the "door."

However, at least rhetorically, the Party must continue to declare that the "door" remains open, since it claims to be a party of the people. The trick lies in ensuring that the "door" is opened in the "correct" way—i.e., with the Party maintaining absolute control throughout the rectification process. Accordingly, the officially endorsed definition of open-door rectification assigns the masses only an auxiliary role. To "open wide the door of rectification" means "letting the masses know who the communist party members are, inviting them to attend rectification meetings, and conducting rectification with the assistance of the masses."[35] In practice, however, what the masses can substantively do is largely limited to providing information to party committees: "the masses have the full right to speak and offer suggestions at party branch meetings."[36] Party leaders are instructed to "mobilize the enthusiasm of the masses and encourage them to expose shortcomings and mistakes in our work and to offer suggestions for its improvement."[37] At the same time, the Party's ultimate authority cannot be shared: "all issues arising in rectification must be discussed and decided by the relevant Party organizations; the erroneous practice of allowing non-party masses to decide intra-party matters must be firmly opposed."[38] Any form of popular participation must therefore remain under party leadership. In more euphemistic terms, the Party describes this arrangement as "an organic combination between mobilizing the masses and strengthening Party leadership," emphasizing that the Mass Line must be distinguished from the so-called "mass-led rectification" (*qunzhong zheng dang*) that once occurred in the Party's history.[39] Indeed, the claim that the masses participate in rectification "as masters of the country," while simultaneously acting "under the leadership of the Party" and following "the requirements, guidelines, and principles set by the Party," appears fundamentally contradictory and preposterous.[40]

Mao's Cultural Revolution can be viewed as the most consequential open-door rectification campaign, one that left an enormous impact on China's political trajectory. Under the banner of Mao's theory of Continuous Revolution, "rebels" from the masses were mobilized and given a free hand to purge the politically unreliable and cleanse the corrupt officialdom. This episode of mass spontaneity left a deep traumatic imprint on many high-ranking party officials, who were first victimized during the mass struggles and later returned to power in the post-Mao era.

Thus, rectification in the reform era left little room for genuine mass participation. Although the spirit of the Mass Line was frequently invoked, the "open door" was never truly opened wide. As noted earlier, the masses were treated primarily as a source of information, while party committees retained exclusive authority over decision-making. Indeed, lessons drawn from the Cultural Revolution were often invoked to reinforce this understanding. In summarizing the 1983–1987 Rectification, Bo Yibo emphasized that the campaign had succeeded in avoiding the mistake of abusing "mass movements."[41] Similarly, when commenting on the Three Talks campaign, Hu Jintao cautioned that "open-door education" meant anything but "big democracy" or "carrying out the revolution with the party committees kicked aside" (*ti kai dang wei nao geming*). Hu further declared that the Three Talks campaign had pioneered a new path for rectification, characterized by "fully mobilizing and relying on the masses without resorting to mass movements, while ensuring that the masses participate actively and effectively under the leadership of party organizations."[42]

Absent downward accountability and meaningful bottom-up input, the effectiveness of reform-era rectification campaigns remains open to question. Although systematic assessments are lacking, official narratives themselves indicate that these rectification efforts were often far from effective. The problems are manifold. First, owing to the persistent issue of information asymmetry, rectification campaigns frequently devolve into mere formality—"going through the motions" (*zou guo chang*). Second, given their limited time and energy, reform-era cadres often had to choose between prioritizing political tasks and developmental projects. Yet it was the latter on which their prospects for political promotion largely depended. This tension further incentivized cadres to go through the motions. It is therefore unsurprising that official documents frequently stipulated that rectification efforts should be "combined with the promotion of current work."

Third, the element of "terror"—i.e., the coercive and punitive dimension of Mao-era rectification—was removed from reform-era campaigns. As a result, cadres appeared to face little real pressure to take rectification seriously. The 1983–1987 Rectification established a clear bottom line: "[we must] guard against repeating the past mistakes of cruel struggle and merciless blows," and "under no circumstances should factionalism be stirred up under the pretext of rectification; nor should factional labels be used to persecute others, nor should false accusations or retaliatory reprisals be allowed."[43] Instead, "positive education and self-education" became the guiding principle. Cadres were encouraged to activate their "inner motivations" for self-improvement and self-cultivation.[44] In addition to self-reflection, a typical instrument of this moral education was the promotion of exemplary models (*dianxing*) for others to emulate.[45]

Finally, party leaders have long recognized that the effects of campaign-style rectification, if any, rarely endure once the campaign ends. In concluding the Three Talks campaign, Hu Jintao acknowledged that "this intensive education can only achieve a limited number of goals within a limited period of time and cannot resolve all problems."[46] Later, Xi Jinping complained about the phenomenon that "the rain only moistens the surface of the ground, and the campaign passes like a gust of wind" (*yu guo dipi shi, huodong yi zhen feng*).[47]

Faced with these systemic flaws, party leaders have continually explored new ways in which top-down measures might fix these problems without opening space for downward accountability. First, the most common and readily available tactic was to strengthen intra-Party supervision—for example, by establishing and dispatching "supervision and guidance teams" (*du dao zu*) and "inspection teams" (*xunhui jiancha zu*).

A second measure was to place greater pressure on party leaders at all levels. In practice, this took the form of a responsibility system. According to official accounts, this mechanism is known as the "leadership responsibility system" (*lingdao zeren zhi*). Under this arrangement, leaders at each level are expected to supervise their subordinates and are held accountable for their misconduct—i.e., "leaders at one level oversee and guide those at the next level down" (*yi ji zhua yi ji*).

Third, it was once proposed, particularly during the Three Talks campaign, that performance in rectification should be incorporated into the evaluation criteria for cadre promotion. Fourth, given that campaign-style rectification could produce at best only short-term results, it seemed natural, if somewhat wishful, to assume that "institutionalizing" the practices introduced during rectification might generate longer-lasting effects. Various terms were used to describe such efforts at routinization, including "regularization" (*jingchang hua*), "institutionalization" (*zhidu hua*), "normalization" (*changtai hua*), and the pursuit of "long-term effectiveness" (*chang xiao hua*). In the case of rectification under Xi Jinping, it was once explicitly claimed that the campaign "is not a campaign." Rather, it was described as "an exploratory effort to integrate thematic education into the routine study and education of leading cadres," and therefore should not be carried out using "the campaign-style approach."[48]

Fifth, new channels were established for ordinary citizens to express their approval or disapproval of local governance. Officially, this mechanism was referred to as a "system of mass supervision and evaluation."[49] Specific techniques included "evaluation by mass representatives" and "random-sample surveys among the masses." Ultimately, however, the authority to reward or punish cadres remained firmly in the hands of party leaders.

Finally, if the masses cannot be granted any substantive role in participation or bottom-up input, party leaders reasoned that sending cadres down to the grassroots and requiring them to remain close to the people might improve local governance. During the Three Talks rectification campaign, cadres were dispatched to "villages that are poor and backward, riddled with conflicts and mass grievances," and were instructed to "eat, live, and work with the masses." This anticipated the Mass Line practices that Bo Xilai would later adopt in Chongqing.[50] Whereas it is usually the masses who seek assistance ***upward*** from state officials (***shang fang***), under this arrangement party cadres were expected to take the initiative to go ***downward*** (***xia fang***) and deliver services to the people.[51]

However, it is doubtful whether these measures could be effective at all. The crux of the matter is that, despite the adoption of various new mechanisms, one fundamental feature has remained unchanged: the Party still ultimately supervises itself. Party leaders are well aware of this. Yet merely asking cadres to "unify upward accountability to superiors with downward accountability to the masses" does not help make such accountability materialized. Likewise, simply refraining from calling a rectification campaign a "campaign" does not make it genuinely institutionalized.

6.5 Bo's Overstep

In sum, the unusual political significance of Bo's political program lies in its invocation of "mass spontaneity." Owing to the Party's persistent vigilance against any uncontrolled bottom-up mass agency, popular participation during the reform era has consistently been conceptualized as a passive response to the Party's top-down guidance. Against this backdrop, an ostensibly non-antagonistic call for mass spontaneity—namely, allowing and encouraging the masses once again to exercise their agency in rectification campaigns—carried unusually strong political symbolism, as it effectively broke with the Party's long-standing routine of political demobilization. The argument is illustrated in Fig. 6.2, in which the shaded area represents the new trend associated with Bo.

Lurking behind the open advocacy of the Mass Line was the populist face of Maoism, which pitted the proletarian masses against revisionist bureaucrats said to be "walking the capitalist road." By invoking this idea,

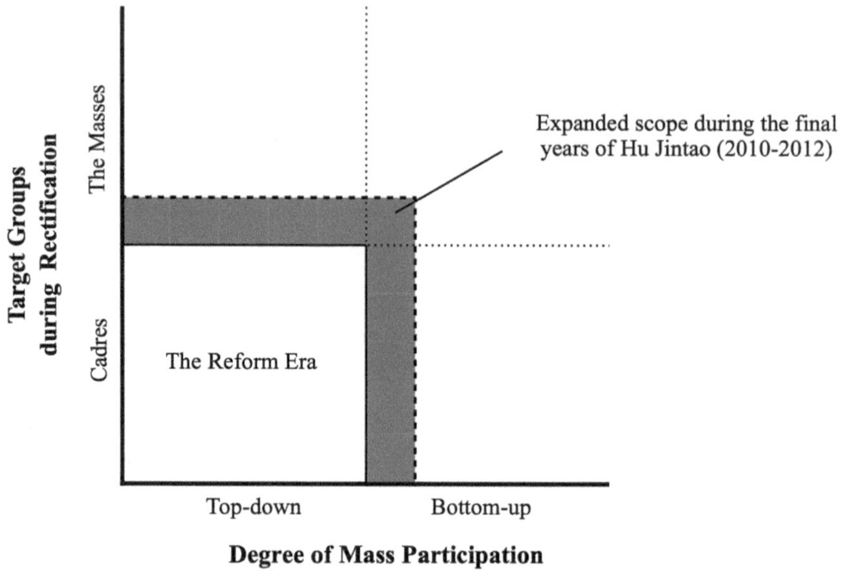

Fig. 6.2 Expanded scope of rectification under Bo

Chinese conservatives effectively issued a political manifesto without stating it explicitly: true communists had a responsibility to struggle against the false ones in defense of the people's interests, i.e., interests that had been gravely harmed, not least by the capitalist path of development.

Notes

1. Melanie Manion, *Corruption by Design: Building Clean Government in Mainland China and Hong Kong* (Harvard University Press, 2004).
2. Frederick C. Teiwes, *Politics and Purges in China: Rectification and the Decline of Party Norms, 1950–1965*, 2nd ed. (M. E. Sharpe, 1993).
3. Ling Li, "The Rise of the Discipline and Inspection Commission, 1927–2012: Anticorruption Investigation and Decision-Making in the Chinese Communist Party," *Modern China* 42, no. 5 (2016): 447–482, https://doi.org/10.1177/0097700416631047; Ling Li, "Politics of Anticorruption in China: Paradigm Change of the Party's Disciplinary Regime, 2012–2017," *Journal of Contemporary China* 28, no. 115 (2019): 47–63, https://doi.org/10.1080/10670564.2018.1497911; Xuezhi Guo, "Controlling Corruption in the Party: China's Central

Discipline Inspection Commission," *The China Quarterly* 219 (2014): 597–624, https://doi.org/10.1017/S0305741014000770.

4. Bruce J. Dickson, "Conflict and Non-Compliance in Chinese Politics: Party Rectification, 1983–1987," *Pacific Affairs* 63, no. 2 (1990): 170–190; Alastair I. Johnston, "Party Rectification in the People's Liberation Army, 1983–1987," *The China Quarterly* 112 (1987): 591–630; Lowell Dittmer, "Party Rectification in Post-Mao China," in *Mainland China: Politics, Economics, and Reform*, ed. Yu-Ming Shaw (Westview Press, 1986), 103–120.
5. See "Zhonggong zhongyang guanyu zheng dang de jueding" [Decision of the Chinese Communist Party Central Committee on Party Rectification], October 11, 1983, in *Di san qi zheng dang zhongyao wenjian yu ziliao* [Important Documents and Materials on the Third Phase of Party Rectification, i.e. *IDMTPPR*] (Renmin chubanshe, 1988), 1–19.
6. Corruption is a broad concept in the Chinese context that may refer to a wide range of misbehaviors in the officialdom. See Xiaobo Lü, *Cadres and Corruption: The Organization Involution of the Chinese Communist Party* (Stanford University Press, 2000).
7. Elizabeth J. Perry, "Challenging the Mandate of Heaven: Popular Protest in Modern China," *Critical Asian Studies* 33, no. 2 (2001): 163–180, https://doi.org/10.1080/14672710122544; Elizabeth J. Perry, "Studying Chinese Politics: Farewell to Revolution?" *The China Journal*, no. 57 (2007): 1–22; Elizabeth J. Perry, "From Mass Campaigns to Managed Campaigns: 'Constructing a New Socialist Countryside,'"" in *Mao's Invisible Hand: The Political Foundations of Adaptive Governance in China*, ed. Sebastian Heilmann and Elizabeth J. Perry (Harvard University Press, 2011), 30–61; Kristen E. Looney, *Mobilizing for Development: The Modernization of Rural East Asia* (Cornell University Press, 2020); Tyrene White, "Postrevolutionary Mobilization in China: The One-Child Policy Reconsidered," *World Politics* 43, no. 1 (1990): 53–76; Tyrene White, *China's Longest Campaign: Birth Planning in the People's Republic, 1949–2005* (Cornell University Press, 2006).
8. Relatedly, it is emphasized that top-down state-led political mobilization in China should be analyzed as a distinct phenomenon, which is to be distinguished from the Western social movement from a contentious politics perspective. See Grzegorz Ekiert and Elizabeth J. Perry, "State-Mobilized Movements: A Research Agenda," in *Ruling by Other Means: State-Mobilized Movements*, ed. Grzegorz Ekiert, Elizabeth J. Perry, and Yan Xiaojun (Cambridge University Press, 2020), 1–23. Some early work on China's mass movement adopted the latter framework. See Wen-hui Tsai, "Mass Mobilization Campaigns in Mao's China," *American Journal of Chinese Studies* 6, no. 1 (1999): 21–48.

9. Xueguang Zhou, "Yundong xing zhili jizhi: Zhongguo guojia zhili de zhidu luoji zai sikao" [Campaign-Style Governance Mechanism: Rethinking the Institutional Logic of China's National Governance], *Kaifang shidai*, no. 9 (2012): 105–125; Xueguang Zhou, *Zhongguo guojia zhili de zhidu luoji: yi ge zuzhi xue yanjiu* [The Institutional Logic of China's National Governance: An Organizational Analysis] (Sanlian shudian, 2017); White, *China's Longest Campaign*.
10. John James Kennedy and Dan Chen, "State Capacity and Cadre Mobilization in China: The Elasticity of Policy Implementation," *Journal of Contemporary China* 27, no. 111 (2018): 393–405, https://doi.org/10.1080/10670564.2018.1410971; Julia C. Strauss, State Formation in China and Taiwan: Bureaucracy, Campaign, and Performance (Cambridge University Press, 2020); Elizabeth J. Perry, "Work Team," in *Afterlives of Chinese Communism: Political Concepts from Mao to Xi*, ed. Christian Sorace, Ivan Franceschini, and Nicholas Loubere (Australian National University Press and Verso, 2019), 325–330; White, "Postrevolutionary Mobilization."
11. Philip Kuhn, *Soulstealer: The Chinese Sorcery Scare of 1768* (Harvard University Press, 1990); Carl Minzner, *End of an Era: How China's Authoritarian Revival Is Undermining Its Rise* (Oxford University Press, 2018).
12. Harry Harding, *Organizing China: The Problem of Bureaucracy, 1949–1976* (Stanford University Press, 1981); Teiwes, *Politics and Purges*.
13. Gordon Bennett, *Yundong: Mass Movement in Chinese Communist Leadership* (Center for Chinese Studies, University of California, 1976); Charles P. Cell, *Revolution at Work: Mobilization Campaigns in China* (Academic Press, 1977); Julia C. Strauss, "Morality, Coercion and State Building by Campaign in the Early PRC: Regime Consolidation and After, 1949–1956," *The China Quarterly* 188 (2006): 891–912, https://doi.org/10.1017/S0305741006000488; Feng Shizheng, "Zhongguo guojia yundong de xingcheng yu bianyi: ji yu zhengti de zhengti xing jieshi" [The Formation and Variation of China's National Movements: A Holistic Explanation Based on Political Regime], *Kaifang shidai*, no. 1 (2011): 73–97.
14. White, *China's Longest Campaign*.
15. Looney, *Mobilizing for Development*.
16. Andrew Mertha, "'Stressing Out': Cadre Calibration and Affective Proximity to the CCP in Reform-Era China," *The China Quarterly* 229 (2017): 64–85, https://doi.org/10.1017/S0305741017000042; Christopher Carothers, *Corruption Control in Authoritarian Regimes: Lessons from East Asia* (Cambridge University Press, 2022).

17. Zhifan Luo, "Discipline the Party: From Rectification Campaigns to Intra-Party Educational Activities in China," *China: An International Journal* 19, no. 4 (2021): 52–74, https://doi.org/10.1353/chn.2021.0041.
18. For example, see Yuan Qian, "Zhongguo gongchandang dang nei jizhong jiaoyu de lishi jincheng, jiben tezheng he dangdai qishi" [The Historical Evolution, Fundamental Characteristics, and Contemporary Implications of the Chinese Communist Party's Internal Education Campaigns], *Qiushi*, no. 6 (2021): 4–13.
19. Lin Le, "Chinese Politics since Hu Jintao and the Origin of Xi Jinping's Strongman Rule: A New Hypothesis," *Texas National Security Review* 6, no. 4 (2023): 37–78, https://doi.org/10.26153/tsw/48844; Lin Le, *China's Conservative Turn: The Origins of Xi Jinping's New Era* (Lynne Rienner Publishers, 2025).
20. "Zhonggong zhongyang guanyu zheng dang de jueding," 1–19.
21. "Zhonggong zhongyang guanyu zai xian ji yi shang dang zheng lingdao banzi, lingdao ganbu zhong shenru kaizhan yi 'jiang xuexi, jiang zhengzhi, jiang zhengqi' wei zhuyao neirong de dangxing dangfeng jiaoyu de yijian" [Opinions of the Central Committee of the Chinese Communist Party on Thoroughly Carrying Out Party Spirit and Party Conduct Education among Leadership Groups and Leading Cadres at the County Level and Above, Focusing on "Talk about Learning, Talk about Politics, and Talk about Integrity"], November 21, 1998, in *Shi wu da yi lai zhongyao wenxian xuan bian* [Selected Important Documents since the Fifteenth Party Congress, i.e. *SID15PC*], vol. 2 (Zhongyang wenxian chubanshe, 2011), 548–555.
22. "Zhonggong zhongyang bangong ting guanyu zai nongcun kaizhan 'san ge daibiao' zhongyao sixiang xuexi jiaoyu huodong de yijian" [Opinions of the General Office of the Central Committee of the Chinese Communist Party on Launching Educational Campaigns in Rural Areas to Study the Important Thought of the "Three Represents"]. November 30, 2000, in *SID15PC*, vol. 2, 580–590.
23. Hu Jintao, "Quanmian guanche 'san ge daibiao' zhongyao sixiang, jin yi bu jiaqiang he gaijin nongcun jiceng zuzhi jianshe" [Fully Implementing the Important Thought of the "Three Represents" and Further Strengthening and Improving the Construction of Grassroots Organizations in Rural Areas], June 24, 2002, in *SID15PC*, vol. 3, 601–620.
24. "Zhonggong zhongyang guanyu zai quan dang kaizhan yi shijian 'san ge daibiao' zhongyao sixiang wei zhuyao neirong de baochi gongchandang yuan xianjin xing jiaoyu huodong de yijian" [Opinions of the Central Committee of the Chinese Communist Party on Carrying Out the Educational Campaign to Maintain the Advanced Nature of Communist

Party Members with the Important Thought of the "Three Represents" as the Main Content], November 7, 2004, in *Shi liu da yi lai zhongyao wenxian xuan bian* [Selected Important Documents since the Sixteenth Party Congress, i.e. *SID16PC*], vol. 2 (Zhongyang wenxian chubanshe, 2011), 413–423.

25. Le, "Chinese Politics since Hu Jintao"; Le, *China's Conservative Turn.*
26. "Zhonggong zhongyang guanyu zai quan dang kaizhan shenru xuexi shijian kexue fazhan guan huodong de yijian" [Opinions of the Central Committee of the Chinese Communist Party on Carrying Out In-Depth Study and Practice of the Scientific Outlook on Development across the Entire Party], September 14, 2008, in *Shi qi da yi lai zhongyao wenxian xuan bian* [Selected Important Documents since the Seventeenth Party Congress, i.e. *SID17PC*], vol. 1 (Zhongyang wenxian chubanshe, 2009), 554–565.
27. Xi Jinping, "Shizhong jianchi he chongfen fahui dang de dute youshi" [Always Upholding and Fully Leveraging the Party's Unique Advantages], June 28, 2012, in *SID17PC*, vol. 3, 1017–1026.
28. "Zhonggong zhongyang guanyu zai quan dang shenru kaizhan dang de qunzhong luxian jiaoyu shijian huodong de yijian" [Opinions of the Central Committee of the Chinese Communist Party on Carrying Out the Party's Mass Line Education and Practice Campaign across the Entire Party], May 9, 2013, in *Shi ba da yi lai zhongyao wenxian xuan bian* [Selected Important Documents since the Eighteenth Party Congress, i.e. *SID18PC*], vol. 1 (Zhongyang wenxian chubanshe, 2014), 283–292.
29. Xi Jinping, "Zai dang de qunzhong luxian jiaoyu shijian huodong zongjie dahui shang de jianghua" [Speech at the Concluding Conference on the Party's Mass Line Education and Practice Campaign], October 8, 2014, in *SID18PC*, vol. 2, 85–102.
30. Le, "Chinese Politics since Hu Jintao"; Le, *China's Conservative Turn.*
31. "Zhonggong zhongyang bangong ting yinfa 'guanyu zai xian chu ji yishang lingdao ganbu zhong kaizhan" san yan san shi "zhuanti jiaoyu fangan' de tongzhi" [Notice from the General Office of the Central Committee of the Chinese Communist Party on Issuing the Plan for Conducting Special Education on the "Three Stricts and Three Earnests" among Leading Cadres at the County and Department Level and Above]. April 10, 2015, in *SID18PC*, vol. 2, 466–472.
32. Li Junru, ed., *Zhongguo gongchandang jianshe shi* [The History of Chinese Communist Party Building], vol. 1 (Haixia chuban faxing jituan and Fujian renmin chubanshe, 2011), 170–172.
33. Nankai University Research and Teaching Office for Marxism and Leninism (NURTOML) and Research and Teaching Team for the Party History (RTTPH), *Zhongguo gongchandang de zheng dang yu zheng feng*

[Rectification of the Chinese Communist Party] (Shandong renmin chubanshe, 1984), 66.
34. Wang Yifan and Chen Mingxian, *Zhongguo gongchandang li ci zheng dang zheng feng* [Previous Rectification Campaigns of the Chinese Communist Party] (Heilongjiang renmin chubanshe, 1985), 91.
35. Wang and Chen, *Zhongguo gongchandang*, 88–89.
36. NURTOML and RTTPH, *Zhongguo gongchandang*, 61.
37. Wang and Chen, *Zhongguo gongchandang*, 13–14.
38. Wang and Chen, *Zhongguo gongchandang*, 13–14.
39. Wang and Chen, *Zhongguo gongchandang*, 13–14.
40. NURTOML and RTTPH, *Zhongguo gongchandang*, 64.
41. Bo Yibo, "Guanyu zheng dang de jiben zongjie he jin yi bu jiaqiang dang de jianshe" [A Basic Summary of Party Rectification and Further Strengthening of Party Building], May 26, 1987, in *IDMTPPR*, 20–41.
42. Hu Jintao, "Zongjie he yunyong 'san jiang' jiaoyu jingyan, nuli kaichuang dang jian gongzuo xin jumian" [Summarizing and Applying the Educational Experience of the "Three Talks" and Striving to Open a New Phase in Party-Building Work], December 16, 2000, in *SID15PC*, vol. 2, 601–619.
43. "Zhonggong zhongyang guanyu zheng dang de jueding," 1–19.
44. Hu, "Quanmian guanche 'san ge daibiao,'" 601–620.
45. "Zhonggong zhongyang guanyu zai xian ji yi shang dang zheng lingdao banzi," 548–555.
46. Hu, "Zongjie he yunyong 'san jiang'," 601–619.
47. Xi, "Zai dang de qunzhong luxian," 85–102.
48. Liu Yunshan, "Zai 'san yan san shi' zhuanti jiaoyu gongzuo zuotanhui shang de jianghua" [Speech at the Symposium on the "Three Stricts and Three Earnests" Special Education Campaign], April 21, 2015, in *SID18PC*, vol. 2, 473–484.
49. "Zhonggong zhongyang guanyu zai quan dang kaizhan yi shijian," 413–423.
50. Hu, "Zongjie he yunyong 'san jiang'," 601–619.
51. Hu, "Quanmian guanche 'san ge daibiao,'" 601–620.

CHAPTER 7

The Party–People Relationship

Bo's strategic use of Maoist campaigns, while effective in signaling his political alignment and conveying political messages, came with significant costs. Those who were mobilized could drift away and exceed the intentions of the mobilizer. Bo's embrace of orthodox Maoism and political conservatism may have been purely instrumental in advancing his political ambitions. Yet many neo-Maoists in China saw it as a sign of his ideological commitment to reviving a radical version of Maoism that advocated Mao-style proletarian "big democracy." This is a long shadow cast by Mao's Proletarian Cultural Revolution, during which his rhetoric of "democracy" and the dictum that "it is right to rebel" enlightened many grassroots revolutionary "rebels" by exposing them to new notions of political participation and political rights.

Mobilizing the masses in authoritarian politics often confronts autocratic elites with the question of how to put awakened democratic aspiration back into dormancy once they no longer have use for it. In an era in which popular sovereignty occupies the moral high ground, one fundamental challenge for authoritarian rulers is how to manage the tension between the de facto "ruler-above-the-subject" relationship and the de jure "people-above-the-state" rhetorical ideal. It is a thorny issue how to maintain authoritarian domination over the ruled while persuading them that they truly possess political sovereignty. In communist China, the Party engineered a chimerical idea of party–people "oneness" to tackle

L. Le, *Revival of Maoism in Reform-Era China*,
https://doi.org/10.1007/978-981-92-4606-9_7

this problem. However, this oneness broke down on several occasions when Chinese autocrats chose to mobilize the masses for political purposes.

By analyzing the party–people relationship, this chapter aims to provide a theoretical perspective for understanding the self-undermining dynamics of Bo's mass mobilization and the backlash it generated.

Sections 7.1, 7.2, and 7.3 describe the party–people relationship in Chinese politics. It comprises three conceptual scenarios: the ruler above the subject, the people above the state, and a peculiar effort to merge the Party with the Chinese people. The conception of party–people relationship presented here draws on multiple Chinese-language sources, including articles from the Chinese liberals' flagship journal *Yan Huang Chun Qiu*,[1] official propaganda materials that elaborate on the Mass Line,[2] and on Jiang Zemin's Three Represents theory.[3] The texts selected are "representative" in the sense that they are not only records of politics but also part of the very politics they document. For this reason, although limited in number, these texts provide sufficient inferential leverage. They serve as the primary sources for establishing the empirical basis of theoretical analysis, even though the narrative they construct does not constitute a comprehensive intellectual history. In other words, the narrative is meant to provide a stylized sketch of the factual bases on which the three conceptual scenarios of the party–people relationship stand, rather than a full and nuanced understanding as to how these ideas evolve over time.

Section 7.4 provides an illustration of the "oneness" that broke down in two historical cases—Mao's Cultural Revolution and the grassroots Neo-Maoist movement that sought to hijack Bo Xilai's Maoist agenda. The Cultural Revolution case relies solely on secondary sources.[4] The Neo-Maoist story builds on various primary sources, including the texts published by the radical wing of the neo-Maoist,[5] by the moderate neo-Maoists who held four symposiums on Bo Xilai and the Chongqing Model,[6] by Zhang Hongliang who was a neo-Maoist opinion leader,[7] and by others who contributed to the discourse.[8]

Section 7.5 concludes with a short comment that points to the hegemonic idea of popular sovereignty as the ideological origin of the dilemma inherent in the party–people relationship for autocratic leaders.

7.1 The Ruler Above the Subject

The political hierarchy of imperial China rested on the principle that the ruler stood naturally above the people, as emperors were divinely sanctioned to govern. This order was structured through *li*, a system of ethical norms that vested supreme political sovereignty in the monarch. Both officials and commoners were required to demonstrate unconditional subservience and loyalty and could not legitimately oppose the emperor's will. This *chen min* (subject) mindset required both officials and commoners to remain unquestioningly loyal, even when the emperor committed injustice. As an old saying put it, "When the emperor orders an official to die, he must die." While the ruler was free to act at will, the subjects possessed only obligations and no rights vis-à-vis the sovereign.

Because the emperor monopolized political power, monarchical authority was the sole source of state authority; the power exercised by aristocrats and officials derived entirely from imperial delegation. The bureaucratic system functioned as an extension of the emperor's rule. The ruler–official relationship was therefore one of master and servants, in which the former dominated the latter at will. At the bottom of this hierarchy stood the commoners, whose lives and fates were subject to the authority of officials and, ultimately, the emperor.

In this imperial political system, which rested on a radically asymmetrical distribution of power, there was no institutionalized accountability. Under the Mandate of Heaven (*tian ming*), the ruler was expected to bring justice, stability, and prosperity to the realm, like a shepherd caring for his flock. In cases where a bad emperor abused his power, the commoners were seen as having a right to revolt, violently if necessary. A successful rebellion that resulted in the enthronement of a new ruler was interpreted as ex post facto evidence that the unworthy predecessor had lost the divine mandate. A new dynastic cycle would then begin, with the ruler remaining on the throne until he failed to fulfill his duties as a divinely sanctioned trustee.

Given the ever-present possibility of mass uprisings, imperial rulers in China were constantly reminded of the paramount importance of securing the commoners' well-being. The ruler–people relationship was often likened to that between water and a boat: "Water can carry the boat, but it can also overturn it." Yet the emperor's recognition of the popular basis of regime security by no means implied that the commoners were thereby elevated in status or granted political rights vis-à-vis the ruler. Mencius's dictum that "the people are the most important, the state the second, and the ruler the least" is often adduced as evidence that people-centeredness (*min ben*) lay at the core of Chinese political culture. Indeed, the Chinese intellectual Hu Shih once remarked that the Mencian idea came close to a notion of popular sovereignty. Yet a distinction must be drawn between political ideal and political reality. On the one hand, imperial rulers foregrounded the idea of people-centeredness to legitimize their rule and to keep themselves vigilant. On the other hand, they simultaneously reinforced a hierarchical political imagination. In terms of institutional design, the idea of people-centeredness was never materialized in the political order of imperial China, and neither the ruler nor state officials were accountable to their subjects.

7.2 The People Above the State

Just as authoritarian rule rests on a hierarchical order in which the ruler presides over the people, Chinese liberals have long advocated a reversal of this relationship—one in which sovereignty belongs to the people as the masters (*zhuren*), and state leaders and officials are merely "public servants" (*gongpu*).

First, according to Chinese liberal thinkers, political reform must begin with a transformation at the level of political cognition and values. A new political imagination must be cultivated through which the people come to understand the meaning of popular sovereignty, namely, not only their rights vis-à-vis state officials but also their reciprocal responsibilities to fellow citizens. Only then can they resist autocratic rulers who enrich themselves through the subjugation of their subjects. The people must learn to defend their own rights actively rather than passively awaiting protection from wise and benevolent rulers. Instead of the state making decisions on behalf of the people (*wei min zuo zhu*), it should follow the will of the people (*you min zuo zhu*).

Second, state power must be constrained so that the people stand above public officials and can hold them meaningfully accountable. In the imperial order, the ruler was checked primarily by a moral code grounded in the presumption of the innate goodness of human nature. The emperor was exhorted to govern benevolently, and failure to do so would trigger the corrective mechanism: the Mandate of Heaven would be withdrawn, as manifested in popular rebellion. In this sense, the ruler was held accountable only ex post facto. By contrast, Chinese liberals insist on the establishment of the rule of law (*fazhi*), under which political power cannot be "privatized" as an instrument of domination, but must instead be exercised within the constraints of law and the constitution.

In practice, a major shift occurred in how Chinese reformers approached political reform under Party rule after 1989.[9] Initially, they sought to constrain state power *through* democratization. This bottom-up strategy assumed that once popular power was activated through expanded political participation and relaxed information control, ordinary citizens would become the ultimate agents of change in overcoming entrenched vested interests. Later, confronted with strong opposition from conservative forces, reformers came to believe that the only viable path to political reform was to constrain power *prior to* democratization, namely, through the creation of constitutional limits. This top-down approach was later crystallized in liberal advocacy for "constitutionalism" (*xian zheng*), which emerged in the final years of Hu Jintao's tenure and extended into the early period of Xi Jinping's rule.

At a time when an explicit denial of democracy's feasibility in China was no longer tenable in an age that treated popular sovereignty and democracy as the ultimate sources of political legitimacy, the Party responded to liberal calls for establishing Western-style democratic institutions in two ways. First, it contended that democracy has no fixed institutional form and that China's unique national conditions required a democratic system "with Chinese characteristics," rather than a mechanical transplantation of Western models. Second, the Party maintained that Western-style democracy is inherently capitalist and therefore incompatible with a socialist polity. An uncritical adoption of foreign practices would generate severe political and social problems.

For all the sophistic defenses advanced by Party conservatives, one major logical hurdle remains: if democracy—however defined and institutionalized—is a universal value (*pushi jiazhi*), in what sense can its universality be reconciled with the alleged uniqueness and class identity (*jieji xing*) of "democracy with Chinese characteristics"? From a technical perspective, the problem lay in the simultaneous inclusion and exclusion of Western capitalists. Politically, it took the form of a dilemma: on the one hand, the Party was unwilling to subject itself to externally defined rules, and on the other hand, it still sought recognition for embodying the highest ideals of humanity. Thus, between the claim to a uniquely Chinese form of democracy and the assertion of democracy as a universal value, a bridge had to be both constructed and dismantled at the same time.

However, the logical weaknesses of this defensive apologia were not fatal. The Party's ideological security has hinged less on refuting the liberal agenda through persuasive argument than on the successful conceptual manipulation of the Party–people relationship. Once the distinction between the Party and the people is made to disappear, potential opposition seeking to pit the ruled against the ruling class is deprived of any Archimedean point from which to launch its challenge.

7.3 The Party–People Oneness

There is a perennial tension between the Party's claim that its rule conforms to the democratic principle of popular sovereignty and the reality that it continues to operate as a quasi-imperial order in which Party leaders exercise near-total control. To square this circle, the Party seeks to blur the distinction between the party-state in power and the people under its yoke, and fuse them into a single political entity. The logic of this strategy of conceptual fusion is most clearly encapsulated in the Party's theory of the Mass Line (*qunzhong luxian*).

Rhetorically, the Party maintains that the proletariat—the Marxist conception of the people—is the sovereign "master" that grants it power. Yet, since this party–people relationship is grounded in Leninist vanguardism, it does not allow the people to exercise their own political agency or to enjoy equal standing vis-à-vis the Party.

7.3.1 The Mass Line

On the one hand, a clear distinction between the Party and the people must be maintained in order to assert the Party's superior status. Party members, as "advanced elements" (*xianjin fenzi*) drawn from the masses, are therefore expected to play a leading role. Given the cognitive gap between the vanguard and ordinary people, only the Party is deemed capable of distinguishing right from wrong. As Mao put it, where the masses hold correct views, the Party must lead them to realize these views in light of changing circumstances; where they hold incorrect ones, the Party must educate them. The masses are thus denied the capacity to determine their own interests. They possess only passive "needs" and "aspirations," which must be discovered and articulated by Party members who engage the masses in order to hear, know, and represent them. In this conception, what the Party calls democracy is the so-called work style of democratism (*minzhu zhuyi zuofeng*)—that is, the practice of *letting* the masses speak (*rang qunzhong jianghua*). The people may speak, but they do not decide, and they may speak only when the Party permits them to do so.

At the core of the Party's Mass Line theory lies a form of paternalistic elitism. Party members are expected to "come from the masses and return to the masses" (*cong qunzhong zhong lai, dao qunzhong zhong qu*). According to this cyclical model of party–people interaction first articulated by Mao, cadres must first gather the opinions and demands of the masses, then process this information through the lens of Marxist theory, and finally return to instruct and mobilize the people—that is, raising their political consciousness by teaching them what is truly in their interests and what they ought to do. Once this round of ideological transformation is completed and policies are implemented, a new cycle of Mass Line interaction begins.

To preempt accusations of imperial-style domination, the Party hastens to add a qualification that its vanguard role does not place it above the people. Party members are said to be not "bosses" or "politicians," but "friends" and "teachers" of the people. Communists are conceptualized as being *of* the masses, rather than standing *above* them.

On the other hand, the Party and the people must be conceptually fused into a "two-in-one" unity, so that potential conflicts of interest and the question of accountability can be obscured and defined away. This move is not incompatible with the vanguardist conception: the solution is to assert that the Party is itself a part of the people. The former can thus "represent" the latter precisely because the two are posited as a single entity. Many analogies are invoked to illustrate this idea of oneness. The relationship between party members and the people is likened to that between "fish" and "water," or between "seeds" and "soil"—i.e., pairs that are understood as inherently created for one another and as mutually constitutive. As Mao put it, Chinese Communists were "rooted" in the Chinese people, and party members were "children" of the people.

Given this concept of oneness, the Party contends that it naturally serves the people's interests wholeheartedly and selflessly. In Mao's formulation, Chinese Communists are depicted as a "special" kind of human beings who never act in their own self-interest.

To keep this party–people chimera viable in practice, cadres must strike an almost impossible balance: remaining accountable both to the people and to the Party. Under ideal conditions, the exemplary cadre is expected to avoid the twin errors of "commandism" (*mingling zhuyi*)—i.e., imposing directives from above that the masses do not understand—and "tailism" (*weiba zhuyi*)—i.e., simply following whatever the masses demand. When reality fails to conform to ideological expectations, responsibility is displaced onto individual cadres. While particular officials can be turned into scapegoats for policy failures and criticized for having lost their revolutionary zeal, the Party as an institution remains unsullied, able to reaffirm its image as the selfless servant of the people.

7.3.2 The Three Represents

Jiang Zemin's theory of the Three Represents (*san ge daibiao*) once posed a serious challenge to the Party's chimerical notion of party–people oneness and, in doing so, revealed what was at stake. Whether intentionally or not, it conceptually undermined this unity by recasting the Party's claim to perfect political representativeness in the mold of a patron–client relationship.

The Three Represents theory was highly controversial within the Party in the first half of the 2000s. The central point of contention was whether private entrepreneurs, or "capitalists," who had become the principal drivers of China's economic development, should be allowed to join the Party that was still nominally a Marxist–Leninist organization committed to the eventual burial of capitalism.

Jiang Zemin and his allies answered in the affirmative. The immediate rationale behind this bold move was the need for the Party to co-opt the rapidly expanding "new social stratum" (*xin de shehui jieceng*), composed largely of the newly wealthy; otherwise, it might consolidate into an autonomous social force. As Jiang himself warned, failure to confront this reality and actively incorporate this group—or, worse, pushing it to the opposite side, whether intentionally or not—would be politically damaging. Ultimately, however, Jiang's objective appeared to have gone beyond mere political co-optation. There is evidence that Jiang sought to modernize the Party and to rationalize its mode of governance by strengthening the regime's "governing capacity" (*zhizheng nengli*), while gradually moving away from the highly politicized and often irrational governing practices rooted in the Party's revolutionary tradition.

To legitimize his initiative, Jiang had to introduce a series of complementary adjustments to the Party's ideological orthodoxy. The first concerned the question: whom does the Party represent? In the reform era, the Party was no longer defined as the vanguard of the working class but was recast as the vanguard of the Chinese people and the Chinese nation. The second concerned the criterion of political worthiness: class identity was to give way to the capacity to contribute to national development. As Jiang put it, whether one belongs to the propertied or the propertyless, and the amount of "capital" one possesses, should not be used as the standard for judging whether a person is politically advanced or backward. Instead, the Party was to open its doors to all the "builders" of socialism with Chinese characteristics. The third concerned the source of political legitimacy. As the Party proclaimed to have transformed from a "revolutionary party" (*geming dang*) into a "governing party" (*zhizheng dang*), the basis of its legitimacy shifted from revolutionary victory to governing performance. This performance-based standard is clearly reflected in the official formulation of the Three Represents.

- [The Party] must always represent the development trend of China's advanced productive forces: ... must continuously improve the living standards of the people through the development of productive forces.
- [The Party] must always represent the orientation of China's advanced culture: ... must continuously enhance ideological and ethical standards, and the scientific and cultural qualities, in order to provide spiritual impetus and intellectual support for China's economic development and social progress.
- [The Party] must always represent the fundamental interests of the overwhelming majority of the Chinese people: ... must enable the people to continuously obtain tangible economic, political, and cultural benefits.

Given these efforts to depoliticize the Party's ideological tenets, Chinese conservatives had strong grounds to resist Jiang Zemin's Three Represents, not least because it appeared to be eroding the Party's Marxist foundations.

However, the real threat that Jiang's initiatives posed to the Party's political survival did not stem from their ideological heterodoxy as such.

Rather, by deactivating class-based representation and installing performance as the primary standard of political legitimacy, the Three Represents conceptually opened the door to holding the Party accountable. First, once the Party claimed to represent not only the proletariat but also capitalists, representation could no longer sustain the ideological fusion that had bound the Party and the Chinese people into a single revolutionary or proletarian body. Second, as this unity dissolved, the Party's self-professed altruism in serving the people rang increasingly hollow. What mattered now was performance. Finally, with revolutionary legitimacy no longer available, there were no "class enemies" to blame for failures in China's development and national rejuvenation. The Party itself had to assume full responsibility when things went wrong.

7.4 The People in Motion

Authoritarian rulers often strategically mobilize the masses for political purposes. When social control is the ruling elite's primary concern, top-down mobilization—whether through bureaucratic hierarchies or the deployment of ad hoc task forces—can enforce compliance and deter opposition by visibly demonstrating state power. When elite infighting disrupts intra-elite unity, mass mobilization can assist a particular faction in the struggle for power, either directly through the sheer physical force of popular participation or indirectly by signaling political strength and resolve to potential allies.

However, in an age in which democracy occupies the moral high ground of political legitimacy, mass mobilization under authoritarian rule always carries the risk that the regime may lose control over the very people it has mobilized. This danger is especially acute when participants are told that they are merely exercising their rights and pursuing their own interests, often under the "guidance" of ostensibly "righteous" political leaders. The power of mass support derives in large part from the movement's scale and momentum. Yet it is precisely this dynamic that provides ordinary people with a rare opportunity to overcome collective action problems and to organize independently of the state. For those who have internalized the official claim that they are the true "masters" of the country, mobilization in the name of sovereign power can become a critical moment of political awakening and enlightenment. For potential activists, faction-driven mass mobilization also supplies a form of political cover under which opposition to the regime can be cautiously pursued.

7.4.1 Political Awakening of the Chinese Masses Under Mao

In this light, the Great Proletarian Cultural Revolution of the 1960s provides a striking example of populist mobilization backfiring on an authoritarian regime. Once awakened, the belief that the People could rule themselves became like a genie released from the bottle—something the authoritarian state could no longer control.

By launching the Cultural Revolution, Mao succeeded in mobilizing the Chinese masses against his political opponents and the Party's bureaucratic apparatus. Yet he soon discovered that he exercised only limited control over the mobilized masses and therefore only partial control over the course of the Revolution itself. The mobilized masses increasingly acted beyond the supreme leader's intention, forcing Mao to rely on the military to bring about demobilization. The unintended ideological crisis it unleashed had an even more profound and lasting impact on China's political development.

Thanks to Mao, a rudimentary democratic notion of popular sovereignty took root in the minds of ordinary Chinese people as a result of the chaotic and freewheeling political mobilization Mao permitted during the Cultural Revolution. Several factors contributed to this political enlightenment. First, regardless of how sincerely Mao himself believed in the principles he advanced, the rhetoric and theories he used to stir mass emotion and enthusiasm resonated deeply with the populace. The idea that the People were entitled to be the Masters of the country and should control their own destiny by supervising state officials and holding them accountable was taken seriously by many participants in the movement. Enshrined as Marxist orthodoxy, Mao's distinctive anti-elitist narratives further catalyzed this popular awakening.

Second, during the Cultural Revolution the Chinese masses briefly experienced an unprecedented degree of political freedom. In the name of Maoist "big democracy" (*da minzhu*), those who participated in the movement could organize, speak, and publish relatively freely, so long as they professed loyalty to Mao. The temporary suspension of Party control, combined with the paralysis of the state bureaucracy and the momentum of mass mobilization, facilitated the spread of an inchoate awareness of popular sovereignty and offered many participants a firsthand experience of putting this principle into practice. Under such circumstances, the long-standing habit of deference to state officials—a mindset deeply rooted in China's imperial political culture—was significantly weakened, as ordinary people learned to challenge and resist official authority.

Third, a profound contradiction existed between Mao's instrumental—even Machiavellian—use of mass mobilization and the moral righteousness and political utopianism it claimed to embody. As shifting dynamics in leadership politics repeatedly altered the political winds, the Cultural Revolution ended up "revolutionizing" the fate of nearly everyone (*ge le suoyou ren de ming*). This universal experience of victimization produced widespread disenchantment among grassroots participants. Such disillusionment, in turn, prompted many to raise fundamental questions about China's political system and the protection of human rights.

Last but not least, the peculiar power structure of the Party during the Cultural Revolution also contributed to the conditions that enabled the political awakening of the masses. Mao set his personal charismatic authority against Party institutions. While this Mao-versus-the-Party configuration greatly enhanced his individual power, it simultaneously weakened the Party's monopoly over the authoritative interpretation of key political doctrines. As the Party's institutional apparatus became temporarily paralyzed, mobilized participants gained direct access to Mao Zedong Thought. Chairman Mao, as a symbolic figure, thus became open to multiple interpretations, and dissenting readings soon emerged. These "heretical" interpretations (*yiduan*), often labeled "radical leftist thinking" (*ji zuo sichao*), were considered radical relative to official party lines because Mao's rhetoric about the people's supreme political status and democracy was deliberately "misrepresented" as a call for genuine popular influence over the state. Such heretical ideas addressed major political questions, including proposals for electoral rights modeled on the Paris Commune, visions of "popular democracy" in which the people would supervise state officials, and the protection of citizens' civil and political rights through an effective legal system.

Admittedly, one should not overstate the extent to which these Cultural Revolution "radicals" or dissenters possessed a clear understanding of what democracy truly is. For many grassroots Maoists, "democracy" meant little more than liberation from bureaucratic domination or popular resistance to autocratic oppression. Nevertheless, the political awakening experienced by some Cultural Revolution participants was a remarkable and spectacular development, precisely because it represented an endogenous breakthrough in political consciousness arising from China's domestic politics itself, rather than from external political influence and intellectual inspiration. In other words, years of turmoil and suffering led some individuals to rethink the meaning and value of being their own masters. This Mao-era enlightenment later became one of the ideological precursors of post-Mao mass activism, including the Democracy Wall movement of 1979–1980 and the Tiananmen protests of 1989.

7.4.2 *The Neo-Maoists and Continuous Revolution After Mao*

By the late 2000s, few people seriously expected to hear calls for another Cultural Revolution. By that time, China had already gone through three decades of Dengist reform. The neo-Maoists—a loosely organized political minority largely composed of grassroots diehards who aspired to restore socialist orthodoxy and advocated a Mao-style "big democracy"—remained something of a living political fossil. Their continued presence testified to the enduring relevance of Maoist political thinking, a long shadow cast by the Cultural Revolution over China's post-Mao political development.

While the neo-Maoists and China's establishment conservatives shared the same socialist vision of a China organized around a command economy and non-Western political institutions, the latter nevertheless regarded the former as a serious threat. This was due in no small part to the neo-Maoists' strong anti-bureaucratic ethos and their peculiar ideal of establishing direct rule by the masses—an outlook shaped by the political "education" they received during Mao's Last Revolution. Confronted with rampant corruption and widening socioeconomic inequality in China's reform era, neo-Maoist activists blamed Dengist reforms for their hardships. More importantly, many concluded that Mao's prophecy had finally come true: Deng Xiaoping and his fellow "revisionists" had recaptured political power through denouncing and delegitimizing Mao, and had quietly restored capitalism in China. The solution, in neo-Maoists' view, was simply to continue the Chairman's unfinished revolution against the "bureaucratic class" accused of walking the capitalist road.

It is worth noting that the neo-Maoist community itself was divided into two camps. The main fault line concerned whether the incumbent Chinese Communist Party had become completely degenerate and beyond redemption, or whether it was merely partially corrupted, with many genuine communists—the "healthy forces within the Party" (*dang nei jiankang liliang*)—still struggling to uphold socialist ideals and fight for the interests of the proletariat. The radical camp accused the moderates of "revolting only against the corrupt officials rather than the emperor." Yet the moderate camp posed no less of a challenge to the Party's conservative elites. Distinguishing "authentic" communists from "fake" ones was no less arbitrary, or politically unsettling, than a wholesale repudiation of the Party itself, and therefore offered little reassurance to the incumbent party leadership. Given their deep suspicion of state officials and their enthusiasm for direct popular oversight of the bureaucracy in the name of Maoist "big democracy," neither camp of neo-Maoists could be tolerated.

In Hu Jintao's final years, as conservative forces within the Party engaged in an intense struggle with the reformist camp,[10] one key strategy was to revive Maoist rhetoric, particularly the slogan "Serve the People." By invoking the political symbolism of Maoism, leftist elites sought to issue a populist appeal to the masses, suggesting that the time had once again come to fight oppression and defend their interests under the leadership of "true" communists—those who claimed to stand in unity with the people against the "revisionists" of the reform era.

However, the strategy of resurrecting Maoist ideology adopted by party conservatives inevitably set free the same genie that had once awakened the Cultural Revolution generation to the people's status as the "Masters" of the Chinese nation. Drawing on the memory of the Cultural Revolution, the ideological blueprint of a Maoist mass democracy, through which the people would exercise direct supervision over state officials and hold them accountable, was readily available to the neo-Maoists. Consistent with earlier strands of "heretic" or "radical" Maoism, a distinctive "democratic" ideal lay at the core of neo-Maoist aspirations. The aim was to establish a form of "proletarian mass democracy" guided by Mao Zedong Thought. Incorporating elements of contemporary populism, neo-Maoist discourse increasingly framed politics in terms of a tension between the people and the "elites" (*jingying*).

When Bo Xilai revived Mao-style mass mobilization in Chongqing, the neo-Maoists promoted the Chongqing Model as a harbinger of socialist rejuvenation and democratization. In their narrative, the Chongqing Model served as the "gateway" to the final, mature "Mao Zedong Model": it signaled the glorious comeback of the People's Democratic Dictatorship, an overdue correction of Dengist reforms, and a sincere return to the principle of "loving the people." Bo Xilai was praised for making mass participation the foundation of policymaking and for allowing ordinary people to supervise local officials. The Chongqing Model was thus portrayed as having discovered a new way to reunite the Party and the masses into one body (*dang qun yi ti hua*).

For all its emphasis on the People's supreme political status, the neo-Maoist conception of "the people running the country as masters" (*ren-min dang jia zuo zhu*) rested less on a substantive commitment to institutional design than on an idealistic faith in the inherent virtue and purity of masses mobilized by wise party leaders. Conflicting ideas thus coexist. On the one hand, neo-Maoists downplayed the role of a supreme leader or strongman rule and championed mass participation as the path to socialist democracy; it is an outlook reinforced by the deification of Mao as an unparalleled leader. On the other hand, they continued to claim that the Party's leadership remained essential: the Party was believed to retain the capacity for "self-reform" or "self-renewal" (*ziwo gengxin*) and could be relied upon so long as its leaders faithfully adhered to the Mass Line.

As with Maoism in the 1960s, the neo-Maoist agenda also had an internationalist dimension. Interpreting the Occupy Wall Street movement in the United States as a precursor to a "general crisis" of capitalism, neo-Maoists envisioned a future in which socialism in China would soon surpass capitalism as the dominant mode of development. In this vision, Mao-style mass democracy served as the political solution, while "common prosperity" constituted the new economic framework. Viewed in context, when Bo Xilai was advancing a Common Prosperity agenda in Chongqing, the neo-Maoist rhetoric about the internationalization of this principle functioned as an indirect way of glorifying Bo's efforts and highlighting his potential historic contribution.

Once again, the genie embodying a rudimentary ideal of popular sovereignty proved unsettling to the party leadership. China's conservatives realized that, in promoting a return to socialist orthodoxy, they had to walk a fine line when restraining the neo-Maoists, or the so-called radical leftists. Hu Jintao's well-known statement—"We must neither revert to the old path of isolation and rigidity, nor stray onto the misguided path of abandoning our [socialist] system"—captured the conservatives' concern about ideological drift, an unintended consequence of leveraging Maoist populism for factional struggle. That's why neo-Maoist organizations and grassroots activism enjoyed no special protection and were often targeted in the same crackdowns that affected other social groups.

As an unstated political ally of the conservative camp, Bo Xilai also appeared vulnerable to being hijacked by radical leftists. As one neo-Maoist opinion leader put it, “Maoist communists” (*mao pai gongchandang ren*) should strive to be “pathbreakers” rather than mere “followers” of the Chongqing Model, since Bo’s political programs still “lagged behind Mao Zedong Thought.” In this view, neo-Maoists should support Bo for both tactical and strategic reasons, while simultaneously seeking to shape the development of the Chongqing Model so that it would move closer to the Mao Zedong Model over time.

Bo Xilai also sought to distance himself from the neo-Maoists. The fact that some neo-Maoists were reportedly given a warm reception by Chongqing’s Public Security Bureau during their visits was often cited as evidence that Bo maintained ties with Utopia (*wu you zhi xiang*), a leading grassroots neo-Maoist organization. Yet the same episode could just as plausibly be interpreted as a discreet measure taken by Bo to monitor, and, if necessary, restrain the radical leftists during their stay in Chongqing. Rhetorically, Su Wei of the Chongqing Party School, Bo’s most important local theoretician, openly accused neo-Maoists of “doing a disservice” (*bang dao mang*). Indeed, Bo was probably not lying when he told the media that his Chongqing policies had nothing to do with Mao’s Cultural Revolution. After all, Cultural Revolution radicalism and socialist fundamentalism are distinct ideas, just as the Party’s official discourse carefully distinguishes Mao Zedong Thought from the so-called erroneous ideas of Mao in his final years. Unfortunately, the Maoism Bo hoped to invoke in pursuit of his political ambitions—mobilizing the masses against political enemies—was inseparable from its radicalized counterpart: awakening the mobilized masses to their political rights vis-à-vis the state.

7.5 Authoritarian Legitimation in the Age of Democracy

Mobilizing the masses often proves to be a double-edged sword for autocrats. Behind this dilemma lies an important ideological factor: the ideas of popular sovereignty and democracy have become the unchallengeable foundations of political legitimacy. This imagery is grounded in empirical reality: even autocrats seek to portray themselves as supported by the people and as ruling in a democratic manner. When autocratic elites struggle for power, they frequently do so in the name of defending the people’s interests against those “enemies” who allegedly do not belong to “the People.”

Given the intrinsic tension between *rhetorically* appealing to the people as the sovereign "Master" and, *in practice*, ruling above them while depriving them of meaningful political autonomy and participation, authoritarian leaders tend to proselytize an authoritarian conception of political representation. In this view, representation is portrayed as legitimate because the ruler or the ruling class either embodies the people or claims to deliver substantial benefits on their behalf, while the process of political authorization is stealthily rendered irrelevant. In other words, the form of representation claimed by authoritarian rulers is one in which the right to govern is effectively transferred to the ruler at the very moment that popular sovereignty is invoked as the ultimate source of legitimacy for exercising that power.

Nonetheless, however autocrats manipulate the meanings of political representation and popular sovereignty, they cannot uproot these normative ideas, for no truly viable alternatives exist. As long as aspirations for democracy and belief in popular sovereignty continue to dominate the contemporary political imagination, any authoritarian appeal to the people must ultimately rest on the language of democratic representation—and thus always carries the seed of popular awakening against authoritarian rule and the possibility that mass mobilization may ultimately backfire on the rulers who initiate it.

Notes

1. The narrative draws on the following articles: Jiang Renbao, "Renmin zhuquan shi zhengzhi wenming de jingsui" [The Essence of Political Civilization Lies in Popular Sovereignty], *Yan Huang Chun Qiu*, no. 8 (2003): 1–4; He Fang, "Zhang Wentian de minzhu zhuiqiu yu shijian—jinian Zhongguo gongchandang dansheng 82 zhounian" [Zhang Wentian's Pursuit and Practice of Democracy: Commemorating the 82nd Anniversary of the Founding of the Chinese Communist Party], *Yan Huang Chun Qiu*, no. 7 (2003): 1–7; Wu Jiang, "Zichan jieji zhengzhi minzhu pingxi (xia)" [An Analysis of Bourgeois Political Democracy, Part II], *Yan Huang Chun Qiu*, no. 6 (2003): 14–16; Yu Guangren, "Shenme shi fengjian zhuyi" [What Is Feudalism?], *Yan Huang Chun Qiu*, no. 2 (2004): 70–73; Yao Songliu, "Cong 'yi ren wei ben' xiang dao de" [Reflections Inspired by the Concept of "People-Centeredness"], *Yan Huang Chun Qiu*, no. 7 (2004): 46–47; Zhang Xushan, "Cong chuantong wenhua jiejian fanfu jingyan shi ge jia mingti" [Drawing on Traditional Culture for Anti-Corruption Practices Is a False Proposition], *Yan Huang*

Chun Qiu, no. 5 (2007): 77–79; Zhang Xushan, "'Ti tian xing dao lun': quanli zhengyi xing de hushenfu" ["The Theory of 'Upholding Justice on Behalf of Heaven': A Shield for the Legitimacy of Power"], *Yan Huang Chun Qiu*, no. 9 (2009): 59–62; Wang Liping, "Zhongguo xuyao yi chang gongmin changshi qimeng yundong" [China Needs an Enlightenment Movement for Civic Common Sense], *Yan Huang Chun Qiu*, no. 8 (2009): 30–31; Liu Zehua, "Cong chenmin yishi xiang gongmin yishi de zhuanbian" [The Transition from Subject Mentality to Civic Consciousness], *Yan Huang Chun Qiu*, no. 4 (2009): 76–81; Dong Jian, "Geren zhuyi yu gongmin shehui" [Individualism and Civil Society], *Yan Huang Chun Qiu*, no. 3 (2010): 4–7.

2. Literature Research Office of the Central Committee of the Chinese Communist Party (LROCCP), *Lun qunzhong luxian—zhongyao lunshu zhaibian* [On the Mass Line—Selected Important Discourses] (Zhongyang wenxian chubanshe and Dangjian duwu chubanshe, 2013); Theoretical Bureau of the Propaganda Department of the Central Committee of the Chinese Communist Party (TBPDCCP), *Lun dang de qunzhong gongzuo—zhongyao lunshu zhaibian* [On the Party's Mass Work—Selected Important Discourses] (Xuexi chubanshe, 2011).
3. Jiang Zemin, "Zai qingzhu Zhongguo gongchandang chengli bashi zhounian dahui shang de jianghua" [Speech at the Conference Commemorating the 80th Anniversary of the Founding of the Chinese Communist Party], in *Jiang Zemin wen xuan* [Selected Works of Jiang Zemin, i.e. *SWJZM*], vol. 3 (Renmin chubanshe, 2006), 264–299; Jiang Zemin, "Kexue duidai Makesi zhuyi" [Approaching Marxism Scientifically], in *SWJZM*, vol. 3 (Renmin chubanshe, 2006), 333–346; Jiang Zemin, "Quanmian jianshe xiaokang shehui, kaichuang Zhongguo tese shehui zhuyi shiye xin jumian" [Building a Moderately Prosperous Society in an All-Round Way and Opening a New Phase in Developing Socialism with Chinese Characteristics], in *SWJZM*, vol. 3 (Renmin chubanshe, 2006), 528–575; Qiu Shi, "Lun 'liang ge xianfeng dui'" [On the "Two Vanguard Teams"], *Qiushi*, no. 3 (2002): 11–16.
4. Roderick MacFarquhar and Michael Schoenhals, *Mao's Last Revolution* (Belknap Press of Harvard University Press, 2006); Yiching Wu, *The Cultural Revolution at the Margins: Chinese Socialism in Crisis* (Harvard University Press, 2014); Gao Gao and Yan Jiaqi, *"Wenhua da geming" shi nian shi* [The Ten-Year History of the Cultural Revolution] (Tianjin renmin chubanshe, 1986); Youyu Xu, *Xing xing se se de zaofan: hong weibing jingshen suzhi de xingcheng ji yanbian* [A Variety of Rebellions: The Formation and Evolution of the Red Guard's Mentality] (Chinese University of Hong Kong Press, 1999); Yongyi Song and Dajin Sun, *Wenhua da geming he ta de yiduan sichao* [Heterodox Thoughts during the

Cultural Revolution] (Tianyuan shuwu, 1997); Hongbiao Yin, *Shizong zhe de zuji: wenhua da geming qijian de qingnian sichao* [The Footprints of the Missing: Youth Ideology during the Cultural Revolution] (Chinese University of Hong Kong Press, 2009).

5. Hongse Zhongguo, "Zhongguo mao pai gongchan zhuyi zhe lianhe qilai—Zhongguo mao pai gongchan zhuyi zhe Luoyang huiyi jiyao" [Chinese Maoist Communists Unite!—Minutes of the Luoyang Meeting of Chinese Maoist Communists], *RedChinaCn*, February 5, 2015, http://redchinacn.net/forum.php?mod=viewthread&tid=13152; Hongse Zhongguo, "Kaichuang shehui zhuyi zai geming de xin jieduan—'Zhongguo mao pai lianhe' er ci huiyi jiyao" [Opening a New Stage of Socialist Re-Revolution—Minutes of the Second Meeting of the "Chinese Maoist Union"], *RedChinaCn*, May 12, 2016, http://www.redchinacn.net/forum.php?mod=viewthread&tid=11634.
6. Wu You Zhi Xiang, "Chongqing moshi de lishi biran xing—Wu You Zhi Xiang di yi ci Chongqing moshi yantao hui jiyao" [The Historical Inevitability of the Chongqing Model—Minutes of the First Wu You Zhi Xiang Seminar on the Chongqing Model], *Wu You Zhi Xiang*, October 25, 2010, http://m.wyzxwk.com/content.php?classid=12&id=196596; Wu You Zhi Xiang, "Wu You Zhi Xiang di er ci 'Chongqing moshi' yantao hui jiyao" [Minutes of the Second Wu You Zhi Xiang Seminar on the "Chongqing Model"], *Wu You Zhi Xiang*, January 8, 2011, http://m.wyzxwk.com/Article/lixiang/2011/01/199909; Wu You Zhi Xiang, "Shijie weiji xia de Chongqing moshi yu Zhongguo weilai—Wu You Zhi Xiang di san ci Chongqing moshi yantao hui jiyao" [The Chongqing Model and China's Future in a World of Crises—Minutes of the Third Wu You Zhi Xiang Seminar on the Chongqing Model], *Wu You Zhi Xiang dianzi ban yue kan*, issue 144, no. 9:2 (2011): 51–57; Wu You Zhi Xiang, "Chongqing moshi shi bimian Hua'erjie geming weiyi zhengque de daolu—Wu You Zhi Xiang 'Chongqing moshi de shijie yiyi' yantao hui jiyao" [The Chongqing Model Is the Only Correct Path to Avoid the Wall Street Revolution—Minutes of the Wu You Zhi Xiang Seminar on the "Global Implications of the Chongqing Model"], *Wu You Zhi Xiang dianzi ban yue kan*, issue 147, no. 11:1 (2011): 21–26.
7. Zhang Hongliang, "Chongqing moshi chengbai yu Zhongguo zhengzhi qianjing" [The Success or Failure of the Chongqing Model and China's Political Future], *Wu You Zhi Xiang dianzi ban yue kan*, issue 141, no. 8:1 (2011): 47–59.
8. Su Wei, "Yu san pi Faguo jizhe tan Chongqing 'chang hong,' 'da hei'"" [A Conversation with Three Groups of French Journalists on Chongqing's "Sing Red" and "Strike Black"], *Wu You Zhi Xiang*, June 21, 2011, https://www.wyzxwk.com/Article/shidai/2011/06/234683.html;

Yang Fan, "Yong fei yishixingtai fangfa yanjiu Zhongguo moshi yu Chongqing moshi" [Studying the China Model and the Chongqing Model Using Non-Ideological Methods], January 5, 2012, https://m.aisixiang.com/data/48866.html.

9. Lin Le, *China's Conservative Turn: The Origins of Xi Jinping's New Era* (Lynne Rienner Publishers, 2025), 185–202.
10. Le, *China's Conservative Turn.*

CHAPTER 8

Conclusion: Another Cultural Revolution?

On March 14, 2012—just one day before Bo Xilai was officially announced to have been removed from office—then Premier Wen Jiabao made a strikingly unexpected public remark, stating that "the pernicious legacy of the mistakes of the Cultural Revolution and the influence of feudalism have not yet been fully eradicated."[1] It was evident that Wen was criticizing Bo Xilai's "Chongqing model" and his campaigns of "Sing Red and Strike Black."

During his tenure in Chongqing, Bo vigorously promoted "red culture," revived the Mass Line and large-scale popular mobilization, and pursued redistributive economic policies that practically relied on taking from the rich and giving to the poor. The strong sense of a Maoist revival stood in sharp contrast to the overarching theme of Dengist reform and opening up. As this book argues, Bo Xilai's leftist turn was part of a central-level power struggle between the left and the right within the Chinese Communist Party (CCP) leadership. In Hu Jintao's final years, conservative forces gained significant momentum, and the reformist agenda was markedly weakened.

Sensing the political winds, Bo Xilai maneuvered accordingly in Chongqing. After assuming leadership there in 2008, he briefly portrayed himself as a follower of the reformist line, only to later reinvent himself as a spokesperson for the Left. With the upcoming party leadership succession

L. Le, *Revival of Maoism in Reform-Era China*,
https://doi.org/10.1007/978-981-92-4606-9_8

in mind, Bo aligned himself with shifting political currents in an attempt to strengthen his own position.

From a theoretical perspective, the dual absence of a political consensus and a dominant faction under authoritarian rule often produces a prolonged tug of war among elites, gradually pushing intra-elite power struggles to the open. Contending elites use public information strategically: by shaping public opinion through propaganda, advancing policy agendas, and mobilizing society, they project political strength, signal political commitments, and coordinate factional alignments.

Wen Jiabao understood that behind Bo Xilai's high-profile promotion of Maoism lay problems rooted in China's political system, rather than merely social and economic grievances—such as distributive injustice, the erosion of trust, and corruption—that had led ordinary people to yearn for an illusory Mao-era ideal of fairness and justice. Wen spoke bluntly about the necessity of political reform, emphasizing in particular "the reform of the Party and state leadership system." Wen stressed that:

> Reform has now entered a critical and difficult stage. Without the success of political reform, economic reform cannot be carried through to the end. The achievements already made in reform and development could even be lost, and newly emerging social problems cannot be fundamentally resolved. Historical tragedies like the 'Cultural Revolution' could occur again.[2]

Today, many people have the sense that Wen Jiabao's words proved prophetic. Over more than a decade of Xi Jinping's rule, the agenda of political reform has all but disappeared, political centralization has been continuously strengthened, and the reform and opening-up agenda have steadily retreated. Ideological controls have tightened, state intervention in the economy has expanded, international trade frictions have intensified, and nationalism has become increasingly radicalized. Wen Jiabao would likely be deeply disappointed. Although Bo Xilai was ultimately purged, the political left turn he championed and the revival of Maoism have not only persisted under Xi Jinping but have expanded. Many of Bo's core policy practices have effectively been replicated under Xi—such as propagating the Party's revolutionary culture, cracking down on criminal organizations, and promoting the ideal of "common prosperity." As some have wryly observed, Xi Jinping appears to be pursuing "a Bo Xilai line without Bo Xilai."[3]

Wen Jiabao's warning about the impasse of reform now appears to have been borne out. But what about the comeback of the Cultural Revolution itself? With the year 2026 marking the 60th anniversary of Mao's launch of the Cultural Revolution, this unnerving question looms large. What lessons, then, does the story of Bo Xilai offer us?

On the one hand, many China observers have offered a range of reasons for concluding that the Cultural Revolution is unlikely to reappear. First, history does not repeat itself with precision. Many of the historical conditions that enabled Mao to launch the Cultural Revolution no longer exist and are unlikely to reemerge. Most importantly, there is no longer a supreme leader like Mao. Although some argue that Xi Jinping's power now exceeds Mao's at the time, Xi does not possess Mao's absolute charismatic authority and political legitimacy, which once allowed Mao to act without meaningful constraint. Second, decades of Dengist reform have fundamentally reshaped Chinese society. The reform fostered more open and modern ways of thinking, turned broad social strata into beneficiaries of continuing reform, and deeply integrated China into the global economy. It is difficult to imagine that another round of Cultural Revolution–style internal upheaval would command widespread support among either officials or the general public. Third, post-Mao China has relied on a strategy of political demobilization as a core mechanism of social control. Launching mass movements to attack political enemies and smash state institutions appears to be an exceptional case, made possible only by Mao's absolute political authority, a historical contingency that would hardly happen again. One of the key lessons drawn from the Cultural Revolution by revolutionary elders who returned to the center of power in the post-Mao era was precisely that genuine political participation and mass mobilization unguided by the state must not be allowed. This is why the Chinese Communist Party has not only repressed democratic activists but has also remained wary of grassroots Maoist groups. For these "radical" Maoists, Maoism is not merely a matter of nostalgia or commemoration; it represents a political blueprint for transforming reality.[4] Particularly unsettling for the Party is the fact that Maoism carries within it Mao's radical anti-bureaucratic theory—i.e., the so-called big democracy. Unsurprisingly, the ability of grassroots Maoist movements to hijack the public discourse around the Chongqing Model became a source of concern for Bo Xilai himself.

That said, the spirit of the Cultural Revolution as a political symbol has never gone away. In the words of Song Yongyi, a prominent scholar of

Mao's Cultural Revolution, "in a certain sense, as long as Mao Zedong's portrait still hangs over Tiananmen, the Cultural Revolution has not truly ended."[5] At this abstract level, the Cultural Revolution refers not to a specific historical campaign, but to the Chinese Communist Party's authoritarian regime—one characterized by unchecked power and repressive social control. In this sense, the continued presence of the Cultural Revolution's spirit has been something the post-Mao Party leadership has found politically necessary. At the same time, because Mao himself embodies the Party's political legitimacy, a thorough repudiation of the Cultural Revolution has never been possible. That is why, in 2016, on the occasion of the 50th anniversary of the Cultural Revolution, a major party mouthpiece stated that it was necessary to "distinguish the 'Cultural Revolution' period from the 'Cultural Revolution' as a political movement, to distinguish the erroneous theories and practices of the 'Cultural Revolution' from the overall history of that decade, and to forcefully rebut misguided views that seek to negate the Party's history, the Party's leadership, and the socialist system by negating the 'Cultural Revolution.' "[6]

On the other hand, what Bo Xilai had accomplished in Chongqing demonstrated that it is possible for the Cultural Revolution's core elements to return in real life. This suggests that a second Cultural Revolution would not replicate the historical details of the original, but would instead appear with its essential components and structures reconstituted in new forms, adapted to a different political context.

First, Bo Xilai emerged as a charismatic leader. Although Mao's physical presence cannot be reproduced, embodiments and spokesmen of Maoism can still arise in response to political demand. This demonstrates the possibility of constructing a supreme leader.

Second, wrapped in Maoist rhetoric, Bo Xilai's policies—"Sing Red," "Strike Black," and "Common Prosperity"—were in essence cases of mass mobilization for the purpose of political infighting. Framed through the lens of class struggle, these policies implied an absolute distinction between friend and enemy, cast one side as the sole representative of justice against the other within a socialist ideological universe, and claimed the moral high ground of carrying the ultimate truth. The political symbolism conveyed by the Chongqing Model was, in fact, a story structurally identical to that of Mao's Cultural Revolution: some good Communist Party members leading the proletariat against the collusion of bad Party members and the bourgeoisie. The Party's conception of party–people oneness renders this form of top-down mobilization—depicting a leader guiding the people toward victory—deeply seductive.

Third, Bo Xilai succeeded in mobilizing Chongqing society in its entirety through administrative means. Whether social groups and officials genuinely identified with the ideological premises of a top-down political movement ultimately mattered little; under coercive command, the movement would proceed regardless. The hierarchical structure of bureaucracies under authoritarian rule thus became an effective organizational instrument. Political directives generated pressures of compliance, forcing individual motivations to align with official priorities. Behind the ostensible "spontaneity" of mass participation promoted in propaganda lay coercion and forced obedience. It turned out that, in the presence of political rewards and material incentives, there would be no shortage of politically active participants eager to carry out the tasks assigned by the leader.

Most importantly, the reemergence of Cultural Revolution elements in Bo Xilai's Chongqing saga was grounded in a specific historical conjuncture whose *structural* nature is very likely to reappear. This is a moment of intense elite power struggle within the Party. A political landscape marked by balance among rival forces and heightened uncertainty during a period of power reconfiguration generated a systematic demand for political competition. This, in turn, made both the partial publicity of elite conflict and the deployment of political mobilization under authoritarian rule possible.

Of course, Bo Xilai's political discourse and mobilization did not display explicit antagonism unlike what happened in the case of Mao's Cultural Revolution. A reasonable explanation is that at the time, intraparty struggles had not escalated to the point of open rupture or violent confrontation among rival factions. Bo Xilai's eventual removal, however, indicates that a dominant political force ultimately emerged, or that a consensus was reached among competing elites, thereby closing off the political space in which Bo's Maoist movement could continue and be sustained.

Nonetheless, Bo Xilai demonstrates that a return of the Cultural Revolution is possible in post-Mao China. Its comeback is ultimately driven by the demands of power holders—specifically, the necessity of elite power struggle. Where such demands exist, there will emerge supplies to meet the demand. The fact that we have not seen any Cultural Revolution–style politics during the Xi era can be explained by the relative stability of power configuration under Xi. Recently, however, signs of change have emerged. Since the Twentieth Party Congress, a spectacular series of political purges and personnel shifts across the party, government, and military have revealed a high degree of uncertainty within the party leadership, and possible political realignment and power redistribution in the making. The future political trajectory of China under Xi therefore remains uncertain. What can be stated with confidence, however, is that the specter of Mao's Cultural Revolution has continued to lurk beneath the surface of post-Mao China. This is because the Cultural Revolution, at its core, was a mode of political struggle in which an autocrat uses mass mobilization to fight political rivals and consolidate power.

Assessing the possibility of a second Cultural Revolution from the standpoint of elite power struggles represents a supply-side perspective. A demand-side perspective, or a perspective of the social conditions that would sustain a Cultural Revolution, suggests that even if the leadership had the political incentive to launch such a movement, it could fail to fully unfold—or might even fizzle out—due to social noncooperation or forms of soft resistance. However, the preconditions for such resistance are highly demanding. They require that the ruled share a set of core values.

First, there must be a genuine concern for the well-being and dignity of every individual human. The power of this belief lies in its capacity to resist the authoritarian directive to inflict harm on others in the name of serving the collective—whether that collective is defined as the state, the nation, or a social class. As critics of China's zero-COVID policy once asked during the pandemic, when the state calls for achieving certain national goals "at any cost," who, exactly, is to be sacrificed as that cost? Behind extreme forms of collective worship lies a deeper theological logic: the human pursuit of eternal life. Individuals are mortal, but life is imagined to endure through the collective.

Second, there must be resistance to the temptation of exercising power under conditions of servitude, and a refusal to serve as an instrument of political control. The stability and security of authoritarian rule necessarily depend on those who are willing to act as agents of repression on behalf of the rulers. Under authoritarian systems, power and material benefits are distributed hierarchically. Compared to their own condition of subjugation, these agents of repression care more about the rewards of power and privilege; by pledging loyalty to the leader, they secure a position above others. They are simultaneously enslaved and enslaving others. The upward drive toward worship of power and the gratification derived from downward oppression together constitute the fundamental incentive structure of authoritarian rule. As Jean-Jacques Rousseau once wrote,

> citizens allow themselves to be oppressed only insofar as they are driven by blind ambition; and looking more below than above them, domination becomes more dear to them than independence, and they consent to wear chains in order to be able to give them in turn to others.[7]

Here, the deeper theological logic lies in human's instinctive desire for glory.

Third, there must be resistance to the illusion of "absolute truth," and a rejection of the incitement to draw rigid black-and-white distinctions between friend and enemy, as well as the deceptive call to follow a so-called messianic leader. The impulse to eliminate dissent entirely and to treat it as irreconcilable hostility stems from an ancient and enduring human desire: the urge to impose one's own views upon others. This corresponds to a theological logic as well: when humans ate the forbidden fruit, their eyes were "opened" and they became "like God, knowing good and evil."[8] Just as "God created man in his own image,"[9] humanity's original sin is often reflected in its desire to mold others in its own image.

Successful enlightenment is difficult, because the challenges it confronts have their roots in enduring weaknesses of human nature. If a Cultural Revolution–style movement were to be relaunched from above, the prospects for bottom-up resistance within Chinese society would not be optimistic. This observation also echoes Wen Jiabao's remarks in 2012 on the crucial role of society in political reform: "I am deeply aware of the difficulty of reform. Above all, any reform must be grounded in the awakening of the people, the support of the people, and the people's initiative and creative spirit."[10]

Notes

1. "Wen Jiabao: Meiyou zhengzhi tizhi gaige de chenggong, Wenge huo hui chongyan" [Wen Jiabao: Without the Success of Political System Reform, the Cultural Revolution May Recur], *Zhongguo gaige xinxi ku*, March 14, 2012, http://www.reformdata.org/2012/0314/22141.shtml.
2. "Wen Jiabao: Meiyou zhengzhi tizhi gaige."
3. "Fangtan: Dangju zai zou meiyou Bo Xilai de Bo Xilai luxian ma?" [Interview: Is the Leadership Following Bo Xilai's Line without Bo Xilai?] *BBC News*, February 10, 2014, https://www.bbc.com/zhongwen/simp/china/2014/02/140210_lse_conference_tong.
4. Lu Zhichao, ed., *Xiangwang Mao Zedong* [Longing for Mao Zedong] (Zhongyang wenxian chubanshe, 2005).

5. "Song Yongyi: Wenge bu keneng chongyan, dan Wenge yijing zai Zhongguo huichao" [Song Yongyi: The Cultural Revolution Will Not Recur, but It Is Already Resurging in China], *Radio Free Asia*, April 19, 2016, https://www.rfa.org/mandarin/yataibaodao/zhengzhi/ck-04192016160346.html.
6. Ren Ping, "Yi shi wei jian shi weile geng hao qianjin" [Using History as a Mirror Is for Better Moving Forward], *Renmin ribao*, May 17, 2016, http://opinion.people.com.cn/n1/2016/0517/c1003-28355143.html.
7. Jean-Jacques Rousseau, *Discourse on the Origin of Inequality*, trans. Donald A. Cress (Hackett, 1992), 66.
8. Genesis 3:4 (ESV).
9. Genesis 1:27 (ESV).
10. "Wen Jiabao: Meiyou zhengzhi tizhi gaige."

Bibliography

Anderlini, Jamil. 2012. Bo Xilai: Power, Death, and Politics. *Financial Times*, July 20. http://www.ft.com/intl/cms/s/2/d67b90f0-d140-11e1-8957-00144feabdc0.html.

Ang, Yuen Yuen. 2018. Domestic Flying Geese: Industrial Transfer and Delayed Policy Diffusion in China. *The China Quarterly* 234:420–443. https://doi.org/10.1017/S0305741018000516.

Arato, Andrew, and Jean L. Cohen. 2022. *Populism and Civil Society: The Challenge to Constitutional Democracy*. Oxford University Press.

Arditi, Benjamín. 2024. *Is There Such a Thing as Populism?: 3 Provocations and 5 1/2 Proposals*. Routledge.

Art, David. 2022. The Myth of Global Populism. *Perspectives on Politics* 20 (3): 999–1011. https://doi.org/10.1017/S1537592720003552.

Barmé, Geremie R. 2012. Red Allure and the Crimson Blindfold. *China Perspectives* 2:29–40.

Bellin, Eva. 2012. Reconsidering the Robustness of Authoritarianism in the Middle East: Lessons from the Arab Spring. *Comparative Politics* 44 (2): 127–149. https://doi.org/10.5129/001041512798838021.

Bennett, Gordon. 1976. *Yundong: Mass Movement in Chinese Communist Leadership*. Center for Chinese Studies, University of California.

Blanchette, Jude. 2019. *China's New Red Guards: The Return of Radicalism and the Rebirth of Mao Zedong*. Oxford University Press.

Bo, Zhiyue. 2015. Were China's Corrupt Officials Plotting a Coup? *The Diplomat*, April 13. https://thediplomat.com/2015/04/were-chinas-corrupt-officials-plotting-a-coup/.

L. Le, *Revival of Maoism in Reform-Era China*,
https://doi.org/10.1007/978-981-92-4606-9

Bo, Zhiyue. 2018. Factional Politics in the Party-State Apparatus. In *Routledge Handbook of the Chinese Communist Party*, edited by Willy Wo-Lap Lam, 122–134. Routledge. https://doi.org/10.4324/9781315543918-8.

Bo, Kuangyi (Guagua). 2024. Bo Xilai as Ned Stark. *X*, December 23. https://x.com/BoKuangyi/status/1871275984621850691.

Bo, Zhiyue, and Chen Gang. 2009. Bo Xilai and the Chongqing Model. *East Asian Policy* 1:42–49.

Boix, Carles, and Milan W. Svolik. 2013. The Foundations of Limited Authoritarian Government: Institutions, Commitment, and Power-Sharing in Dictatorships. *The Journal of Politics* 75 (2): 300–316. https://doi.org/10.1017/S0022381613000029.

Broadhurst, Roderic, and Peng Wang. 2014. After the Bo Xilai Trial: Does Corruption Threaten China's Future? *Survival* 56 (3): 157–178. https://doi.org/10.1080/00396338.2014.920148.

Brown, Kerry, and Simone van Nieuwenhuizen. 2016. *China and the New Maoists*. Zed Books.

Brownlee, Jason. 2007. *Authoritarianism in an Age of Democratization*. Cambridge University Press.

Brownlee, Jason, Tarek E. Masoud, and Andrew Reynolds. 2015. *The Arab Spring: Pathways of Repression and Reform*. Oxford University Press.

Bueno de Mesquita, Bruce, Alastair Smith, Randolph M. Siverson, and James D. Morrow. 2003. *The Logic of Political Survival*. MIT Press.

Cairns, Christopher. 2019. Microblog Dissent and Censorship During the 2012 Bo Xilai Scandal. In *Handbook of Protest and Resistance in China*, edited by Teresa Wright, 361–376. Edward Elgar Publishing. https://doi.org/10.4337/9781786433787.00037.

Carothers, Christopher. 2022. *Corruption Control in Authoritarian Regimes: Lessons from East Asia*. Cambridge University Press.

Carter, Erin Baggott, and Brett L. Carter. 2023. *Propaganda in Autocracies: Institutions, Information, and the Politics of Belief*. Cambridge University Press.

Cartier, Carolyn, and Luigi Tomba. 2012. Symbolic Cities and the 'Cake Debate'. In *China Story Yearbook 2012*, edited by Geremie R. Barmé, chap. 2. Australian Centre on China in the World.

Casper, Brett Allen, and Scott A. Tyson. 2014. Popular Protest and Elite Coordination in a Coup d'État. *The Journal of Politics* 76 (2): 548–564. https://doi.org/10.1017/S0022381613001485.

Cell, Charles P. 1977. *Revolution at Work: Mobilization Campaigns in China*. Academic Press.

Central Committee of the Chinese Communist Party Steering Committee for Party Rectification Work. 1988. *Di san qi zheng dang zhongyao wenjian yu ziliao* [Important Documents and Materials on the Third Phase of Party Rectification, i.e. **IDMTPPR**], Renmin chubanshe.

Chan, Alfred L. 2022. *Xi Jinping: Political Career, Governance, and Leadership, 1953–2018*. Oxford University Press.

Chen, Chunhua, and Bruce Dickson. 2018. Coping with Growth in China: Comparing Models of Development in Guangdong and Chongqing. *Journal of Chinese Governance* 3 (2): 197–222. https://doi.org/10.1080/23812346.2018.1430998.

Cheng, Joseph Y. S. 2013. The 'Chongqing Model': What It Means to China Today. *Journal of Comparative Asian Development* 12 (3): 411–442. https://doi.org/10.1080/15339114.2013.862919.

Cheung, Olivia. 2023. *Factional-Ideological Conflicts in Chinese Politics: To the Left or to the Right?* Amsterdam University Press. https://doi.org/10.5117/9789463720298.

Chongqing Association for Social Sciences. 2009. *Chongqing "hi "jiefang sixiang, kuoda kaifang" da taolun da xing wenji* [A Complete Anthology of Chongqing's Grand Discussion on "Emancipating the Mind and Expanding the Scope of Opening-Up"]. Sichuan chuban jituan/Sichuan kexuejishu chubanshe.

Chongqing guo zi: di san caizheng shijian [State-Owned Assets in Chongqing: The Practice of the Third Source of Fiscal Revenue]. 2010. *Liaowang*, No. 67.

Chongqing Leading Small Group for Internet Regulation (CLSGIR), External Propaganda Office of Chongqing Party Committee (EPOCPC), and Chongqing Center for Internet News Research (CCINR). 2010. *Yu lun 2009* [Public Opinion in Chongqing 2009]. Self-published.

Chongqing Ribao [Chongqing Daily]. 2008–2012. Chongqing: Chongqing Municipal Committee of the Chinese Communist Party. Various issues.

Chou, Mark, Benjamin Moffitt, and Octavia Bryant. 2020. *Political Meritocracy and Populism: Cure or Curse?* Routledge.

Chwe, Michael Suk-Young. 2001. *Rational Ritual: Culture, Coordination, and Common Knowledge*. Princeton University Press.

CLSGIR, EPOCPC and CCINR. 2011. *Yu lun 2010* [Public Opinion in Chongqing 2010]. Self-publish.

Connery, Christopher. 2019. The Chongqing Way. *boundary 2* 46 (2): 163–188. https://doi.org/10.1215/01903659-7497088.

Dai, Yaoyao, and Zijie Shao. 2016. Populism and Authoritarian Survival in China: Concept and Measurement. *Comparative Politics Newsletter* 26 (2): 31–39.

Deng, Xiaoping. 1993. *Deng Xiaoping wen xuan* [Selected Works of Deng Xiaoping, i.e. *SWDXP*], vol. 3. Renmin chubanshe.

Deng, Bin, Peng Weimin, and Huang Xiaohua. 2012. 'Chongqing moshi yu Zhongguo tese shehui zhuyi' xueshu yantao hui shuyao [A Summary of the Academic Seminar on the "Chongqing Model and Socialism with Chinese Characteristics"]. *Tansuo* 1:179–181.

Dickson, Bruce J. 1990. Conflict and Non-Compliance in Chinese Politics: Party Rectification, 1983–1987. *Pacific Affairs* 63 (2): 170–190.

Dimitrov, Martin K. 2023. *Dictatorship and Information: Authoritarian Regime Resilience in Communist Europe and China*. Oxford University Press.

Dittmer, Lowell. 1986. Party Rectification in Post-Mao China. In *Mainland China: Politics, Economics, and Reform*, edited by Yu-Ming Shaw, 103–120. Westview Press.

Downie, Edmund. 2014. One City, Many Models: The Chinese Left's Debates over Chongqing. Academia.edu, April 14. https://www.academia.edu/8919324/One_City_Many_Models_The_Chinese_Left_s_Debates_over_Chongqing.

Duckett, Jane, and Ana Inés Langer. 2013. Populism versus Neoliberalism: Diversity and Ideology in the Chinese Media's Narratives of Health Care Reform. *Modern China* 39 (6): 653–680. https://doi.org/10.1177/0097700413492602.

Dukalskis, Alexander. 2017. *The Authoritarian Public Sphere: Legitimation and Autocratic Power in North Korea, Burma, and China*. Routledge.

Eaton, Sarah, and Armin Müller. 2024. Varieties of Chinese Populism: Mapping the Mindsets of Pro- and Anti-System Populists. In *Three Faces of Populism in Asia: Populism as a Multifaceted Political Practice*, edited by Shiru Wang, 44–64. Routledge.

Ekiert, Grzegorz, and Elizabeth J. Perry. 2020. State-Mobilized Movements: A Research Agenda. In *Ruling by Other Means: State-Mobilized Movements*, edited by Grzegorz Ekiert, Elizabeth J. Perry, and Yan Xiaojun, 1–23. Cambridge University Press.

External Propaganda Office of the Chongqing Party Committee (EPOCPC) and Chongqing Center for Internet News Research (CCINR). 2009. *Yu lun 2008* [Public Opinion in Chongqing 2008]. Self-published.

Fangtan: Dangju zai zou meiyou Bo Xilai de Bo Xilai luxian ma? [Interview: Is the Leadership Following Bo Xilai's Line without Bo Xilai?]. 2014. *BBC News*, February 10. https://www.bbc.com/zhongwen/simp/china/2014/02/140210_lse_conference_tong.

Feng, Shizheng. 2011. Zhongguo guojia yundong de xingcheng yu bianyi: ji yu zhengti de zhengti xing jieshi [The Formation and Variation of China's National Movements: A Holistic Explanation Based on Political Regime]. *Kaifang shidai* 1:73–97.

Fewsmith, Joseph. 2008. The 17th Party Congress: Informal Politics and Formal Institutions. *China Leadership Monitor*, No. 23 (Winter).

Fewsmith, Joseph. 2010. Bo Xilai Takes on Organized Crime. *China Leadership Monitor*, No. 32 (Spring).

Fewsmith, Joseph. 2012. Bo Xilai and Reform: What Will Be the Impact of His Removal? *China Leadership Monitor*, No. 38 (Summer).

Fewsmith, Joseph. 2021. *Rethinking Chinese Politics*. Cambridge University Press.

FlorCruz, Jaime A. 2013. China's Bo Xilai Trial: A Show or Serious Test of Communist Party Reforms? *CNN*, August 18. https://www.cnn.com/2013/08/18/world/asia/china-bo-xilai-trial-analysis.

Gallagher, Mary E. 2023. China's Struggle for Common Prosperity. *China Leadership Monitor*, No. 75 (Spring).

Gallagher, Mary E., and Jonathan K. Hanson. 2015. Power Tool or Dull Blade? Selectorate Theory for Autocracies. *Annual Review of Political Science* 18:367–385. https://doi.org/10.1146/annurev-polisci-071213-041224.

Gandhi, Jennifer. 2008. *Political Institutions under Dictatorship*. Cambridge University Press.

Gao, Xiang. 2024. Patriotic Songs and Populism in Chinese Politics. In *The Routledge Handbook of Populism in the Asia Pacific*, edited by D. B. Subedi, Howard Brasted, Karin von Strokirch, and Alan Scott, 330–342. Routledge.

Gao, Gao, and Yan Jiaqi. 1986. *"Wenhua da geming" shi nian shi* [The Ten-Year History of the Cultural Revolution]. Tianjin renmin chubanshe.

Garnaut, John. 2012. *The Rise and Fall of the House of Bo*. Penguin.

Geddes, Barbara. 2006. Why Parties and Elections in Authoritarian Regimes? Paper Presented at the Annual Meeting of the American Political Science Association, Philadelphia, PA, August 31–September 3.

Geddes, Barbara, Joseph George Wright, and Erica Frantz. 2018. *How Dictatorships Work: Power, Personalization, and Collapse*. Cambridge University Press.

Gewirtz, Julian. 2022. *Never Turn Back: China and the Forbidden History of the 1980s*. Harvard University Press.

Godement, François, Yang Chan, Jean-Pierre Cabestan, Jérôme Doyon, and Romain Lafarguette. 2011. *One or Two Chinese Models? China Analysis*. European Council on Foreign Relations.

Gongyang, ed. 2003. *Si chao: Zhongguo "xin zuo pai" ji qi yingxiang* [Trends of Thought: China's "New Left" and Its Influence]. Zhongguo shehui kexue chubanshe.

Gore, Lance L. P. 2012. The Fall of Bo Xilai and the Seduction of the Chongqing Model. *East Asian Policy* 4 (2): 53–61.

Gregory, Paul Roderick. 2012. Making Sense of China's Bo Xilai Earthquake. *Forbes*, April 10. https://www.forbes.com/sites/paulroderickgregory/2012/04/10/making-sense-of-chinas-bo-xilai-earthquake/.

Guan, Tianru, and Yilu Yang. 2021. Rights-Oriented or Responsibility-Oriented? Two Subtypes of Populism in Contemporary China. *International Political Science Review* 42 (5): 672–689. https://doi.org/10.1177/0192512120925555.

Gueorguiev, Dimitar D., and Paul J. Schuler. 2016. Keeping Your Head Down: Public Profiles and Promotion under Autocracy. *Journal of East Asian Studies* 16 (1): 87–116. https://doi.org/10.1017/jea.2015.1.

Guo, Hong. 2010. Chongqing guanfang cu 75 wan daxuesheng zai xue 'gong, nong, bing' [The Chongqing Government Urging 750,000 University

Students to Learn from Workers, Peasants, and Soldiers Once Again]. *Zhongguo xinwen wang*, November 9. http://www.chinanews.com.cn/edu/2010/11-09/2644946.shtml.

Guo, Xuezhi. 2014. Controlling Corruption in the Party: China's Central Discipline Inspection Commission. *The China Quarterly* 219:597–624. https://doi.org/10.1017/S0305741014000770.

Guo, Bei, and Ying Jiang. 2015. Analyzing the Coexistence of Emerging Transparency and Tight Political Control on Weibo: Case Study of Weibo Broadcast of the Bo Xilai Trial. *The Journal of International Communication* 21 (1): 78–108. https://doi.org/10.1080/13216597.2014.998700.

Harding, Harry. 1981. *Organizing China: The Problem of Bureaucracy, 1949–1976*. Stanford University Press.

He, Kun, Scott A. Eldridge II, and Marcel Broersma. 2021. Conceptualizing Populism: A Comparative Study between China and Liberal Democratic Countries. *International Journal of Communication* 15:3006–3024.

He, Kun, Scott A. Eldridge II, and Marcel Broersma. 2023. Who Are the People? Populists' Articulation of 'the People' in Contemporary China. *Chinese Journal of Communication* 16 (3): 267–284. https://doi.org/10.1080/17544750.2023.2183970.

Ho, Norman P. 2016. Addressing Corruption and the Trial of Bo Xilai: Historical Continuities, Rule of Law Implications. In *China's Socialist Rule of Law Reforms Under Xi Jinping*, edited by John Garrick and Yan Chang Bennett, 109–121. Routledge.

Ho, Pin, and Wenguang Huang. 2013. *Zhongguo quangui de siwang youxi: Bo Xilai shijian mimi baogao* [A Death in the Lucky Holiday Hotel: Murder, Money, and an Epic Power Struggle in China]. Translated by Li Tianxin. Lingxiu chubanshe.

Hollyer, James R., B. Peter Rosendorff, and James Raymond Vreeland. 2019. Why Do Autocrats Disclose? Economic Transparency and Inter-Elite Politics in the Shadow of Mass Unrest. *Journal of Conflict Resolution* 63 (6): 1488–1516. https://doi.org/10.1177/0022002718792602.

Hongse Zhongguo. 2015. Zhongguo mao pai gongchanzhuyi zhe lianhe qilai—Zhongguo mao pai gongchanzhuyi zhe Luoyang huiyi jiyao [Chinese Maoist Communists Unite!—Minutes of the Luoyang Meeting of Chinese Maoist Communists]. *RedChinaCn*, February 5. http://redchinacn.net/forum.php?mod=viewthread&tid=13152.

Hongse Zhongguo. 2016. Kaichuang shehui zhuyi zai geming de xin jieduan—'Zhongguo mao pai lianhe' er ci huiyi jiyao [Opening a New Stage of Socialist Re-Revolution—Minutes of the Second Meeting of the "Chinese Maoist Union"]. *RedChinaCn*, May 12. http://www.redchinacn.net/forum.php?mod=viewthread&tid=11634.

Hou, Huiqin, and Xin Xiangyang, eds. 2011. *Wenhua minsheng de shidai jiedu—Chongqing "chang du jiang chuan" huodong kao* [A Contemporary Interpretation of Culture and People's Livelihoods: An Investigation of Chongqing's "Sing, Read, Say, Spread" Activities]. Renmin chubanshe.

Hu, Angang, ed. 2010. *Kexue fazhan guan de fangfa lun: yi Chongqing wei li* [The Methodology of the Scientific Outlook on Development: A Case Study of Chongqing]. Dangjian duwu chubanshe.

Hu Jintao zhongyao pishi zai daxuesheng 'cun guan' zhong yinqi qianglie fanxiang [Hu Jintao's Important Directive Sparks Strong Response among University Student "Village Officials"]. 2008. *Xinhua*, December 23. http://www.gov.cn/ldhd/2008-12/23/content_1185163.htm.

Hu, Angang, Yan Longyi, and Wei Xing. 2011. *2030 Zhongguo mai xiang gongtong fuyu* [China Marching toward Common Prosperity in 2030]. Zhongguo renmin daxue chubanshe.

Huang, Philip C. C. 2011. Chongqing: Equitable Development Driven by a 'Third Hand'? *Modern China* 37 (6): 569–622. https://doi.org/10.1177/0097700411419966.

Huang, Chengju. 2014. Power, Ambition, and Arrogance: Lessons of Bo Xilai's 'Singing Red Song' Campaign as a Political Communication Project. *Global Media Journal (Australian Edition)* 8 (1): 1–13.

Huang, Haifeng. 2015. Propaganda as Signaling. *Comparative Politics* 47 (4): 419–444. https://doi.org/10.5129/001041515816103220.

Ji, Shuoming. 2009. Chongqing moshi chuang Zhongguo jingji fangong xin lujing [The Chongqing Model Created a New Path for China's Economic Comeback]. *Yazhou Zhoukan*, No. 6.

Ji, Shuoming. 2010. Chongqing tanxun Zhongguo gongtong fuyu moshi xin lujing [Chongqing Is Exploring a New Path for China's Model of Common Prosperity]. *Yazhou Zhoukan*, No. 12.

Jiang, Zemin. 2006. *Jiang Zemin wen xuan* [Selected Works of Jiang Zemin, i.e. ***SWJZM***], vols. 1–3. Renmin chubanshe.

Jiang, Junyan, Tianyang Xi, and Haojun Xie. 2024. In the Shadows of Great Men: Retired Leaders and Informal Power Constraints in Autocracies. *British Journal of Political Science* 54 (4): 1088–1114. https://doi.org/10.1017/S0007123424000012.

Jinri Chongqing [Chongqing Today]. 2008–2012. Chongqing: Propaganda Department of the Chongqing Municipal Committee of the Chinese Communist Party. Various Issues.

Johnson, Ian. 2012. China's Falling Star. *The New York Review of Books*, April 26. https://www.nybooks.com/articles/2012/04/26/chinas-falling-star/.

Johnston, Alastair I. 1987. Party Rectification in the People's Liberation Army, 1983–1987. *The China Quarterly* 112:591–630.

Junker, Andrew. 2020. Left Populism in a Communist Civil Sphere: The Lesson of Bo Xilai. In *Populism in the Civil Sphere*, edited by Jeffrey C. Alexander et al., 232–250. Polity Press.

Kahn, Joseph. 2007. Bo Yibo, 98, Leader Who Helped Reshape Chinese Economy. *The New York Times*, January 17. https://www.nytimes.com/2007/01/17/world/asia/17bo.html.

Kaltwasser, Cristóbal Rovira. 2012. The Ambivalence of Populism: Threat and Corrective for Democracy. *Democratization* 19 (2): 184–208. https://doi.org/10.1080/13510347.2011.572619.

Keller, Franziska Barbara. 2016. Moving Beyond Factions: Using Social Network Analysis to Uncover Patronage Networks among Chinese Elites. *Journal of East Asian Studies* 16 (1): 17–41. https://doi.org/10.1017/jea.2015.3.

Kennedy, John James, and Dan Chen. 2018. State Capacity and Cadre Mobilization in China: The Elasticity of Policy Implementation. *Journal of Contemporary China* 27 (111): 393–405. https://doi.org/10.1080/10670564.2018.1410971.

King, Gary, Jennifer Pan, and Margaret E. Roberts. 2013. How Censorship in China Allows Government Criticism but Silences Collective Expression. *American Political Science Review* 107 (2): 326–343. https://doi.org/10.1017/S0003055413000014.

King, Gary, Jennifer Pan, and Margaret E. Roberts. 2017. How the Chinese Government Fabricates Social Media Posts for Strategic Distraction, Not Engaged Argument. *American Political Science Review* 111 (3): 484–501. https://doi.org/10.1017/S0003055417000144.

Kuhn, Philip. 1990. *Soulstealer: The Chinese Sorcery Scare of 1768.* Harvard University Press.

Kuran, Timur. 1991. Now Out of Never: The Element of Surprise in the East European Revolution of 1989. *World Politics* 44 (1): 7–48. https://doi.org/10.2307/2010422.

Lam, Willy Wo-Lap. 2012. The Maoist Revival and the Conservative Turn in Chinese Politics. *China Perspectives* 2:5–15. https://doi.org/10.4000/chinaperspectives.5851.

Lam, Willy Wo-Lap. 2015. *Chinese Politics in the Era of Xi Jinping: Renaissance, Reform, or Retrogression?* Routledge.

Landry, Pierre F., Xiaobo Lü, and Haiyan Duan. 2018. Does Performance Matter? Evaluating Political Selection along the Chinese Administrative Ladder. *Comparative Political Studies* 51 (8): 1074–1105. https://doi.org/10.1177/0010414017730078.

Le, Lin. 2023. Chinese Politics since Hu Jintao and the Origin of Xi Jinping's Strongman Rule: A New Hypothesis. *Texas National Security Review* 6 (4): 37–78. https://doi.org/10.26153/tsw/48844.

Le, Lin. 2025. *China's Conservative Turn: The Origins of Xi Jinping's New Era*. Lynne Rienner Publishers.

Leber, Andrew, Christopher Carothers, and Matthew Reichert. 2023. When Can Dictators Go It Alone? Personalization and Oversight in Authoritarian Regimes. *Politics & Society* 51 (1): 66–107. https://doi.org/10.1177/00323292221078661.

Lee, Francis L. F. 2018. Political Scandals under Responsive Authoritarianism: The Case of the Bo Xilai Trial in China. *International Journal of Communication* 12:3048–3066.

Li, Xiguang. 2010. Kexue fazhan guan shiye de Chongqing shijian [The Chongqing Practice from the Perspective of the Scientific Outlook on Development]. *Gaige* 7:6–15.

Li, Junru, ed. 2011a. *Zhongguo gongchandang jianshe shi* [The History of Constructing the Chinese Communist Party]. Haixia chuban faxing jituan and Fujian renmin chubanshe.

Li, Shenming, ed. 2011b. *Gongtong fuyu yu Zhongguo tese shehui zhuyi* [Common Prosperity and Socialism with Chinese Characteristics]. Zhongguo shehui kexue chubanshe.

Li, Cheng. 2012. The Bo Xilai Crisis: A Curse or a Blessing for China? *Brookings Institution*, April 18. https://www.brookings.edu/on-the-record/the-bo-xilai-crisis-a-curse-or-a-blessing-for-china/.

Li, He. 2015. *Political Thought and China's Transformation: Ideas Shaping Reform in Post-Mao China*. Springer.

Li, Cheng. 2016a. *Chinese Politics in the Xi Jinping Era: Reassessing Collective Leadership*. Brookings Institution Press.

Li, Ling. 2016b. The Rise of the Discipline and Inspection Commission, 1927–2012: Anticorruption Investigation and Decision-Making in the Chinese Communist Party. *Modern China* 42 (5): 447–482. https://doi.org/10.1177/0097700416631047.

Li, Ling. 2019. Politics of Anticorruption in China: Paradigm Change of the Party's Disciplinary Regime, 2012–2017. *Journal of Contemporary China* 28 (115): 47–63. https://doi.org/10.1080/10670564.2018.1497911.

Li, He. 2021. Populism in China. In *The Routledge Handbook of Chinese Studies*, edited by Chris Shei and Weixiao Wei, 376–388. Routledge.

Li, Hongbin, and Li-An Zhou. 2005. Political Turnover and Economic Performance: The Incentive Role of Personnel Control in China. *Journal of Public Economics* 89 (9–10): 1743–1762. https://doi.org/10.1016/j.jpubeco.2004.06.009.

Lianjie Chongqing—Shi qi da yi lai Chongqing shi tuijin fanfu changlian jianshe de tansuo yu shijian [Clean Chongqing: Exploration and Practice of Anti-Corruption and Clean Governance in Chongqing since the 17th Party Congress]. 2011. Hongqi chubanshe.

Liebman, Benjamin L. 2011. A Return to Populist Legality? Historical Legacies and Legal Reform. In *Mao's Invisible Hand: The Political Foundations of Adaptive Governance in China*, edited by Sebastian Heilmann and Elizabeth J. Perry, 165–200. Harvard University Press.

Lim, Kean Fan, and Niv Horesh. 2017. The Chongqing vs Guangdong Developmental 'Model' in Post-Mao China: Regional and Historical Perspectives on the Dynamics of Socioeconomic Change. *Journal of the Asia Pacific Economy* 22 (3): 372–395. https://doi.org/10.1080/13547860.2016.1263044.

Literature Research Office of the Central Committee of the Chinese Communist Party (LROCCP). 2004. *Deng Xiaoping nianpu 1975–1997* [The Chronicle of Deng Xiaoping, 1975–1997], vols. 1–2. Zhongyang wenxian chubanshe.

Liu, Yawei. 2011. Bo Xilai's Campaign for the Standing Committee and the Future of Chinese Politicking. *China Brief* 11 (21): 8–11.

Liu, Kang, Zhang Guilin, and Tang Yaoguo. 2010. Zhuanxing Zhongguo de Chongqing tupo [The Chongqing Breakthrough in a Transforming China]. *Liaowang*, April 19.

Liu, Sida, Lily Liang, and Terence C. Halliday. 2014. The Trial of Li Zhuang: Chinese Lawyers' Collective Action against Populism. *Asian Journal of Law and Society* 1 (1): 79–97. https://doi.org/10.1017/als.2013.9.

Liu, Laura Xiaolei, Haibing Shu, and K. C. John Wei. 2017. The Impacts of Political Uncertainty on Asset Prices: Evidence from the Bo Scandal in China. *Journal of Financial Economics* 125 (2): 286–310. https://doi.org/10.1016/j.jfineco.2017.05.011.

Looney, Kristen E. 2020. *Mobilizing for Development: The Modernization of Rural East Asia*. Cornell University Press.

Lorentzen, Peter. 2014. China's Strategic Censorship. *American Journal of Political Science* 58 (2): 402–414. https://doi.org/10.1111/ajps.12065.

Lorentzen, Peter. 2017. Designing Contentious Politics in Post-1989 China. *Modern China* 43 (5): 459–493. https://doi.org/10.1177/0097700416688895.

LROCCP. 2009–2013. *Shi qi da yi lai zhongyao wenxian xuan bia*n [Selected Important Documents since the 17th Party Congress, i.e. *SID17PC*], vols. 1–3. Zhongyang wenxian chubanshe.

LROCCP. 2011a. *Shi wu da yi lai zhongyao wenxian xuan bian* [Selected Important Documents since the 15th Party Congress, i.e. *SID15PC*], vols. 1–3. Zhongyang wenxian chubanshe.

LROCCP. 2011b. *Shi liu da yi lai zhongyao wenxian xuan bian* [Selected Important Documents since the 16th Party Congress, i.e. *SID16PC*], vols. 1–3. Zhongyang wenxian chubanshe.

LROCCP. 2013 *Lun qunzhong luxian—zhongyao lunshu zhaibian* [On the Mass Line—Selected Important Discourses]. Zhongyang wenxian chubanshe and Dangjian duwu chubanshe.

LROCCP. 2014–2018. *Shi ba da yi lai zhongyao wenxian xuan bian* [Selected Important Documents since the 18th Party Congress, i.e. *SID18PC*], vols. 1–3. Zhongyang wenxian chubanshe.

Lü, Xiaobo. 2000. *Cadres and Corruption: The Organization Involution of the Chinese Communist Party*. Stanford University Press.

Lu, Zhichao, ed. 2005. *Xiangwang Mao Zedong* [Longing for Mao Zedong]. Zhongyang wenxian chubanshe.

Luo, Zhifan. 2021. Discipline the Party: From Rectification Campaigns to Intra-Party Educational Activities in China. *China: An International Journal* 19 (4): 52–74. https://doi.org/10.1353/chn.2021.0041.

Ma, Guochuan. 2013. *Zou chu weiwen niandai: 2008–2013 Zhongguo shehui sixiang jiaofeng* [Moving Beyond the Age of Stability Maintenance: Clashing Social Thoughts in China, 2008–2013]. Hong Kong Zhonghe chuban.

MacFarquhar, Roderick, and Michael Schoenhals. 2006. *Mao's Last Revolution*. Belknap Press of Harvard University Press.

Magaloni, Beatriz. 2006. *Voting for Autocracy: Hegemonic Party Survival and Its Demise in Mexico*. Cambridge University Press.

Magaloni, Beatriz. 2008. Credible Power-Sharing and the Longevity of Authoritarian Rule. *Comparative Political Studies* 41 (4–5): 715–741. https://doi.org/10.1177/0010414007313124.

Magaloni, Beatriz, and Ruth Kricheli. 2010. Political Order and One-Party Rule. *Annual Review of Political Science* 13:123–143. https://doi.org/10.1146/annurev.polisci.031908.220529.

Manion, Melanie. 2004. *Corruption by Design: Building Clean Government in Mainland China and Hong Kong*. Harvard University Press.

Mao, Zedong. 1963. Ren de zhengque sixiang shi cong nali lai de? [Where Do Correct Ideas Come From?]. May. https://marxistphilosophy.org/maozedong/mx8/061.htm.

McAdam, Doug, Sidney Tarrow, and Charles Tilly. 2001. *Dynamics of Contention*. Cambridge University Press.

Mei, Xiao. 2017a. *Chongqing's Red Culture Campaign: Simulation and Its Social Implications*. Routledge.

Mei, Xiao. 2017b. Why Chongqing's Red Culture Campaign Was Not a Real Mass Campaign. *International Journal of Politics, Culture, and Society* 30:63–81. https://doi.org/10.1007/s10767-016-9217-7.

Meisner, Maurice. 1971. Leninism and Maoism: Some Populist Perspectives in Marxism-Leninism in China. *The China Quarterly* 45:2–36. https://doi.org/10.1017/S0305741000010407.

Meng, Dongfang. 2011. Chongqing shi kaizhan 'san jin san tong' huodong de sikao [Reflections on Chongqing's "Three Enters and Three Togethers" Activities]. In *Chongqing lan pi shu: Zhongguo Chongqing fazhan baogao* [The Blue Book on Chongqing: A Report on Development in Chongqing, China], edited by Chongqing Academy of Social Sciences and Center for Development Research of the Chongqing Government, 46–58. Chongqing chubanshe.

Meng, Bingchun. 2016. Political Scandal at the End of Ideology? The Mediatized Politics of the Bo Xilai Case. *Media, Culture & Society* 38 (6): 811–826. https://doi.org/10.1177/0163443716635858.

Meng, Anne. 2020. *Constraining Dictatorship: From Personalized Rule to Institutionalized Regimes.* Cambridge University Press.

Meng, Anne, Jack Paine, and Robert Powell. 2023. Authoritarian Power Sharing: Concepts, Mechanisms, and Strategies. *Annual Review of Political Science* 26:153–173. https://doi.org/10.1146/annurev-polisci-052121-020406.

Mertha, Andrew. 2017. 'Stressing Out': Cadre Calibration and Affective Proximity to the CCP in Reform-Era China. *The China Quarterly* 229:64–85. https://doi.org/10.1017/S0305741017000042.

Miao, Michelle. 2013. Capital Punishment in China: A Populist Instrument of Social Governance. *Theoretical Criminology* 17 (2): 233–250. https://doi.org/10.1177/1362480613476788.

Miao, Ying. 2020. Can China Be Populist? Grassroot Populist Narratives in the Chinese Cyberspace. *Contemporary Politics* 26 (3): 268–287. https://doi.org/10.1080/13569775.2020.1727398.

Miller, Alice. 2006. The Problem of Hu Jintao's Successor. *China Leadership Monitor*, No. 19 (Fall).

Miller, Alice. 2008. China's New Party Leadership. *China Leadership Monitor*, No. 23 (Winter).

Miller, Alice. 2009. The Case of Xi Jinping and the Mysterious Succession. *China Leadership Monitor*, No. 30 (Fall).

Miller, Alice. 2010. The 18th Central Committee Politburo: A Quixotic, Foolhardy, Rashly Speculative, But Nonetheless Ruthlessly Reasoned Projection. *China Leadership Monitor*, No. 33 (Summer).

Miller, Alice. 2011. The Politburo Standing Committee Under Hu Jintao. *China Leadership Monitor*, No. 35 (Summer).

Miller, Alice. 2012. The Bo Xilai Affair in Central Leadership Politics. *China Leadership Monitor*, No. 38 (Summer).

Miller, Alice. 2015. The Trouble with Factions. *China Leadership Monitor*, No. 46 (Winter).

Miller, Alice. 2018. Valedictory: Analyzing the Chinese Leadership in an Era of Sex, Money, and Power. *China Leadership Monitor*, No. 57 (Fall).

Minzner, Carl. 2018. *End of an Era: How China's Authoritarian Revival Is Undermining Its Rise.* Oxford University Press.

Mudde, Cas. 2004. The Populist Zeitgeist. *Government and Opposition* 39 (4): 541–564. https://doi.org/10.1111/j.1477-7053.2004.00135.x.

Mudde, Cas. 2017. Populism: An Ideational Approach. In *The Oxford Handbook of Populism*, edited by Cristóbal Rovira Kaltwasser et al., 27–47. Oxford University Press.

Mudde, Cas, and Cristóbal Rovira Kaltwasser, eds. 2012. *Populism in Europe and the Americas: Threat or Corrective for Democracy?* Cambridge University Press.

Müller, Jan-Werner. 2016. *What Is Populism?* University of Pennsylvania Press.

Mulvad, Andreas. 2015. Competing Hegemonic Projects within China's Variegated Capitalism: 'Liberal' Guangdong vs. 'Statist' Chongqing. *New Political Economy* 20 (2): 199–227. https://doi.org/10.1080/13563467.2014.914160.

Myerson, Roger B. 2008. The Autocrat's Credibility Problem and Foundations of the Constitutional State. *American Political Science Review* 102 (1): 125–139. https://doi.org/10.1017/S0003055408080076.

Nadiri, Khalid. 2007. China's Peasant Populism: A Look Inland. *SAIS Review* 27 (1): 125–126. https://doi.org/10.1353/sais.2007.0017.

Nankai University Research and Teaching Office for Marxism and Leninism (NURTOML), and Research and Teaching Team for the Party History (RTTPH). 1984. *Zhongguo gongchandang de zheng dang yu zheng feng* [Rectification of the Chinese Communist Party]. Shandong renmin chubanshe.

Naughton, Barry. 2021. 'Common Prosperity' as Revealed in the Documents. *Interpret: China*. Center for Strategic and International Studies. https://interpret.csis.org/common-prosperity.

Ostiguy, Pierre. 2017. Populism: A Socio-Cultural Approach. In *The Oxford Handbook of Populism*, edited by Cristóbal Rovira Kaltwasser et al., 73–97. Oxford University Press.

Pappas, Takis S. 2019. *Populism and Liberal Democracy: A Comparative and Theoretical Analysis*. Oxford University Press.

PDCPC. 2008a. *Shan cheng lun jian: "jiefang sixiang, kuoda kaifang" dianshi bianlun sai shilu* [A Contest at the City of Hills: A Documentary of the TV Debate on "Emancipating the Mind and Expanding the Scope of Opening-Up"]. Chongqing chubanshe.

PDCPC. 2008b. *Kaifang luntan yanjiang ji* [A Collection of Speeches at the 2008 Open Forum]. Chongqing chubanshe.

PDCPC. 2008c. *Tanlu chengxiang tongchou* [Exploring the Way toward Urban–Rural Integration]. Chongqing chubanshe.

PDCPC. 2009. *Kexue fazhan xin zhuiqiu* [The New Pursuits of Scientific Development]. Chongqing chubanshe.

PDCPC. 2010. *Chengshi hangbiao: Chongqing chengshi jingshen tanxun* [Beacons for Urban Development: Searching for Chongqing's City Spirit]. Xinan shifan daxue chubanshe.

PDCPC. 2012a. *Chongqing zhuiqiu* [Chongqing's Pursuit]. Chongqing chubanshe.

PDCPC. 2012b. *Qian fada jieduan, qian fada diqu: kaiqi "kexue fazhan, fu min xing Yu" xin zheng cheng* [A Phase and an Area of Underdevelopment: Starting a New Journey Toward "Scientific Development, Enriching the People and Prospering Chongqing"]. Chongqing chubanshe.

PDCPC and Chongqing Office of Internet and Information (COII). 2012. *Chongqing yuqing huibian*, vol. 8 [Collection of Chongqing's Public Opinion, vol. 8]. Self-published.

Pei, Minxin. 2021. The Origins and Implications of Xi Jinping's 'Common Prosperity' Agenda. *China Leadership Monitor*, No. 70 (Winter).

Perry, Elizabeth J. 2001. Challenging the Mandate of Heaven: Popular Protest in Modern China. *Critical Asian Studies* 33 (2): 163–180. https://doi.org/10.1080/14672710122544.

Perry, Elizabeth J. 2007. Studying Chinese Politics: Farewell to Revolution? *The China Journal* 57:1–22.

Perry, Elizabeth J. 2011. From Mass Campaigns to Managed Campaigns: 'Constructing a New Socialist Countryside'. In *Mao's Invisible Hand: The Political Foundations of Adaptive Governance in China*, edited by Sebastian Heilmann and Elizabeth J. Perry, 30–61. Harvard University Press.

Perry, Elizabeth J. 2019. Work Team. In *Afterlives of Chinese Communism: Political Concepts from Mao to Xi*, edited by Christian Sorace, Ivan Franceschini, and Nicholas Loubere, 325–330. Australian National University Press and Verso.

Peters, B. Guy, and Jon Pierre. 2020. A Typology of Populism: Understanding the Different Forms of Populism and Their Implications. *Democratization* 27 (6): 928–946. https://doi.org/10.1080/13510347.2020.1751615.

Profile: Bo Xilai. 2013. *BBC*, September 22. https://www.bbc.com/news/world-asia-china-19709555.

Propaganda Department of Chongqing Party Committee (PDCPC). 2006. *Goujian hexie Chongqing* [Building a Harmonious Chongqing]. Chongqing chubanshe.

Przeworski, Adam. 1991. *Democracy and the Market: Political and Economic Reforms in Eastern Europe and Latin America*. Cambridge University Press.

Qiu Shi. 2012. Chuang xian zheng you huodong de shenhou shijian jichu he jianshi lilun zhicheng [The Deep Practical Foundation and Firm Theoretical Support for the "Chuang Xian Zheng You" Activities]. *Qiushi* 9:41–44.

Quan guo chuang xian zheng you huodong zongjie jiaoliu hui guanche Hu Jintao zhongyao pishi [The Summary and Exchange Conference on the National "Chuang Xian Zheng You" Campaign Emphasized the Implementation of Hu Jintao's Important Directives]. 2012 October 15. https://www.gov.cn/jrzg/2012-10/15/content_2244332.htm.

Renmin Luntan [People's Tribune]. 2011. Beijing: People's Daily Press.

Renmin University Project Team on Chongqing (RUPTC). 2011. *Chongqing xin shi* [New Things in Chongqing]. Zhongguo renmin daxue chubanshe.

Roberts, Margaret E. 2018. *Censored: Distraction and Diversion Inside China's Great Firewall.* Princeton University Press.

Rosenfeld, Bryn, and Jeremy Wallace. 2024. Information Politics and Propaganda in Authoritarian Societies. *Annual Review of Political Science* 27:263–281. https://doi.org/10.1146/annurev-polisci-041322-035951.

Rousseau, Jean-Jacques. 1992. *Discourse on the Origin of Inequality.* Translated by Donald A. Cress. Hackett.

Saich, Tony. 2021. *From Rebel to Ruler: One Hundred Years of the Chinese Communist Party.* Harvard University Press.

Schedler, Andreas. 2013. *The Politics of Uncertainty: Sustaining and Subverting Electoral Authoritarianism.* Oxford University Press.

Schedler, Andreas, and Bert Hoffmann. 2016. Communicating Authoritarian Elite Cohesion. *Democratization* 23 (1): 93–117. https://doi.org/10.1080/13510347.2015.1095181.

Schroeder, Ralph. 2020. Political Power and the Globalizing Spread of Populist Politics. *Journal of Political Power* 13 (1): 22–40. https://doi.org/10.1080/2158379X.2020.1720101.

Self, Ben. 2015. The Bo Xilai Trial and China's Struggle with the Rule of Law. *Washington University Global Studies Law Review* 14 (1): 155–180.

Shambaugh, David. 2021. *China's Leaders: From Mao to Now*. Polity.

Shi, Zhongquan. 2011. Jixu jianjue geili yufang he chengzhi fubai [Continuing to Firmly Strengthen the Prevention and Punishment of Corruption]. In *Jinian Zhongguo gongchandang chengli 90 zhounian dang jian lilun yu shijian Chongqing yantao hui lunwen ji* [Papers of the Chongqing Symposium on Party Building Theories and Practices in Commemoration of the Chinese Communist Party's 90th Anniversary], vol. 1, 71–80. Dangjian duwu chubanshe.

Shih, Victor. 2016. Contentious Elites in China: New Evidence and Approaches. *Journal of East Asian Studies* 16 (1): 1–15. https://doi.org/10.1017/jea.2015.2.

Shih, Victor, Wei Shan, and Mingxing Liu. 2010. Gauging the Elite Political Equilibrium in the CCP: A Quantitative Approach Using Biographical Data. *The China Quarterly* 201:79–103. https://doi.org/10.1017/S0305741009991081.

Shih, Victor, Christopher Adolph, and Mingxing Liu. 2012. Getting Ahead in the Communist Party: Explaining the Advancement of Central Committee Members in China. *American Political Science Review* 106 (1): 166–187. https://doi.org/10.1017/S0003055411000566.

Shirk, Susan. 2022. *Overreach: How China Derailed Its Peaceful Rise.* Oxford University Press.

Shum, Desmond. 2021. *Red Roulette: An Insider's Story of Wealth, Power, Corruption, and Vengeance in Today's China*. Scribner.

Slater, Dan. 2010. *Ordering Power: Contentious Politics and Authoritarian Leviathans in Southeast Asia*. Cambridge University Press.

Song, Yafei, ed. 2013. *Bo Xilai tingshen shilu* [The Bo Xilai Trial Transcript]. Xin shijie chuanmei.

Song, Yongyi, and Sun Dajin. 1997. *Wenhua da geming he ta de yiduan sichao* [Heterodox Thoughts During the Cultural Revolution]. Tianyuan shuwu.

Song Yongyi: Wenge bu keneng chongyan, dan Wenge yijing zai Zhongguo huichao [Song Yongyi: The Cultural Revolution Will Not Recur, But It Is Already Resurging in China]. 2016. *Radio Free Asia*, April 19. https://www.rfa.org/mandarin/yataibaodao/zhengzhi/ck-04192016160346.html.

Steinbock, Dan. 2012. Guangdong and Chongqing: Two Sides of the Same Coin. *China US Focus*, December 11. http://www.chinausfocus.com/uncategorized/guangdong-and-chongqing-two-sides-of-the-same-coin/.

Strauss, Julia C. 2006. Morality, Coercion and State Building by Campaign in the Early PRC: Regime Consolidation and After, 1949–1956. *The China Quarterly* 188:891–912. https://doi.org/10.1017/S0305741006000488.

Strauss, Julia C. 2020. *State Formation in China and Taiwan: Bureaucracy, Campaign, and Performance*. Cambridge University Press.

Stromseth, Jonathan R., Edmund J. Malesky, Dimitar D. Gueorguiev, Hairong Lai, Wang Xixin, and Carl Brinton. 2017. *China's Governance Puzzle: Enabling Transparency and Participation in a Single-Party State*. Cambridge University Press.

Su, Wei. 2010. Lun xin de lishi qidian shang de Chongqing xinzheng yu Chongqing moshi [On the New Policies of Chongqing and the Chongqing Model at a New Historical Starting Point]. *Tansuo* 4:21–28.

Su, Wei. 2011. Yu san pi faguo jizhe tan Chongqing 'chang hong', 'da hei' [A Talk with Three Groups of French Journalists About Chongqing's "Sing Red" and "Strike Black"]. *Wu You Zhi Xiang*, June 21. https://www.wyzxwk.com/Article/shidai/2011/06/234683.html.

Su, Wei. 2012. 'Chongqing moshi' shi zenyang bei wudu de [How the "Chongqing Model" Has Been Misinterpreted]. *Guancha zhe wang*, February 2. https://www.guancha.cn/politics/2012_02_02_64993.shtml.

Su, Wei, Yang Fan, and Liu Shiwen. 2011. *Chongqing moshi* [The Chongqing Model]. Zhongguo jingji chubanshe.

Sun, Xin. 2022. *Decoding China's "Common Prosperity" Drive*. LSE IDEAS.

Svolik, Milan W. 2012. *The Politics of Authoritarian Rule*. Cambridge University Press.

Szelenyi, Ivan. 2011. Third Ways. *Modern China* 37 (6): 672–683. https://doi.org/10.1177/0097700411420799.

Tai, Zixue. 2015. Networked Resistance: Digital Populism, Online Activism, and Mass Dissent in China. *Popular Communication* 13 (2): 120–131. https://doi.org/10.1080/15405702.2015.1021469.

Tang, Wenfang. 2016. *Populist Authoritarianism: Chinese Political Culture and Regime Sustainability*. Oxford University Press.

Tarrow, Sidney G. 2011. *Power in Movement: Social Movements and Contentious Politics*. 3rd ed. Cambridge University Press.

Teiwes, Frederick C. 1993. *Politics and Purges in China: Rectification and the Decline of Party Norms, 1950–1965*. 2nd ed. M. E. Sharpe.

Teiwes, Frederick C. 2015. The Study of Elite Political Conflict in the PRC: Politics Inside the 'Black Box'. In *Handbook of the Politics of China*, edited by David S. G. Goodman, 21–41. Edward Elgar Publishing.

Theoretical Bureau of the Propaganda Department of the Central Committee of the Chinese Communist Party (TBPDCCP). 2011. *Lun dang de qunzhong gongzuo—zhongyao lunshu zhaibian* [On the Party's Mass Work—Selected Important Discourses]. Xuexi chubanshe.

Townsend, James R. 1977. Chinese Populism and the Legacy of Mao Tse-Tung. *Asian Survey* 17 (11): 1003–1015. https://doi.org/10.2307/2643349.

Tsai, Wen-hui. 1999. Mass Mobilization Campaigns in Mao's China. *American Journal of Chinese Studies* 6 (1): 21–48.

Urbinati, Nadia. 2019. Political Theory of Populism. *Annual Review of Political Science* 22:111–127. https://doi.org/10.1146/annurev-polisci-050317-070753.

Wang, Weiguang, and Zhao Jianying. 2009. Kexue fazhan guan wei shenme, shi shenme, zenme ban [The Scientific Outlook on Development: Why, What, and How]. In *Zhongguo makesi zhuyi yanjiu qianyan 2008* [Frontier of Marxism Research in China, 2008], edited by Zhao Jianying, Wu Bo, and Zheng Xiangfu, 25–36. Zhongguo shehui kexue chubanshe.

Wang, Yifan, and Chen Mingxian. 1985. *Zhongguo gongchandang li ci zheng dang zheng feng* [Previous Rectification Campaigns of the Chinese Communist Party]. Heilongjiang renmin chubanshe.

Wang, Chu, and Liu Taishan. 2007. Wang Yang: Zheng dang shijian kexue fazhan guan de paituobing [Wang Yang: Striving to Be the Vanguard in Practicing the Scientific Outlook on Development]. *Renmin ribao*, December 29.

Wang, Zhengxu, and Anastas Vangeli. 2016. The Rules and Norms of Leadership Succession in China: From Deng Xiaoping to Xi Jinping and Beyond. *The China Journal* 76:24–40. https://doi.org/10.1086/686141.

Wang Yang: bei wudu de 'dangao lun' [Wang Yang: The Misinterpreted "Cake Theory"]. 2011. *Liaowang Dongfang Zhoukan*, July 25. https://news.sohu.com/20110725/n314471558.shtml.

Wen Jiabao: fen hao shehui caifu zhe ge 'dangao' shi zhengfu de liangzhi [Wen Jiabao: The Conscience of the Government Requires that the "Cake" of Social

Wealth Be Divided Fairly]. 2010. *Zhongguo zhengfu wang*, February 27. http://www.gov.cn/zlft2010/content_1543394.htm.

Wen Jiabao: Meiyou zhengzhi tizhi gaige de chenggong, Wenge huo hui chongyan [Wen Jiabao: Without the Success of Political System Reform, the Cultural Revolution May Recur]. 2012. *Zhongguo gaige xinxi ku*, March 14. http://www.reformdata.org/2012/0314/22141.shtml.

Weyland, Kurt. 2001. Clarifying a Contested Concept: Populism in the Study of Latin American Politics. *Comparative Politics* 34 (1): 1–22. https://doi.org/10.2307/422412.

Weyland, Kurt. 2017. Populism: A Political-Strategic Approach. In *The Oxford Handbook of Populism*, edited by Cristóbal Rovira Kaltwasser et al., 48–72. Oxford University Press.

White, Tyrene. 1990. Postrevolutionary Mobilization in China: The One-Child Policy Reconsidered. *World Politics* 43 (1): 53–76.

White, Tyrene. 2006. *China's Longest Campaign: Birth Planning in the People's Republic, 1949–2005.* Cornell University Press.

Wintrobe, Ronald. 1998. *The Political Economy of Dictatorship.* Cambridge University Press.

Wu, Yiching. 2014. *The Cultural Revolution at the Margins: Chinese Socialism in Crisis.* Harvard University Press.

Wu, Guoguang. 2022. *China's Common Prosperity Program: Causes, Challenges, and Implications.* Asia Society Policy Institute.

Wu You Zhi Xiang. 2010. Chongqing moshi de lishi biran xing—Wu You Zhi Xiang di yi ci Chongqing moshi yantao hui jiyao [The Historical Inevitability of the Chongqing Model—Minutes of the First Wu You Zhi Xiang Seminar on the Chongqing Model]. *Wu You Zhi Xiang*, October 25. http://m.wyzxwk.com/content.php?classid=12&id=196596.

Wu You Zhi Xiang. 2011a. Wu You Zhi Xiang di er ci 'Chongqing moshi' yantao hui jiyao [Minutes of the Second Wu You Zhi Xiang Seminar on the "Chongqing Model"]. *Wu You Zhi Xiang*, January 8. http://m.wyzxwk.com/Article/lixiang/2011/01/199909.

Wu You Zhi Xiang. 2011b. Shijie weiji xia de Chongqing moshi yu Zhongguo weilai—Wu You Zhi Xiang di san ci Chongqing moshi yantao hui jiyao [The Chongqing Model and China's Future in a World of Crises—Minutes of the Third Wu You Zhi Xiang Seminar on the Chongqing Model]. *Wu You Zhi Xiang dianzi ban yue kan*, issue 144, 9 (2): 51–57.

Wu You Zhi Xiang. 2011c. Chongqing moshi shi bimian Hua'erjie geming weiyi zhengque de daolu—Wu You Zhi Xiang 'Chongqing moshi de shijie yiyi' yantao hui jiyao [The Chongqing Model Is the Only Correct Path to Avoid the Wall Street Revolution—Minutes of the Wu You Zhi Xiang Seminar on the "Global Implications of the Chongqing Model"]. *Wu You Zhi Xiang dianzi ban yue kan*, issue 147, 11 (1): 21–26.

Wu, Baotong, Hu Zhaolin, and Jin Xianfeng. 2010. 'Shi da xingdong' feng sheng shui qi tongyi zhanxian fenli qianxing—2010 nian Zhongyang tong zhan bu shishi 'shi da xingdong' zongshu [The "Ten Major Initiatives" Gaining Momentum and the United Front Moving Forward—A Summary of the Implementation of the "Ten Major Initiatives" by the Central United Front Department in 2010]. *Zhongguo tongyi zhanxian* 12:14–21.

Xi, Jinping. 2021. Zhashi tuijin gongtong fuyu [Solidly Promoting Common Prosperity]. *Qiushi*, No. 20. http://www.qstheory.cn/dukan/qs/2021-10/15/c_1127959365.htm.

Xiang, Lanxing. 2012. The Bo Xilai Affair and China's Future. *Survival* 54 (3): 59–68. https://doi.org/10.1080/00396338.2012.690979.

Xu, Youyu. 1999. *Xing xing se se de zaofan: hong weibing jingshen suzhi de xingcheng ji yanbian* [A Variety of Rebellions: The Formation and Evolution of the Red Guard's Mentality]. Chinese University of Hong Kong Press.

Xu, Ben. 2001. Chinese Populist Nationalism: Its Intellectual Politics and Moral Dilemma. *Representations* 76 (1): 120–140. https://doi.org/10.1525/rep.2001.76.1.120.

Xu, Chenggang. 2011. The Fundamental Institutions of China's Reforms and Development. *Journal of Economic Literature* 49 (4): 1076–1151. https://doi.org/10.1257/jel.49.4.1076.

Xu, Zhun. 2012. The Chongqing Event and Its Implications. *Economic and Political Weekly* 47 (16): 12–14.

Xu, Qingquan. 2018. 'Ba lao' yu 1980 niandai zhengtan gaoceng geju [The "Eight Immortals" and the Political Structure of Top Leadership in the 1980s]. *Duli zhongwen bihui*, July 29. https://www.chinesepen.org/blog/archives/107417.

Yan Huang Chun Qiu [China Through the Ages]. 2003–2016. Beijing. Monthly journal. Various issues.

Yang, Jisheng. 2010. *Zhongguo gaige niandai de zhengzhi douzheng* [The Political Struggles during China's Reform Era]. Tiandi tushu youxian gonsi.

Yang, Fan. 2012. Yong fei yishixingtai fangfa yanjiu Zhongguo moshi yu Chongqing moshi [Studying the China Model and the Chongqing Model Using Non-Ideological Methods]. January 5. https://m.aisixiang.com/data/48866.html.

Yang Lujun: ri zhao Chongqing—Bo Xilai yu 'Chongqing moshi' [Yang Lujun: The Sun Shines on Chongqing—Bo Xilai and "The Chongqing Model"]. 2010 December 8. https://m.aisixiang.com/data/37711.html.

Yi, Xiaoguang. 2012. *Pojie Zhongguo fazhan zhi kunju: Chongqing shijian lun* [Cracking the Problem of Development in China: A Thesis on Chongqing's Practices]. Zhongguo jingji chubanshe.

Yin, Hongbiao. 2009. *Shizong zhe de zuji: wenhua da geming qijian de qingnian sichao* [The Footprints of the Missing: Youth Ideology During the Cultural Revolution]. Chinese University of Hong Kong Press.

Yu, Yunyao. 2011. Chongqing shi de 'san xiang zhidu' yu xin xingshi xia de qunzhong gongzuo [Chongqing's "Three Institutions" and Mass-Related Work under New Circumstances]. In *Jinian Zhongguo gongchandang chengli 90 zhounian dang jian lilun yu shijian Chongqing yantaohui lunwen ji* [Papers of the Chongqing Symposium on Party Building Theories and Practices in Commemoration of the Chinese Communist Party's 90th Anniversary], vol. 1, 22–23. Dangjian duwu chubanshe.

Yuan, Qian. 2021. Zhongguo gongchandang dang nei jizhong jiaoyu de lishi jincheng, jiben tezheng he dangdai qishi [The Historical Evolution, Fundamental Characteristics, and Contemporary Implications of the Chinese Communist Party's Internal Education Campaigns]. *Qiushi* 6:4–13.

Zakharzhevskaya, Anna. 2017. The Chongqing Model—Socialist Alternative or Propaganda Cliché? *Research in Political Economy* 32:227–252. https://doi.org/10.1108/S0161-723020170000032013.

Zang, Dongsheng. 2010. Rise of Political Populism and the Trouble with the Legal Profession in China. *Harvard China Review* 6:79–99. https://digitalcommons.law.uw.edu/faculty-articles/830.

Zhang, Hongliang. 2011. Chongqing moshi chengbai yu Zhongguo zhengzhi qianjing [The Success or Failure of the Chongqing Model and China's Political Future]. *Wu You Zhi Xiang dianzi ban yue kan*, issue 141, 8 (1): 47–59.

Zhang, Chenchen. 2020a. Right-Wing Populism with Chinese Characteristics? Identity, Otherness and Global Imaginaries in Debating World Politics Online. *European Journal of International Relations* 26 (1): 88–115. https://doi.org/10.1177/1354066119850253.

Zhang, Yueran. 2020b. The Chongqing Model One Decade On. *Made in China Journal* 3:31–39. https://madeinchinajournal.com/2021/01/11/the-chongqing-model-one-decade-on/.

Zhang, Xinhua, and Song Yingjun, eds. 2011. *"Zhongguo daolu" yu "Chongqing shijian"* [The "Chinese Path" and the "Chongqing Practice"]. Chongqing daxue chubanshe.

Zhao, Qizheng. 2011. Guanyu Chongqing chuangxin yiyi de ganhuai [Reflections on the Significance of Chongqing's Innovation]. In *Gongtong fuyu yu Zhongguo tese shehui zhuyi* [Common Prosperity and Socialism with Chinese Characteristics], edited by Li Shenming, 14–18. Zhongguo shehui kexue chubanshe.

Zhao, Yuezhi. 2012. The Struggle for Socialism in China: The Bo Xilai Saga and Beyond. *Monthly Review* 64 (5): 1–17.

Zhonggong zhongyang bangong ting yinfa [The General Office of the Chinese Communist Party Central Committee Issued "Opinions on Comprehensively

Carrying Out the Learn from Lei Feng Campaign"]. 2012 March 2. http://www.moe.gov.cn/jyb_xxgk/moe_1777/moe_1778/201203/t20120314_132124.html.

Zhou, Ruijin. 2008. 'Di san ci sixiang jiefang' yao jiejue liu da wenti ["The Third Wave of Mind Emancipation" Needs to Address Six Major Questions]. *Xin jing bao*, March 17. http://www.chinanews.com.cn/gn/news/2008/03-17/1193735.shtml.

Zhou, Xueguang. 2012. Yundong xing zhili jizhi: Zhongguo guojia zhili de zhidu luoji zai sikao [Campaign-Style Governance Mechanism: Rethinking the Institutional Logic of China's National Governance]. *Kaifang shidai* 9:105–125.

Zhou, Xueguang. 2017. *Zhongguo guojia zhili de zhidu luoji: yi ge zuzhi xue yanjiu* [The Institutional Logic of China's National Governance: An Organizational Analysis]. Sanlian shudian.

Zhou, Yang. 2018. Do Ideology Movements and Legal Intervention Matter: A Synthetic Control Analysis of the Chongqing Model. *European Journal of Political Economy* 51:44–56. https://doi.org/10.1016/j.ejpoleco.2017.03.010.

Index[1]

[1] Note: Page numbers followed by 'n' refer to notes.

L. Le, *Revival of Maoism in Reform-Era China*,
https://doi.org/10.1007/978-981-92-4606-9

Kolibri 360 GmbH
Ferdinand-Jühlke-Straße 7
99095 Erfurt, Deutschland
produktsicherheit@kolibri360.de